The Idea of Human Rights

The Idea of Human Rights

FOUR INQUIRIES

Michael J. Perry

New York Oxford ◆ Oxford University Press 1998

Oxford University Press

Oxford   New York

Athens   Auckland   Bangkok   Bogota   Bombay   Buenos Aires
Calcutta   Cape Town   Dar es Salaam   Delhi   Florence   Hong Kong
Istanbul   Karachi   Kuala Lumpur   Madras   Madrid   Melbourne
Mexico City   Nairobi   Paris   Singapore   Taipei   Tokyo   Toronto   Warsaw

and associated companies in
Berlin   Ibadan

Copyright © 1998 Oxford University Press, Inc.

Published by Oxford University Press, Inc.
198 Madison Avenue, New York, New York 10016

Library of Congress Cataloging-in-Publication Data
Perry, Michael J.
The idea of human rights : four inquiries / by Michael J. Perry.
p.   cm.
Includes index.
ISBN 0-19-511636-4
1. Human rights—Religious aspects.
2. Human rights—Philosophy.   I. Title.
BL65.H78P47   1998
323'.01—dc21   97-12764

1 3 5 7 9 8 6 4 2
Printed in the United States of America
on acid-free paper

For my children,
Daniel James Perry O'Leary
and
Gabriel Francis Perry O'Leary.

May the idea of human rights become,
in their lifetime,
an ever more tangible reality.

Contents

The Idea of Human Rights

INTRODUCTION

The Idea of Human Rights

It is often stressed that the idea of human rights is of recent origin, and that this is enough to dismiss its claims to timeless validity. In its contemporary form, the doctrine is certainly new, though it is arguable that it is a modern version of the natural law theory, whose origins we can trace back at least to the Stoic philosophers and, of course, to the Judaic and Christian sources of European culture. There is no substantial difference between proclaiming "the right to life" and stating that natural law forbids killing. Much as the concept may have been elaborated in the philosophy of the Enlightenment in its conflict with Christianity, the notion of the immutable rights of individuals goes back to the Christian belief in the autonomous status and irreplaceable value of the human personality.

—Leszek Kolakowski[1]

I

During the last days of 1987 and the first days of 1988, I visited El Salvador with friends from a church in Chicago with which I was then associated. El Salvador was in the grip of its terrible civil war. The violations of human rights by both sides in the war, but especially by the government, were many and horrible.[2] A searing passage from Mark Danner's book, *The Massacre at El Mozote: A Parable of the Cold War* (1994), comes to mind:

> There was one in particular the soldiers talked about . . . : a girl on La Cruz whom they had raped many times during the course of the afternoon, and through it all, while the other women of El Mozote had screamed and cried as if they had never had a man, this girl had sung hymns, strange evangelical songs, and she had kept right on singing, too, even after they had done what had to be done, and shot her in the chest. She had lain there on La Cruz with the blood flowing from her chest, and had kept on singing—a bit weaker than before, but still singing. And the soldiers, stupefied, had watched and pointed. Then they had grown tired of the game and had shot her again, and she sang still, and their wonder began to turn to fear—until finally they had unsheathed their machetes and hacked through her neck, and at last the singing had stopped.

After quoting this passage in his review of Danner's "parable", Christopher Lehmann-Haupt wrote: "Throughout the remainder of this overwhelming book, you keep straining hopelessly to hear the sound of that singing."[3]

By the time I returned, dazed, from El Salvador, the issues I had first addressed in *Morality, Politics, and Law*—issues to which I return in this book—had become, for me, both more concrete and more urgent.[4] Issues that had been, for me, primarily intellectual had become profoundly existential. This book is one legacy—alas, a pale one—of that brief but transforming journey to El Salvador.[5] The Salvadoran civil war ended before I began drafting this book. But other, no less awful events—in Bosnia-Herzogovina, for example—quickly erupted. The real world is endlessly fertile in its yield of sobering, wrenching, clarifying contexts for thinking about the idea of human rights.

II

The name of the state where I was born and raised—Kentucky—derives from a Native American word meaning "a dark and bloody ground".[6] An apt name for this century in which we have been born and raised—this century now ending—is the dark and bloody time: The twentieth century has surely been as unrelentingly dark and bloody as any in human history. In the midst of the countless grotesque inhumanities of the twentieth century, however, there is a heartening story, amply recounted elsewhere:[7] the emergence in international law, in the period since the end of the Second World War, of the idea of human rights and the protection by international law of what many consider to be basic human rights. ("Until World War II, most legal scholars and governments affirmed the general proposition, albeit not in so many words, that international law did not impede the natural right of each equal sovereign to be monstrous to his or her subjects."[8]) As important and hopeful as the story is, however, there is little reason to believe that many basic human rights are really any more secure now than they were before 1945.[9] In this final decade of the twentieth century, the furious slaughter of innocents continued—most famously, perhaps, in Rwanda and in the former Yugoslavia. Even slavery, thought by many to have died with the nineteenth century, remains alive and well at the end of the twentieth—especially the enslavement of women and children.[10] Torture, too, remains pervasive.[11] Nonetheless, the emergence in international law of the idea of human rights and the attendant rhetoric of human rights so pervasive in world today, especially in the Western world, present an important occasion, in my view, for addressing several fundamental questions about the idea of human rights.

Let me begin with a statement of the idea of human rights, followed by two general observations about the idea. As I explain in this book, the idea of human rights consists of two parts. According to the first part, each and every human being is sacred—each and every human being is "inviolable", has "inherent dignity and worth", is "an end in himself", or the like. According to the second part of the idea, *because* every human being is sacred (and given all other relevant information), certain choices should be made and certain other choices rejected; in particular, certain things ought not to be done to any human being and certain other things ought to be done for every human being.

Now, two general observations about the idea of human rights. First: Although its emergence in international law is a relatively recent development, the idea of human rights itself is not new. In one form or another, the idea is very old—as the passage by Kolakowski that I have put at the beginning of this introduction suggests. Second: While the idea of human rights is not, for those who accept it, the whole of morality, it is a fundamental part. However it is that I, as one human being, ought to live my life, I ought not to live it in a way that negates the idea of human rights or violates human rights. However it is that we, as a community of human beings—in particular, as a political community—ought to live our collective life, our life in common, we ought not to live it in a way that negates the idea of human rights or violates human rights. Thus, for those who accept it, the idea of human rights operates as a fundamental moral limit on how we human beings, both individually and collectively, may live our lives, on what choices we may make.

I pursue, in this book, four fundamental inquiries about the idea of human rights. I begin, in chapter 1, with what is perhaps the most fundamental of the four inquiries: Is there any intelligible secular version of the claim that every human being is sacred—or, instead, is the claim inescapably religious and the idea of human rights, therefore, ineliminably religious? (I distinguish the terms "religious" and "secular" in chapter 1.) I conclude that there is, finally, no intelligible (much less persuasive) secular version of the conviction that every human being is sacred; the only intelligible versions are religious. (To say that the only intelligible versions of the conviction are religious is not to say that any religious version is persuasive or even plausible.) The conviction that every human being is sacred is, in my view, inescapably religious—and the idea of human rights, therefore, ineliminably religious.[12] Contrary to what some might think, I do not load the dice by using the term "sacred"; the word "inviolable" would do as well. As Ronald Dworkin has explained, and as I emphasize in chapter 1, the conviction that every human being is sacred "may be, and commonly is, interpreted in a secular as well as in a conventionally religious way."[13]

In the course of inquiring, in chapter 1, if the idea of human rights is ineliminably religious, I comment on a number of matters implicated by the question. For example, I explain why Ronald Dworkin's conception of what it means to say that a human life is "sacred" is deeply problematic.[14] Further along, I indicate why Richard Rorty's dismissal of "human rights foundationalism"—his dismissal of the effort to provide a foundation for human rights claims—is profoundly subversive of Rorty's (and anyone else's) commitment to what he calls "our Eurocentric human rights culture".[15]

In chapter 2, I address two questions about the language or vocabulary of "rights", which is the principal language in which, in this century, claims about what ought not to be done to any human being and claims about what ought to be done for every human being have come to be expressed: What does "rights talk" mean—how does the rhetoric of rights function—both in the discourse of the international law of human rights and in the moral, especially the political-moral, discourse that underlies and shapes the international-legal discourse? And, as it functions in that twofold discourse, is rights talk problematic? I conclude that rights talk (as it functions in that twofold discourse) is not at all problematic. Along the way, I explain why any effort to extend Mary Ann Glendon's recent critique of rights talk beyond her intended target—beyond what Glendon calls "our current American rights talk"[16]—to international human rights talk is deeply misconceived.

In chapters 3 and 4, I turn to the second part of the idea of human rights: the claim that because every human being is sacred, certain things ought not to be done to any human being and certain other things ought to be done for every human being. The central inquiry, in chapter 3, is whether human rights are truly universal. The principal position I address in chapter 3, which I call "the relativist challenge", holds that whether or not every human being is sacred—and, so, even if every human being *is* sacred—there are no things that ought not to be done (not even any things that *conditionally rather than unconditionally* ought not to be done) to any human being and no things that ought to be done (not even any things that *conditionally* ought to be done) for every human being. That is, no putatively "human" right is truly a *human* right: no such right is the right of *every* human being; in that sense, no such right—no such "ought" or "ought not"—is truly universal. In chapter 3, I contend against this relativist challenge to the (second part of the) idea of human rights; I also identify and address various other "relativisms" that are relevant to the idea of human rights or are implicated by debates about what human rights, if any, human beings have.

"Moral relativism" is a phrase that is often used and, even by those who use the phrase, often misunderstood. One of my principal goals, in chapter 3, is to clarify and address the unusually murky subject of "moral relativism"—and to do so from the perspective of what can properly be called "natural law". "In so far as any common core can be found to the principal versions of the natural law theory, it seems to amount to the statement that the basic principles of morals and legislation are, *in some sense or other*, objective, accessible to reason and based on human nature."[17] As I explain in chapter 3, the "natural law" conception of the subject matter of morality, the "natural law" conception of what moral knowledge is knowledge of or about—namely, the requirements of authentic human flourishing—unites such otherwise diverse moral thinkers as Martha Nussbaum and Pope John Paul II.

In chapter 4, the central inquiry—again, an inquiry about the second part of the idea of human rights—is whether human rights are absolute or unconditional. Assuming that every human being is sacred, are there some things that ought *never* (i.e., under any circumstances or conditions) to be done to any human being or some things that ought *always* (under all conditions) to be done for every human being? Or, instead, are there only things that *conditionally* ought not to be done to any human being and things that *conditionally* ought to be done for every human being—things that ought not to be done, and things that ought to be done, under some, even most, conditions, but not under every imaginable condition? My answer, in chapter 4, is mixed. No one claims that *all* human rights are, either as moral rights or as legal rights, absolute. Many human rights are, both as moral rights and as legal rights, conditional, not unconditional. The serious claim is that *some* human rights are, as moral rights, absolute. I argue, in chapter 4, to the contrary. (John Finnis is a prominent and persistent defender of the claim that some human rights are absolute; I explain, in chapter 4, why I reject his position.) I also argue, however, that even if *no* human rights are, as moral rights, absolute, *some* human rights, as international-legal rights, should be—and, happily, are—absolute.

⁂

Of all the influential—indeed, formative—moral ideas to take center stage in the twentieth century, like democracy and socialism, the idea of human rights (which, again, in one form or another, is an old idea) is, for many, the most difficult. It is the most difficult in the sense that it is, for many, the hardest of the great moral ideas to integrate, the hardest to square, with the reigning intellectual assumptions of the age, especially what Bernard Williams has called "Nietzsche's thought": "[T]here is, not only no God, but no metaphysical order of any kind . . . ."[18] For those who accept "Nietzsche's thought", can the idea of human rights possibly be more than a kind of aesthetic preference? In a culture in which it was widely believed that there is no God or metaphysical order of any kind, on what basis, if any, could the idea of human rights long survive?[19] I take up such questions in chapter 1. The other dominant intellectual assumption of the age with which it is difficult to integrate the idea of human rights is actually a collection of related assumptions or positions, all of which are "relativist" in one or another sense. I disaggregate and address these various relativisms in chapter 3. My overarching aim, in this book, is to understand, or to better understand, the difficult idea of human rights.

I do not imagine, however, that I have achieved closure with respect to the difficult issues I address in this book. Such an imagining would be, *for anyone,* hallucinatory; after all, each of the four basic issues I address here is, in one or another version, perennially controversial. Indeed, I do not imagine even that I have succeeded in developing as fully as I should the basic positions I present and defend in this book. In part thanks to those persons who have commented on earlier versions of this work, I am acutely aware that more needs to be done. Nonetheless, I hope that, notwithstanding its incompleteness, this book will advance both our understanding of and our discourse about the important and difficult idea of human rights.

III

One of my most vivid memories of El Salvador (aided by some wonderful photographs) is of all the children who greeted and surrounded us while we were there, both in the city of San Salvador and in the countryside—children relentlessly uprooted and multiply savaged by the civil war. I think of them now[20] as I dedicate this book to my own children, in the hope that the idea of human rights becomes, in my children's lifetime, an ever more tangible reality.

Acknowledgments. I wrote this book during the period I was the Howard J. Trienens Chair in Law at Northwestern University. (In September 1997, I became the University Distinguished Chair in Law at Wake Forest University.) I am grateful to many friends, colleagues, and students at Northwestern University, and elsewhere, for helpful comments. I am especially grateful to the Northwestern University law students who, at one time or another in the last several years, discussed with me, in my "Human Rights" course, both the questions I address in, and draft chapters of, this book. For financial support during the summer of 1996, when I was completing this book, I am grateful to the Clemens and Jane Werner Faculty Enrichment Fund of the Northwestern University Law School.

I am grateful to the faculty and students—and especially to Professor Gary Leedes—of the T.C. Williams School of Law, University of Richmond, with whom I discussed an earlier version of chapter 1 while, in April 1993, I was in residence at the T.C. Williams School of Law as the Visiting George E. Allen Professor of Law. I presented earlier versions of chapter 1 as the 1995 Kamm Lecture at Wheaton College, Illinois, and at St. John's University School of Law while, in March 1996, I was Scholar-in-Residence. In March 1994, I presented an earlier version of chapter 2 at the Suffolk University Law School as a part of the Donahue Lecture Series. For their helpful comments, I am grateful to the audiences at Wheaton, St. John's, and Suffolk.

Finally, I am deeply grateful to the men and women with whom I traveled in El Salvador almost ten years ago, during the week of December 26, 1987 to January 2, 1988. This book took root during that trip. I remember standing in the airport in New Orleans on the afternoon of January 2, 1988, shortly after our flight from San Salvador had landed. I was somewhat dazed. The experience we had just lived through was, for me, disorienting. But it was also, for me, profoundly orienting. As I stood there, I began to realize that, happily, I had fallen into the grip of the idea of human rights.

At many points in this book, I cite or quote various human rights documents, like the Universal Declaration of Human Rights. Those documents may be found in *Basic Documents on Human Rights*, edited by Ian Brownlie (Oxford University Press, 3rd ed., 1992).

CHAPTER I

≈≈≈

Is the Idea of Human Rights
Ineliminably Religious?

*The essence of all morality is this: to believe that every human being is of infinite
importance, and therefore that no consideration of expediency can justify the
oppression of one by another. But to believe this it is necessary to believe in God.*

— R.H. Tawney[1]

*We almost all accept . . . that human life in all its forms is sacred. . . . For some
of us, this is a matter of religious faith; for others, of secular but deep philosophical
belief.*

— Ronald Dworkin[2]

*The conception of human rights, based upon the assumed existence of a human
being as such, broke down at the very moment when those who professed to
believe in it were for the first time confronted with people who had indeed lost all
other qualities and specific relationships—except that they were still human. The
world found nothing sacred in the abstract nakedness of being human.*

— Hannah Arendt[3]

The idea of human rights—the idea that has emerged in international law in
the period since the Second World War—is complex. In this book, I mean to
explore all the main constituents of the idea. In this chapter, however, I am interested only in one constituent—albeit, a foundational one: the conviction
that every human being is sacred.

Who is right: those, like R.H. Tawney, who believe that the conviction that
every human being is sacred is inescapably religious, or those, like Ronald
Dworkin, who believe that there can be secular versions of the conviction as
well as religious ones? For reasons I develop in this chapter, I conclude that
Tawney is right and Dworkin, wrong: There is no intelligible (much less persuasive) secular version of the conviction that every human being is sacred; the
only intelligible versions are religious. (To say that the only intelligible versions

of the conviction are religious is not to say that any religious version is persuasive or even plausible.) The conviction that every human being is sacred is, in my view, inescapably religious—and the idea of human rights is, therefore, ineliminably religious.

The passages by Tawney and Dworkin that I have put at the beginning of this chapter speak to the question that is the title and central inquiry of the chapter. The passage by Hannah Arendt speaks to a different, and darker, question: Does anyone really take seriously the conviction that every human being is sacred? We should neither doubt nor forget, as we pursue the inquiry of this chapter, that the sacredness of every human being has been, at best, a merely intellectual affirmation much more often than it has been a truly existential one.

I

"The International Bill of Human Rights", as it is sometimes called, consists of three documents. The first of these, the Universal Declaration of Human Rights (1948), speaks, in the Preamble, of "the inherent dignity . . . of all members of the human family" and of "the dignity and worth of the human person". In Article I, the Declaration proclaims: "All human beings . . . should act towards one another in a spirit of brotherhood." The second and third documents are the International Covenant on Civil and Political Rights (1976) and the International Covenant on Economic, Social and Cultural Rights (1976). The preamble common to both covenants echoes the Universal Declaration in speaking of "the inherent dignity . . . of all members of the human family". The preamble then states: "[T]hese rights derive from the inherent dignity of the human person. . . ." The Vienna Declaration and Programme of Action, adopted on June 25, 1993, by the UN-sponsored World Conference on Human Rights,[4] reaffirms this language in insisting that "all human rights derive from the dignity and worth inherent in the human person . . . ."

A regional human rights document, the American Declaration of the Rights and Duties of Man (1948), begins: "The American peoples have acknowledged the dignity of the individual. . . . The American states have on repeated occasions recognized that the essential rights of man are not derived from the fact that he is a national of a certain state, but are based upon attributes of his human personality." The preamble to the American Declaration proclaims: "All men . . . should conduct themselves as brothers to one another." Another regional document, the American Convention on Human Rights (1978), echoes the American Declaration in stating, in the preamble, that "the essential rights of man are not derived from one's being a national of a certain state, but are based upon attributes of the human personality." Similarly, the African [Banjul] Charter on Human and Peoples' Rights (1986) says, in the preamble, that "fundamental human rights stem from the attributes of human beings."

The idea of human rights that informs these various international human rights documents (and many others) is, then, in part, the idea that *there is something about each and every human being, simply as a human being, such that certain choices should be made and certain other choices rejected; in particular, certain things ought not to be done to any human being and certain other things ought to be done for every human being.*[5] The "every human being, simply as a human being," is represented in the Universal Declaration of Human Rights (Article 2) by this language: "Everyone is entitled to all the rights and freedoms set forth in this Declaration, without distinction of any kind, such as race, colour, sex, language, religion, political or other opinion, national or social origin, property, birth or other status."[6] Both the International Covenant on Economic, Social and Cultural Rights and the International Covenant on Civil and Political Rights contain identical language.

What, precisely, is that "something about each and every human being, simply as a human being"—what is it about us "simply as human beings"— such that, in particular, certain things ought not to be done to us and certain other things ought to be done for us? To ask the question in the words of the American Declaration, the American Convention, and the African Charter, what are the relevant "attributes" of each and every human being—the attributes on which "the essential rights of man" are based? The principal such attribute, according to the documents of the International Bill of Human Rights, is "the inherent dignity of all members of the human family" (from which, according to the documents, human rights derive).

What are we to make of such talk: talk about "the inherent dignity" of all human beings—about all human beings as members of one "family"—and about the importance, therefore, of all human beings acting toward one another "in a spirit of brotherhood"?[7] It is easy enough to understand such talk as *religious* talk.[8] (More about that later.) But is it possible, finally, to understand such talk in a nonreligious ("secular") sense? Is there, at least, a nonreligious equivalent for such talk—and, if so, what is it? Or must we conclude that the idea of human rights is indeed ineliminably religious, that a fundamental constituent of the idea, namely, *the conviction that every human being is sacred—that every human being is "inviolable",*[9] *has "inherent dignity", is "an end in himself", or the like*—is inescapably religious?[10]

II

What does it means to say that a conviction (belief, idea, worldview, etc.) is or is not "religious"?[11]

In *Sources of the Self: The Making of the Modern Identity*, Charles Taylor observes that "[t]he problem of the meaning of life is . . . on our agenda, however much we may jibe at the phrase".[12] The problem of the meaning of life does not arise for everyone, it is not on everyone's agenda (even if, as Taylor says, it is on "our" agenda). But it does arise for many. The problem can even arise *again* for someone, after it had been resolved, or repressed—someone who had been convinced of the meaningfulness of life, but whose conviction has gradually been eroded or has suddenly been shattered. A principal occasion of its arising (or arising again)—at least, of its arising in an existential, as distinct from merely intellectual, way—is a searing encounter with such a common but elemental event as sickness, old age, or death. Another principal occasion is an encounter, whether personal or vicarious, with evil and the terrible, primal suffering that evil causes. Such experiences, and experiences of other kinds, can leave one with a feeling that she is, or might be, a stranger, an alien, an exile, homeless, anxious, vulnerable, threatened, in a world, a universe, that is, finally and radically, unfamiliar, hostile, perhaps even pointless, absurd. Albert Camus wrote: "What, then, is that incalculable feeling that deprives the mind of the sleep necessary to life? A world that can be explained even with bad reasons is a familiar world. But, ... in a universe suddenly divested of illusions and lights, man feels an alien, a stranger. His exile is without remedy since he is deprived of the memory of a lost home or the hope of a promised land. This divorce between man and his life, the actor and his setting, is properly the feeling of absurdity."[13]

Because of its radically alienating character, any such experience can be an occasion of existential confrontation with the problem of meaning: *Am I indeed an alien, an exile, homeless, in a world, a universe, that is strange, hostile, pointless, absurd? Or, instead, is the world, finally and radically, familiar, even gracious; does the world have a point, is it a project; is the world, in that sense, meaningful: meaningfull, full of meaning rather than bereft of it (and therefore meaning-less, absurd)? In particular, is the world hospitable to me in my deep yearning to be at home, rooted, connected?*[14] For the person deep in the grip of, the person claimed by, the problem of meaning, "[t]he cry for meaning is a cry for ultimate relationship, for ultimate belonging", wrote Abraham Heschel. "It is a cry in which all pretensions are abandoned. Are we alone in the wilderness of time, alone in the dreadfully marvelous universe, of which we are a part and where we feel forever like strangers? Is there a Presence to live by? A Presence worth living for, worth dying for? Is there a way of living in the Presence? Is there a way of living compatible with the Presence?"[15]

One fundamental response to the problem of meaning is "religious": the trust that the world is finally meaningful, meaningful in a way hospitable to our deepest yearnings. The word "religion" derives from the Latin verb "religare", which means to bind together again that which was once bound but has since been torn or broken; to heal.[16] A "religious" vision, then, etymologically understood, is a vision of final and radical reconciliation, a set of beliefs about how one is or can be bound or connected to the world—to the "other" and to "nature"—and, above all, to Ultimate Reality in a profoundly intimate way. If a worldview is not grounded or embedded in a vision of the finally or ultimately meaningful nature of the world and of our place in it, it is a confusion, on the understanding of religion I am presenting here, to think of that worldview as "religious"—even if the worldview, like Marxism, is all-encompassing.[17]

Throughout human history it has been the religious "mystics" who have trusted most deeply and affirmed most passionately the ultimate meaningfulness of reality.[18] Although her experience that the world is ultimately meaningful is deeply personal, the religious mystic denies that the experience is reducible to an idiosyncratic, perhaps even pathological, psychological state. Notwithstanding its noetic quality, however, and for all its power, the mystical experience is often, if not invariably, transitory.[19] Moreover, not everyone is graced by such experience (or graced as often, or to the same degree). In the aftermath of mystical experience, therefore, or in its absence, fundamental questions about the meaningfulness of human existence—questions that so thoroughly pervade, and so relentlessly subvert, our lives—remain in need of answers that are intellectually satisfying and emotionally resonant. In Milan Kundera's *The Unbearable Lightness of Being*, the narrator, speaking of "the questions that had been going through Tereza's head since she was a child", says that "the only truly serious questions are ones that even a child can formulate. Only the most naive of questions are truly serious. They are the questions with no answers. A question with no answer is a barrier that cannot be breached. In other words, *it is questions with no answers that set the limits of human possibilities, describe the boundaries of human existence*."[20] Communities, especially historically extended communities—"traditions"—are the principal matrices and repositories of religious answers to such questions:[21] Who are we? Where did we come from; what is our origin, our beginning? Where are we going; what is our destiny, our end?[22] What is the meaning of suffering? Of evil? Of death? And there is the cardinal question, the question that comprises many of the others: Is the world ultimately meaningful or, instead, ultimately bereft of meaning, meaning-less, absurd? If any questions are fundamental, *these* questions—"religious or limit questions"[23]—are fundamental. Such questions—"naive" questions, "questions with no answers", "barriers that cannot be breached"—are "the most serious and difficult . . . that any human being or society must face. . . . To formulate such questions honestly and well, to respond to them with passion and rigor, is the work of all theology. . . . Religions ask and respond to such fundamental questions. . . . Theologians, by definition, risk an intellectual life on the wager that religious traditions can be studied as authentic responses to just such questions."[24]

※※※

To say that a conviction is "religious", therefore, is to say that the conviction is embedded in a religious vision or cosmology, that it is an aspect, a constituent, of such a vision: a vision according to which the world is ultimately meaningful (in a way hospitable to our deepest yearnings). (Not every religious tradition tells the same story about the way in which the world is ultimately meaningful; often the stories are different, even if sometimes the stories are quite similar.) To ask if the conviction that every human being is sacred—the conviction that every human being is "inviolable", has "inherent dignity", is "an end in himself", or the like—is inescapably religious is to ask if the conviction can be embedded in, if it can be supported by—or, at least, if it can cohere with—either an antireligious cosmology, according to which the world is, at the end of the day, not meaningful but meaningless, or a cosmological agnosticism that neither affirms nor denies the ultimate meaningfulness of the world.

Real moralities—the moralities that various human communities have actually lived—have always been cosmologically embedded: In every human community across time and space, "moral norms are closely linked to beliefs about the facts of human life and the world in which human life is set. . . . To know what people find good in human action, we must know something about the powers and vulnerabilities they find characteristically human, and about how they explain the constraints that nature, power, finitude, and mortality impose on persons. . . . [W]hen they formulate moral norms and impose them on themselves and others[, persons] are trying to formulate relationships between realities and human purposes that allow them 'to live as [they] would in a world that is the way it is.'"[25] The conviction that every human being is sacred is cosmologically embedded; it is (as we will see) embedded in a religious cosmology.[26] Indeed, in one or another version the conviction is embedded in more than one religious cosmology.[27] The question before us is whether the conviction can be embedded in (or if it can cohere with) either an antireligious cosmology or, at least, a cosmological agnosticism.

III

As I said, it is easy to understand talk about "the inherent dignity" of all human beings and related talk—for example, about all human beings as members of one "family"—as *religious* talk. But can we understand such talk in a secular sense? I now want to present a religious version of talk about the inherent dignity of all human beings; that is, I want to present a religious version—the Christian version, or at least *a* Christian version—of the conviction that every human being is sacred. We will then be in a better position to discern whether there is—indeed, whether there can be—an intelligible secular version of the conviction.

For Christians, the basic shape of the good life is indicated by the instruction given by Jesus at a Passover seder on the eve of his execution: "I give you a new commandment: love one another; you must love one another just as I have loved you."[28] The "one another" is radically inclusive: "You have heard how it was said, You will love your neighbor and hate your enemy. But I say this to you, love your enemies and pray for those who persecute you; so that you may be children of your Father in heaven, for he causes his sun to rise on the bad as well as the good, and sends down rain to fall on the upright and the wicked alike. For if you love those who love you, what reward will you get? Do not even the tax collectors do as much? And if you save your greetings for your brothers, are you doing anything exceptional? Do not even the gentiles do as much? You must therefore set no bounds to your love, just as your heavenly Father sets none to his."[29]

But, *why* should we "love one another"? The answer, in the vision of Judaism and Christianity, a vision nourished by what David Tracy has called "the analogical imagination",[30] is that the Other (the outsider, the stranger, the alien), too, no less than oneself and the members of one's family or of one's tribe or nation or race or religion, is a "child" of God—God the creator and sustainer of the universe, imag(in)ed, analogically, as loving "parent"[31]—and therefore a "sister"/"brother". As Hilary Putnam has written, the moral image central to what Putnam calls the Jerusalem-based religions "stresse[s] equality and also fraternity, as in the metaphor of the whole human race as One Family, of all women and men as sisters and brothers."[32] (At the beginning of its "Pastoral Letter on Catholic Social Teaching and the U.S. Economy", titled *Economic Justice for All*, the National Conference of Catholic Bishops wrote: "This letter is a personal invitation to Catholics to use the resources of our faith, the strength of our economy, and the opportunities of our democracy to shape a society that better protects the dignity and basic rights of *our sisters and brothers both in this land and around the world.*"[33]) In a recent essay on "The Spirituality of the Talmud", Ben Zion Bokser and Baruch M. Bokser state: "From this conception of man's place in the universe comes the sense of the supreme sanctity of all human life. 'He who destroys one person has dealt a blow at the entire universe, and he who sustains or saves one person has sustained the whole world.'"[34] They continue:

> The sanctity of life is not a function of national origin, religious affiliation, or social status. In the sight of God, the humble citizen is the equal of the person who occupies the highest office. As one talmudist put it: "Heaven and earth I call to witness, whether it be an Israelite or pagan, man or woman, slave or maidservant, according to the work of every human being doth the Holy

Spirit rest upon him." . . . As the rabbis put it: "We are obligated to feed non-Jews residing among us even as we feed Jews; we are obligated to visit their sick even as we visit the Jewish sick; we are obligated to attend to the burial of their dead even as we attend to the burial of the Jewish dead."[35]

Friedrich Nietzsche was relentlessly critical of what he called "the concept of the 'equal value of men before God' ". That concept, he wrote,

> is extraordinarily harmful; one forbade actions and attitudes that were in themselves among the prerogatives of the strongly constituted—as if they were in themselves unworthy of men. One brought the entire tendency of the strong into disrepute when one erected the protective measures of the weakest (those who were weakest also when confronting themselves) as a form of value.
>
> Confusion went so far that one branded the very virtuosi of life (whose autonomy offered the sharpest antithesis to the vicious and unbridled) with the most opprobrious names. Even now one believes one must disapprove of a Cesare Borgia; that is simply laughable. The church has excommunicated German emperors on account of their vices: as if a monk or priest had any right to join in a discussion about what a Frederick II may demand of himself. A Don Juan is sent to hell: that is very naive. Has it been noticed that in heaven all interesting men are missing?— Just a hint to the girls as to where they can best find their salvation.— If one reflects with some consistency, and moreover with a deepened insight into what a "great man" is, no doubt remains that the church sends all "great men" to hell—it fights *against* all "greatness of man."
>
>   . . .
>
> The degeneration of the rulers and the ruling classes has been the cause of the greatest mischief in history! Without the Roman Caesars and Roman society, the insanity of Christianity would never have come to power.
>
> When lesser men begin to doubt whether higher men exist, then the danger is great! And one ends by discovering that there is *virtue* also among the lowly and subjugated, the poor in spirit, and that *before God* men are equal—which has so far been the *non plus ultra* of nonsense on earth! For ultimately, the higher men measured themselves according to the standard of virtue of slaves—found they were "proud," etc., found all their higher qualities reprehensible.
>
> When Nero and Caracalla sat up there, the paradox arose: "the lowest man is worth more than the man up there!" And the way was prepared for an image of God that was as remote as possible from the image of the most powerful—the god on the cross![36]

One might respond to the religious vision sketched here, if not like Nietzsche, then this way: "Even if I assume, for the sake of argument, that the Other is a 'child' of God and therefore my 'sister/brother', still, why should I love the Other? In particular, why should I give a damn about the well-being of her or him who is, in some deep sense, my sister or my brother?" For us—or, at least, for most of us—it is a fundamental conviction, born not merely of our own experience, but of the experience of the historically extended communities ("traditions") that for many of us have been formative, that an important constituent of one's own well-being—of one's authentic flourishing as a human being—is concern for the well-being of one's sisters and brothers. We believe, based on that experience, that a life of loving connection to one's sisters and brothers is, to that extent, a flourishing life and that a life of unloving—uncaring—alienation from one's sisters and brothers is, to that extent, a withering life. This fundamental conviction about human good—about what it means to be (truly, fully) human, about what is of real and ultimate value in life, about what makes a life most deeply meaningful[37]—is, for us, bedrock; this is where our spade is turned.[38] There might be little of resonance for us to say, if indeed there is anything, *to* one who rejects the conviction—which, it bears emphasis, is not necessarily, for a person whose conviction it is, a religious conviction. But there is this to say *about* one who rejects it: He is, by our lights, no less in the grip of a pathology of estrangement than if he were to reject that an important constituent of one's own well-being is concern for the well-being of one's child, or spouse, or parent.[39] The serious question among us—some of whom count ourselves religious, but others of whom do not—is not whether a life of loving connection to our sisters and brothers is (to that extent) a flourishing life, but this: "Who is my sister? Who is my brother?"[40] Or, in a different but spiritually equivalent terminology: "Who is my neighbor?"[41]—which is the very question to which, according to Luke's Gospel, Jesus responded with the Parable of the Good Samaritan.[42] "Plato got moral philosophy off on the wrong foot. He led moral philosophers to concentrate on the rather rare figure of the psychopath, the person who has no concern for any human being other than himself. Moral philosophy has systematically neglected the much more common case: the person whose treatment of a rather narrow range of featherless bipeds is morally impeccable, but who remain indifferent to the suffering of those outside this range, the ones he or she thinks of as pseudohumans."[43]

One response to the "who is my sister/brother" question, a religious response, is that the Other, too, is, in the deepest possible sense—i.e., as a child of God—your sister/brother. To fail to "see" the Other as sister/brother is (according to this religious response) to succumb to a kind of blindness: blindness to the true nature or being both of the Other and of oneself, which nature/being consists partly in a profound kinship (connection, relatedness) between self and Other. And to fail to love the Other as sister/brother—worse, to hate the Other—is to succumb to the pathology of estrangement; it is, to that extent, to wither as a human being rather than to flourish.[44] That the estrangement is radical—indeed, that it is estrangement even from "the Lord your God"[45]—and involves the most fundamental and enduring failure to achieve human well-being, is emphasized in the searing "Last Judgment" passage of Matthew:

> When the Son of man comes in his glory, escorted by all the angels, then he will take his seat on his throne of glory. All nations will be assembled before him and he will separate people from one another as the shepherd separates sheep from goats. He will place the sheep on his right hand and the goats on his left. Then the King will say to those on his right hand, "Come, you whom my Father has blessed, take as your heritage the kingdom prepared for you since the foundation of the world. For I was hungry and you gave me food, I was thirsty and you gave me drink, I was a stranger and you made me welcome, lacking clothes and you clothed me, sick and you visited me, in prison and you came to see me." Then the upright will say to him in reply, "Lord, when did we see you hungry and feed you, or thirsty and give you drink? When did we see you a stranger and make you welcome, lacking clothes and clothe you? When did we find you sick or in prison and go to see you?" And the King will answer, "In truth I tell you, in so far as you did this to one of the least of these brothers of mine, you did it to me." Then he will say to those on his left hand, "Go away from me, with your curse upon you, to the eternal fire prepared for the devil and his angels. For I was hungry and you never gave me food, I was thirsty and you never gave me anything to drink, I was a stranger and you never made me welcome, lacking clothes and you never clothed me, sick and in prison and you never visited me." Then it will be their turn to ask, "Lord, when did we see you hungry or thirsty, a stranger or lacking clothes, sick or in prison, and did not come to your help?" Then he will answer, "In truth I tell you, in so far as you neglected to do this to one of the least of these, you neglected to do it to me." And they will go away to eternal punishment, and the upright to eternal life.[46]

The response of the Gospel to "Who is my sister/brother/neighbor?"—and kindred responses—are religious in the fundamental sense that such a response is embedded in a religious vision of the world and of our place in it. There are differences among religious visions within the relevant range—sometimes large differences, sometimes small. The analogical imagination does not yield precisely the same vision in every time or in every place. How a person or a community arrives at a religious vision is a difficult question—as is the question how one brings another to such a vision. Moreover, different religious traditions, and even different theologies within the same broad religious tradition, proffer different answers to such questions.

It bears emphasis that a theistic religious vision does not necessarily include (though some conventional theistic religious visions do include) a conception of "God" as a kind of divine legislator, issuing directives for human conduct.[47] Indeed, a religious person might well believe that such a "God"—such an idol—is dead.[48] The imperative to "love one another as I have loved you" can be understood (and in my view should be understood) not as a piece of divine legislation, but as a (truly, fully) human response to the question of how to live. However, to say that the response is a human one does not entail that it is not also a religious response. What makes the imperative a *religious* human response and not merely a secular one is that the response is the existential yield of a religious conviction about how the world (including we-in-the-world) hangs together: in particular, the conviction that the Other is, finally, one's own sister/brother—and should receive, therefore, the gift of one's loving concern.[49]

Indeed, a theistic religious vision is not necessarily attended by confident, much less dogmatic, God-talk. (I have developed the point elsewhere.[50]) If that statement seems strange, consider what one scholar has recently stressed about Thomas Aquinas, perhaps the greatest Christian theologian: "[M]uch of [Aquinas's] doctrine about talking about God is in truth a carefully qualified *via negativa*. . . . Aquinas would simply agree with modern antitheists that we cannot say what God is; and that human language is inadequate to the claimed reality of God; and that there is something improper even in saying that God is a being. But not only does Aquinas think that none of these admissions disqualifies him from theism; he actually thinks that the theist should make these admissions."[51] As Aquinas understood, to insist that we cannot say what God is—that we can only follow a *via negativa* and say what God is not—is not to deny that we can try to mediate our experience of Ultimate Reality analogically—for example, by speaking of God as *like* a loving "parent", and of the Other as *like* a "sister"/"brother". In addition to his "carefully qualified *via negativa* . . . Aquinas also has, of course, a *via positiva* about God-talk, namely, the 'doctrine of analogy.' . . ."[52] However, to insist, with Aquinas, that in talking about God we must either follow a *via negativa* or speak analogically is *not* to say that God-talk is merely metaphorical or figurative or poetic. Aquinas was, after all, a committed theological realist.[53]

❦

To forestall predictable misunderstanding, let me make two points. First, in sketching a religious version of the conviction that every human being is sacred, I have relied on the religious materials I know best. In relying primarily on Christian materials, however, I do not mean to suggest that there are not ample materials in other religious traditions out of which one can construct, or reconstruct, a relevantly similar version of the conviction. Just as there are differences among the precise religious visions adhered to by different sects within Christianity, there are differences among the precise visions adhered to by different world religions. (Again, the analogical imagination does not yield precisely the same vision in every time or place.) But such differences as there are ought not to obscure the fact that the experience of all human beings as sacred is widely shared among different sects and religions, albeit expressed—

mediated—differently in different traditions. And that common ("ecumenical") ground helps to explain the emergence of the idea of human rights as a point of convergence among peoples from different religious traditions.[54]

Second, in presenting a religious version of the conviction that every human being is sacred, and in relying primarily on Christian materials in doing so, I do not mean to deny that the lived practice, as distinct from the professed ideals, of every religious tradition, including Christianity, offers at best equivocal support for what many of us consider to be basic human rights.[55] Indeed, I do not mean to deny even that the professed ideals of religious traditions—at least on some quite plausible construals of those ideals—fail to support, and even oppose, some such rights. Christianity is a conspicuous example.[56] There has been an obvious tendency on the part even of the world's "great" religious traditions to tribalism, racism, and sexism—and worse. ("[T]he great religious ages were notable for their indifference to human rights in the contemporary sense. They were notorious not only for acquiescence in poverty, inequality, exploitation and oppression but for enthusiastic justifications of slavery, persecution, abandonment of small children, torture, genocide."[57]) No person who takes seriously the resources of one or another religious tradition should deny "the brokenness and ambiguity of every tradition" or repress "one's own inevitably ambivalent relationship to [the tradition]."[58] A self-critical attitude toward one's own tradition is "the route to liberation from the negative realities of [the] tradition."[59] As David Tracy has emphasized,

> For believers to be unable to learn from secular feminists on the patriarchal nature of most religions or to be unwilling to be challenged by Feuerbach, Darwin, Marx, Freud, or Nietzsche is to refuse to take seriously the religion's own suspicions on the existence of those fundamental distortions named sin, ignorance, or illusion. The interpretations of believers will, of course, be grounded in some fundamental trust in, and loyalty to, the Ultimate Reality both disclosed and concealed in one's own religious tradition. But fundamental trust, as any experience of friendship can teach, is not immune to either criticism or suspicion. A religious person will ordinarily fashion some hermeneutics of trust, even one of friendship and love, for the religious classics of her or his tradition. But, as any genuine understanding of friendship shows, friendship often demands both critique and suspicion. A belief in a pure and innocent love is one of the less happy inventions of the romantics. A friendship that never includes critique and even, when appropriate, suspicion is a friendship barely removed from the polite and wary communication of strangers. As Buber showed, in every I-Thou encounter, however transient, we encounter some new dimension of reality. But if that encounter is to prove more than transitory, the difficult ways of friendship need a trust powerful enough to risk itself in critique and suspicion. To claim that this may be true of all our other loves but not true of our love for, and trust in, our religious tradition makes very little sense either hermeneutically or religiously.[60]

IV

The religious-cosmological context of the conviction that every human is sacred—the context I sketched in the preceding section—is not appealing to everyone. It was very unappealing to Nietzsche. And even for one to whom it is greatly appealing, it might not be credible. It is not credible, for example, to Jürgen Habermas, who has written: "[By confronting] the conscientious question about deliverance for the annihilated victims[,] we become aware of the limits of that transcendence from within which is directed to this world. But this does not enable us to ascertain the *countermovement* of a compensating transcendence from beyond. That the universal covenant of fellowship would be able to be effective retroactively, toward the past, only in the weak medium of our memory . . . falls short of our moral need. But the painful experience of a deficit is still not a sufficient argument for the assumption of an 'absolute freedom which saves in death.'"[61]

Even if one finds incredible the religious-cosmological context of the conviction that every human being is sacred, the question persists whether the religious version of the conviction isn't finally the only intelligible version. Can there be an intelligible secular version—an intelligible version not finally rooted in a religious vision of the world and of our place in it? Can the conviction be embedded in, or even cohere with, either an antireligious cosmology or a cosmological agnosticism? Consider Glenn Tinder's statement:

> Nietzsche's stature is owing to the courage and profundity that enabled him to make all this unmistakably clear. He delineated with overpowering eloquence the consequences of giving up Christianity, *and every like view of the universe and humanity*. His approval of those consequences and his hatred of Christianity give force to his argument. Many would like to think that there are no consequences—that we can continue treasuring the life and welfare, the civil rights and political authority, of every person without believing in a God who renders such attitudes and conduct compelling. Nietzsche shows that we cannot. We cannot give up the Christian God—*and the transcendence given other names in other faiths*—and go on as before. We must give up Christian morality too. If the God-man is nothing more than an illusion, the same thing is true of the idea that every individual possesses incalculable worth. The standard of *agape* collapses. It becomes explicable only on Nietzsche's terms: as a device by which the weak and failing exact from the strong and distinguished a deference they do not deserve. Thus the spiritual center of Western politics fades and vanishes.[62]

(Tinder's emphasis on the Christian tradition will surely and understandably be, for some non-Christians, a provocative distraction from his fundamental point. Tinder's (and Nietzsche's) point loses nothing, however, if the emphasis is placed not on the Christian tradition but on the Jewish, for example. Recall the comment on the Talmud quoted earlier in this chapter.[63])

Is Tinder right? We might agree with Charles Larmore that morality is now widely understood (or, at least, understood by many of us, religious or not, who read books like this one) to be independent of God conceived of as the supreme moral legislator.[64] But is it plausible to think that morality can be independent of *any* cosmological convictions—any convictions about how the world (including we-in-the-world) hangs together? After Nietzsche, we may ask if it is plausible to think that a morality embedded in religious convictions about how the world hangs together can be more or less equivalent to a morality embedded in the conviction that the world is nothing but a great cosmic process utterly bereft of ultimate meaning and therefore, from a human point of view, absurd.[65] Nietzsche declared: " 'Naiveté: as if morality could survive when the *God* who sanctions it is missing! The 'beyond' absolutely necessary if faith in morality is to be maintained."[66] Writing of "anthropocentrism, [which] by abolishing all horizons of significance, threatens us with a loss of meaning and hence a trivialization of our predicament", Charles Taylor has said: "At one moment, we understand our situation as one of high tragedy, alone in a silent universe, without intrinsic meaning, condemned to create value. But at a later moment, the same doctrine, by its own inherent bent, yields a flattened world, in which there aren't very meaningful choices because there aren't any crucial issues."[67]

Consider a cosmology according to which the world is, finally and radically, meaningless—or, even if meaningful in some sense, not meaningful in a way hospitable to our deepest yearnings for what Heschel called "ultimate relationship, ultimate belonging".[68] Consider, for example, Clarence Darrow's bleak vision (as recounted by Paul Edwards):

> Darrow, one of the most compassionate men who ever lived, . . . concluded that life was an "awful joke." . . . Darrow offered as one of his reasons the apparent aimlessness of all that happens. "This weary old world goes on, begetting, with birth and with living and with death," he remarked in his moving plea for the boy-murderers Loeb and Leopold, "and all of it is blind from the beginning to the end." Elsewhere he wrote: "Life is like a ship on the sea, tossed by every wave and by every wind; a ship headed for no port and no harbor, with no rudder, no compass, no pilot; simply floating for a time, then lost in the waves." In addition to the aimlessness of life and the universe, there is the fact of death. "I love my friends," wrote Darrow, "but they all must come to a tragic end." Death is more terrible the more one is attached to things in the world. Life, he concludes, is "not worthwhile," and he adds . . . that "it is an unpleasant interruption of nothing, and the best thing you can say of it is that it does not last long."[69]

One prominent contemporary proponent of a Darrowian cosmology, the physicist (and Nobel laureate) Steven Weinberg, "finds his own world-view 'chilling and impersonal'. He cannot understand people who treat the absence of God and of God's heaven as unimportant."[70]

Where is the place in a cosmological view like Weinberg's for the conviction that every human being is sacred—the conviction that every human being is inviolable, has inherent dignity, is an end in himself, and so on—to gain a foothold? Indeed, embedded in the view that the world is merely a process devoid of ultimate meaning, what would the conviction that every human being is sacred even mean? If the only intelligible version of the conviction is religious, then cosmological agnosticism, which neither affirms nor denies the ultimate meaningfulness of the world, entails agnosticism about the sacredness *vel non* of human beings.

❦

In writing recently about abortion and euthanasia, Ronald Dworkin has asserted that "[w]e almost all accept, as the inarticulate assumption behind much of our experience and conviction, that human life in all its forms is *sacred*."[71] Dworkin then observes that "[f]or some of us, [the sacredness of human life] is a matter of religious faith; for others, of secular but deep philosophical belief."[72] Now, many folks who believe that every human being is sacred do not count themselves religious; some of them even embrace antireligious views like Weinberg's. The question nonetheless persists whether there is an intelligible secular version of the conviction about the sacredness of every human being. Imagine a nonreligious person—a person who is either antireligious or religiously agnostic—saying: "That every human being is sacred is not, for me, a religious tenet; it is a secular but deep philosophical belief." We can ask: "Please tell us something about the constellation of views—views about how the world, including we-in-the-world, hangs together—in which, for you, that philosophical belief is embedded." Imagine this answer: "For me the conviction that every human being is sacred is not only axiomatic; it is unconnected to any of my views about how the world hangs together." (Perhaps the answer includes this statement: "I have no confident views about how the world hangs together. I'm agnostic about all such 'religious' or 'cosmological' matters.") It seems, then, that the premise that every human being is sacred is, for our nonreligious interlocutor, less a conviction about (a part of) the world than a kind of free-floating aesthetic preference. In Dworkin's view, however, the premise is, even for most nonreligious persons who hold it, much more than an aesthetic preference.

In his book on abortion and euthanasia, Dworkin writes that "one of [his] main claims [is] that there is a secular as well as a religious interpretation of the idea that human life is sacred."[73] Dworkin purports to explain, in his book, how the conviction that every human being (or, as Dworkin says, "life") is sacred "may be, and commonly is, interpreted in a secular as well as in a conventionally religious way."[74] To say that a human life is sacred is partly to say, according to Dworkin, "that it has *intrinsic* and *objective* value quite apart from any value it might have to the person whose life it is."[75] Emphasizing in particular the notion of "intrinsic" value, Dworkin writes: "[M]uch of our life is based on the idea that objects or events can be valuable in themselves. . . . [T]he idea that some events or objects are valuable in and of themselves . . . is . . . a familiar part of our experience. . . . The idea of intrinsic value is commonplace, and it has a central place in our shared scheme of values and opinions. . . . Something is intrinsically valuable . . . if its value is *independent* of what people happen to enjoy or want or need or what is good for them."[76]

Dworkin's comments about "intrinsic" value obscure rather than clarify that value is always and everywhere value *for* someone(s) or something(s). The notion that something is valuable independently of a beneficial relation to anyone or anything—whether a human being, a nonhuman but living entity, or God—is perfectly opaque. Putting aside things that are values either for nonhuman entities or for God, "the category of values is anthropocentric, in that it corresponds to interests which can only take root in creatures with something approaching our own affective make-up. . . . [V]alues are only ascribable from points of view constituted by human patterns of affective response. A wholly dispassionate eye would be as blind to them as a black-and-white camera to chromatic colors."[77] The relevant distinction here is between "intrinsic" value and "instrumental" value. To say that something has intrinsic value is to say, not that something has value even if it has no value for anyone (not even God) or anything—what would *that* mean?—but that something has value for someone (or something) *not merely as a means to an end but as an end in itself.* And to say that something has "objective" value and not (or not merely) "subjective" value is to say that something has value for someone (for example, that it is good for her, that it is conducive to or perhaps even constitutive of her flourishing) *even if she is unaware that it has value for her—indeed, even if she believes that it has disvalue for her.*[78] Now, that something has both objective and intrinsic value for someone does not mean that it is sacred. An end to my itch has both objective and intrinsic value for me, but it is not thereby sacred. For some persons who count themselves religious, to say that every human being is sacred is to say (speaking analogically) that every human being is the beloved child of God (God who is love). For persons who do not count themselves religious, what does it mean to say that every human being is sacred?

According to Dworkin, "[T]he nerve of the sacred lies in the value we attach to a process or enterprise or project rather than to its results considered independently from how they were produced."[79] The sacredness of human beings is rooted, for nonreligious persons, in two basic facts about human beings (argues Dworkin). First, every human being is "the highest product of natural creation. . . . [T]he idea that human beings are special among natural creations is offered to explain why it is horrible that even a single human individual life should be extinguished."[80] Second, "each developed human being is the product not just of natural creation, but also of the kind of deliberative human creative force that we honor in honoring art."[81] "The idea that each individual human life is inviolable is therefore rooted . . . in two combined and intersecting bases of the sacred: natural *and* human creation."[82]

> The life of a single human organism commands respect and protection, then, no matter in what form or shape, because of the complex creative investment it represents and because of our wonder at the . . . processes that produce new lives from old ones, at the processes of nation and community and language through which a human being will come to absorb and continue hundreds of generations of cultures and forms of life and value, and, finally, when mental life has begun and flourishes, at the process of internal personal creation and judgment by which a person will make and remake himself, a mysterious, inescapable process in which we each participate, and which is therefore the most powerful and inevitable source of empathy and communion we have with every other creature who faces the same frightening challenge. The horror we feel in the willful destruction of a human life reflects our shared inarticulate sense of the intrinsic importance of each of these dimensions of investment.[83]

This, then, is Dworkin's rendering of a secular version of the conviction that every human being is sacred. Even if in truth the world is nothing but a process bereft of ultimate meaning, every human being is nonetheless sacred, according to Dworkin, because "each human being . . . is a creative masterpiece"[84]— a masterpiece of "natural *and* human creation."[85]

Does Dworkin succeed in portraying an intelligible secular version of the conviction that every human being is sacred? Important questions need to be answered—or so it seems to me. How does the fact that something is a masterpiece of natural and human creation make that something not merely a creative masterpiece but sacred? What is the precise sense of "sacred" in play in Dworkin's portrayal? Let us agree that every human being is a creative masterpiece and, as such, inspires (or should inspire) awe in us. That something justifiably inspires awe in us, however—James Joyce's *Ulysses*, for example— entails neither that we believe it to be sacred nor that it is sacred.

To say that every human being is sacred is ordinarily to say something about (what is believed to be) the true nature of every human being. Something might inspire awe in us, and we might therefore value it—it might have value for us, both objective value and intrinsic value—because it is sacred (or, at least, because we believe it to be sacred). But to suggest, as in his book Dworkin at least sometimes does, that something is sacred *because* it inspires awe in us, because we value it, is to reverse the ordinary order of things. (Recall, for example, Dworkin's statement that "the nerve of the sacred lies in the value we attach to a process or enterprise or project rather than to its results considered independently from how they were produced."[86] Or his statement that "[t]he life of a single human organism commands respect and protection . . . because of our wonder at the . . . processes that produce new lives from old ones . . ."[87]) Dworkin seems to be using "sacred" in what we can call a weak, or "subjective", sense—something (e.g., a human life) is sacred *because,* or *in the sense that,* it inspires awe in us and we attach great value to it—rather than in the strong, or "objective", sense—something is sacred and *therefore* it inspires awe in us and we attach great value to it. Moreover, in using "sacred" in the weak or subjective sense, Dworkin is trading on the greater strength of the objective sense in which the word is ordinarily used.

That rhetorical strategy, however, is problematic. The premise that every human being is sacred-in-the-subjective-sense cannot begin to bear the weight of the premise that every human being is sacred-in-the-objective-sense. Imagine someone saying to a Bosnian Serb: "The Bosnian Muslim, too, no less than you, is sacred. It is wrong for you to rape her." If "sacred" is meant in the subjective sense, the Bosnian Serb can reply: "Sacred to you and yours, perhaps, but not to me and mine. In the scheme of things, we happen not to attach much value to her life." By contrast, "sacred" in the objective sense is not fundamentally a matter of "sacred to you" or "sacred to me"; it is, rather, a matter of how things really are. (One might disbelieve the ontology, but that a different problem.) If every human being is sacred in the objective sense, then, in violating the Bosnian Muslim, the Bosnian Serb does not merely violate what some of us attach great value to; he violates the very order of creation.

Now, Dworkin might insist that he's been misunderstood. He might insist that he means "sacred" in the objective sense, and that on his account of "sacred" the Bosnian Serb is indeed violating the very order of creation. He might say that the Bosnian Muslim has intrinsic value even for the Bosnian Serb—and objective value too: that the welfare of the Bosnian Muslim is an intrinsic good for the Bosnian Serb even if the Bosnian Serb will remain forever unaware of that fact. But if Dworkin wants to respond in some such way, then he must forswear any explanation of the sacredness of someone or something in terms of, or by reference to, "the value we attach to" that someone or something. He must explain it solely in other terms. It is not clear, however, what that other explanation might be; in particular, it is not obvious that either a secular cosmology or cosmological agnosticism can yield the requisite conviction about how things really are. How do we get from "the universe is (or might be) nothing but a cosmic process bereft of ultimate meaning" to "every human being is nonetheless sacred (in the strong or objective sense)"? Even in an absurd universe, a universe bereft of transcendent meaning, there can be creative masterpieces. But, again, that something is a creative masterpiece and understandably inspires awe in us entails neither that it is sacred nor even that we believe it to be sacred (in the strong sense).

Has Dworkin identified an intelligible secular version of the conviction that every human being is sacred? It seems not, if "sacred" is meant in the objective sense. If, however, "sacred" is meant in the subjective sense, perhaps Dworkin has identified an intelligible secular version. But if he has, Dworkin's secularized claim that every human being is sacred is a substantially weaker claim—it claims much less—than the paradigmatic claim about the sacredness of all human beings. In any event, Dworkin has said nothing to diminish suspicion that the conviction that every human being is sacred—*sacred in the strong/objective sense, sacred because of how the world really is, and not because of what we attach value to in the world*—is inescapably religious. The challenge is to identify an intelligible secular version of *that* conviction. In his review of Dworkin's book for the *Times Literary Supplement*, Robert Grant concluded that "[i]n *Life's Dominion*, Professor Dworkin makes considerable play with, indeed frankly exploits, the idea of the sacred, but shows no understanding of it."[88]

V

If—*if*—the conviction that every human being is sacred is inescapably religious, it follows that the idea of human rights is ineliminably religious, because the conviction is an essential, even foundational, constituent of the idea. The possibility that the idea of human rights is ineliminably religious poses a problem for the secular enthusiast of human rights, whether she be antireligious or only agnostic. One response to the problem is to try to defend human rights claims, not by relying on the conviction that every human being is sacred, but by means of a justificatory strategy that avoids reliance on that conviction— that avoids reliance, therefore, on "the idea of human rights". I now want to identify and comment briefly on two such strategies.[89]

A. The Definitional Strategy

> *[T]here is today no way of "proving" that napalming babies is bad except by asserting it (in a louder and louder voice), or by defining it as so, early in one's game, and then later slipping it through, in a whisper, as a conclusion.*[90]

The idea of human rights, again, is that because every human being is, simply as a human being, sacred, certain choices should be made and certain other choices rejected; in particular, certain things ought not to be done to any human being and certain other things ought to be done for every human being. The definitional strategy is a different way of trying to defend human rights claims—especially claims about what ought not to be done to any human being or about what ought to be done for every human being (or about both)—in particular, a way that does not rely on the premise that human beings are sacred. According to the definitional strategy, certain things ought not to be done to any human being and certain other things ought to be done for every human being simply because "the moral point of view"—understood as the "impartial" or "universal" point of view—requires it. In commenting on "that sort of impartiality that constitutes the moral point of view", James Griffin has written that "[w]e all agree that to look at things morally is to look at them, in some sense or other, impartially, granting every person some sort of equal status. Of course, we should have to make this notion of equal status more determinate—say through one interpretation or other of the Ideal Observer or Ideal Contractor. In any case, principles of equality can be principles of impartiality in this sense: they can express the spirit with which one will, if one is moral, consider the facts of the matter."[91] As Bernard Williams has observed, "[I]t is often thought that no concern is truly moral unless it is marked by this universality. For morality, the ethical constituency is always the same: the universal constituency. An allegiance to a smaller group, the loyalties to family or country, would have to be justified from the outside inward, by an argument that explained how it was a good thing that people should have allegiances that were less than universal."[92]

The definitional strategy is deeply problematic, because it fails even to address what David Tracy has called the "limit-question" of morality: "Why be moral at all?"[93] (Richard Rorty has contrasted the "the rational egoist's question 'Why should I be moral?'" to "the much more frequently posed question 'Why should I care about a stranger, a person who is no kin to me, a person whose habits I find disgusting?'"[94] But, given the conventional understanding of the "moral" point of view as the "impartial" or "universal" point of view, the question "Why should I be moral?" just *is* the question "Why should I care about a stranger?") The definitional strategy fails to respond to this fundamental challenge:

> You claim that we ought not to do certain things to any human being, and that we ought to do certain other things for every human being. We ask why. You say that the moral (impartial, universal) point of view requires it. For the sake of argument we will stipulate to your definition of "moral". Our challenge remains, but now we'll express it this way: Why ought we to adopt "the moral point of view"; why ought we to be "moral" in the stipulated sense? Why ought we to give a damn about being "moral" or doing the "moral" thing? We are right back where we started: What reasons—what real-world, flesh-and-blood reasons—are there for doing for every human being those certain things that the moral point of view requires be done for every human being and for not doing to any human being those certain other things that the moral point of view forbids be done to any human being?

The fundamental challenge to each and every human rights claim—in particular, to each and every claim about what ought not to be done to any human being or what ought to be done for every human being—is a demand for reasons. James Nickel has distinguished between two different interpretations of the demand: one according to which it is "a demand for prudential reasons" and another according to which it is "a request for moral reasons".[95] (The distinction between "prudential" and "moral" is deeply problematic, at least for anyone with an Aristotelian understanding of morality.[96] But let's move on.) The second interpretation, Nickel suggests, "assumes that one's audience has transcended egoism and is prepared to accept arguments that appeal directly to what is reasonable from the moral point of view, whether or not it can be shown that adopting this perspective is likely to promote the long-term interests of the individual."[97] But the problem is larger, much larger, than "egoism": One might favor, not just oneself, or even just one's family, but just one's tribe or nation or race or religion. The assumption that those to whom human rights claims are addressed have "transcended" such favoritism is wildly implausible.[98] The fundamental challenge to human rights claims is a real-world challenge: Many to whom such claims are addressed have conspicuously not adopted anything like "the moral (impartial, universal) point of view". The moral point of view is not a justificatory basis for human rights claims—at least, not a fundamental basis. The moral point of view is itself in dire need of justification, especially in a world—*our* world, the *real* world—that is often fiercely partial/ local rather than impartial/universal. The real world is full of what Primo Levi called "us-ism": "Those on the Rosenstrasse who risked their lives for Jews did not express opposition to antisemitic policies per se. They displayed primarily what the late Primo Levi, a survivor of Auschwitz, called 'selfishness extended to the person closest to you . . . us-ism.' In most of the stories that I have heard of Aryans who risked their lives for Jews to whom they were married, they withdrew to safety, one by one, the moment their loved ones were released. Their protests bring home to us the iron limits, the tragically narrow borders, of us-ism."[99]

The question remains: What reasons are there for adopting "the moral point of view"? Charles Taylor, commenting critically on moral theories that are variations on the definitional strategy—in particular, theories that exclude discourse about human well-being—has put the point this way:

> [Such theories] leave us with nothing to say to someone who asks why he should be moral. . . . But this could be misleading, if we seemed to be asking how we could convince someone who saw none of the point of our moral beliefs. There is nothing we can do to 'prove' we are right to such a person. But imagine him to be asking another question: he could be asking us to make plain the point of our moral code, in articulating what's uniquely valuable in cleaving to these injunctions [e.g., act 'impartially']. Then the implication of these theories is that we have nothing to say which can impart insight. We can wax rhetorical and propagandize, but we can't say what's good or valuable about [the injunctions], or why they command assent.[100]

The definitional strategy is unavailing. A strategy is not definitional if it explains "the moral point of view" on the basis of a cosmological vision that yields something like the premise that every human being is sacred. But then we're back to the question whether such a premise isn't inescapably religious.[101]

B. The Self-Regarding Strategy

The self-regarding strategy is yet another way—a way that does not rely on anything like the premise that human beings are sacred—of trying to defend human rights claims. According to the self-regarding strategy, it is good for oneself or for one's family/tribe/nation/race/religion/etc. that certain things not be done to any human being and certain other things be done for every human being. This strategy needs to be distinguished from (lest it collapse into) the different (and inescapably religious?) strategy according to which every human being is sacred and it is good for everyone to recognize that fact and act accordingly. According to the self-regarding strategy, it is good for oneself or for one's nation/etc. that certain things not be done and certain other things be done even if it is not the case that every human being is sacred.

The fundamental problem with the self-regarding strategy, *as a strategy for defending human rights claims*, is twofold. First, it is not clear how much more than "a mere nonaggression treaty"[102]—a treaty among persons who either fear one another or, at least, think that one day they might have reason to fear one another—the self-regarding strategy can support. A recent, prominent self-regarding strategy is David Gauthier's contractarian argument. Let's put aside the question whether the argument works[103] and look simply at the aim of the argument, which, according to Gauthier, is to show "that rational persons will recognize a role for constraints, both unilateral and mutual, in their choices and decisions, that rational persons would agree ex ante on certain mutual constraints were they able to do so, and that rational persons will frequently comply with those mutual constraints in their interactions."[104] In particular, Gauthier's self-regarding argument does not aim to justify anything close to the range of rights established in international law—in the International Bill of Human Rights, for example. As one commentator has observed, "[Gauthier's] main interest is to give an account of rational and impartial constraints on conduct. If this does not capture the traditional conception of morality, so much the worse for the traditional conception. Rationality—not morality—is the important notion for him."[105]

Second, whatever rights beyond "a mere nonaggression treaty" a strategy like Gauthier's can support, it is not clear that such a strategy can support them as *human* rights—as rights of every human being. It might be able to support them only as rights among persons who fear one another (or think that one day they might have reason to fear one another) or who need one another's cooperation (or think that one day they might need one another's cooperation). Nietzsche wrote: "Justice (fairness) originates among those who are approximately *equally powerful*, as Thucydides . . . comprehended correctly. . . . [J]ustice is repayment and exchange on the assumption of an approximately equal power position. . . . Justice naturally derives from prudent concern with self-preservation; that means, from the egoism of the consideration: 'Why should I harm myself uselessly and perhaps not attain my goal anyway?'"[106] Even if you are not within the circle of those I happen to respect and for whom I happen to have concern, if you are my neighbor I might fear your aggression or need your cooperation. But if you are a Somalian, or a Bosnian Muslim, we (as North Americans) might not fear *your* aggression or even think that one day we might have reason to fear your aggression; and we might not need *your* cooperation or even think that one day we might need your cooperation. Indeed, even if you live among us but are, say, severely handicapped, we might not think that you have anything to offer us.

> [Gauthier's contractarian] view of the relationship between the individual and society has some implications about which even the most committed contractarians are uneasy. If justice is wholly a matter of reciprocity, do we have any obligation to support people who are so severely handicapped that they can offer us nothing in return? . . . Gauthier has to concede that the handicapped lie "beyond the pale of morality tied to mutuality"; if we have moral duties in these cases, [Gauthier's] theory cannot account for them. Each of us may feel *sympathy* for the handicapped, and if so, the welfare of the handicapped will be among the ends we pursue; but this is a matter of preference, not moral obligation.[107]

Perhaps it is the case, however, that even if you are only a lowly inhabitant of an alien, distant, and weak community, we or some of those who happen to be within the circle of our respect and concern might eventually suffer in ways not always easy to predict or even foresee if we fail to act toward you as if you too were within the circle of our respect and concern—if, in that sense, we fail to take you into the circle of our respect and concern. Although, again, their principal justificatory reliance is on the idea of human rights—although, that is, their principal argument is other-regarding—even the Universal Declaration of Human Rights and the other documents of the International Bill of Human Rights contain at least a hint of a self-regarding argument, namely: If you want to enjoy the fruits of peace in the world, you must extend your respect and concern to all human beings. The Universal Declaration, the International Covenant on Economic, Social and Cultural Rights, and the International Covenant on Civil and Political Rights all state, in their preambles, that "recognition . . . of the equal and inalienable rights of all members of the human family is the foundation of freedom, justice *and peace* in the world" (emphasis added). Similarly, the European Convention for the Protection of Human Rights and Fundamental Freedoms (1953) states that the "Fundamental Freedoms" it affirms "are the foundation of justice *and peace* in the world" (emphasis added).

As a matter of domestic political debate—as a matter of domestic *Realpolitik*—plausible self-regarding ("pragmatic") reasons for our nation taking even the lowliest of the low into the circle of those it happens to respect and for whom it happens to have concern are undoubtedly an important complement to the other-regarding argument (i.e., the idea of human rights) for our nation doing so.[108] Addressing the World Conference on Human Rights in June 1993, U.S. Secretary of State Warren Christopher included self-regarding reasons in his argument that the nations of the world should take seriously the cause of human rights, including the cause of democracy: "A world of democracies would be a safer world. . . . States that respect human rights and operate on democratic principles tend to be the world's most peaceful and stable. On the other hand, the worst violators of human rights tend to be the world's aggressors and proliferators. These states export threats to global security, whether in the shape of terrorism, massive refugee flows, or environmental pollution. Denying human rights not only lays waste to human lives; it creates instability that travels across borders."[109]

It seems quite doubtful, however, that self-regarding reasons can by themselves bear all the weight. Put another way, it seems doubtful that any domestic political argument that is not at least partly other-regarding—that does not appeal at least in part to the conviction that every human being is sacred—can do the required work. The self-regarding reasons are, after all, abstract and highly speculative; their applicability to many concrete contexts is either just barely plausible or not plausible at all. Consider, in that regard, Jerome Shestack's catalogue of such reasons (see note).[110] As one human rights scholar has concluded, self-regarding "arguments are hard to prove and not fully persuasive. Despite considerable effort, it has been difficult to construct a wholly convincing 'selfish' rationale for major U.S. national commitments to promote the human rights of foreigners."[111] How confident are we that we Americans will eventually suffer if we fail to take the Bosnian Muslims, for example, or the Tibetan Buddhists, into the circle of our respect and concern? Confident enough to incur the costs of taking them in (if we do not also believe that they and all human beings are sacred)? In any event, no political argument for our nation taking the human rights of distant peoples seriously will begin to have the power of an argument that appeals at least in part to the conviction that all human beings are sacred. That conviction, after all, is partly constitutive of the American identity.[112]

Moreover, in the Declaration of Independence, the conviction is presented in a religious version: "We hold these truths to be self-evident, that all men are created equal, that they are endowed by their Creator with certain inalienable Rights, that among these are Life, Liberty and the pursuit of Happiness." What becomes of that proclamation—a proclamation that has been formative of our national identity[113]—if we abandon our belief in the "Creator"? Is there an intelligible secular version of the proclamation? Whatever the answer, for most Americans the power of the conviction that all human beings are sacred, and the power of an argument that appeals to that conviction, derive substantially from the fact that for them, the conviction that human beings are sacred is a religious conviction, even if for others the conviction is not religious—indeed, even if the conviction is not inescapably religious. For most Americans, the religious language of the Declaration ("all men are *created* equal, . . . they are endowed by their *Creator* . . .") remains a resonant language, even if for others it is an antique language from an irretrievable past.

Unlike the definitional strategy, the self-regarding strategy for insisting that certain things not be done to any human being and that certain other things be done for every human being should not be dismissed. But the self-regarding strategy is probably availing only or mainly as a buttress, a complement, to the strategy that relies on the idea of human rights—on the conviction that every human being, even the lowliest inhabitant of the most alien, distant, and weak community, is sacred. Significantly, neither individually nor even cumulatively can self-regarding reasons by themselves begin to account for the passionate other—regarding character of most discourse in support of human rights claims.

VI

To suggest that the idea of human rights is ineliminably religious—that there is, finally, no intelligible secular version of the idea of human rights, that the conviction that human beings are sacred is inescapably religious—is *not* to deny that one can take human rights very seriously indeed without being religious, that agnostics, too, even atheists, can take human rights seriously, that they, too, can love the Other.[114] *Undeniably*, atheists—like Albert Camus[115]—can take human rights seriously; *undeniably*, they and other nonreligious persons can love the Other. Indeed, if the Other really is, in some deep sense, one's sister/brother, then it would be surprising if every nonreligious person were existentially disconnected from that truth.[116] But as the example of Camus attests, to be connected to that truth existentially, as Camus certainly was, is not necessarily to affirm it intellectually.

(And, alas, as countless depressing examples illustrate, to affirm intellectually the truth—if it is a truth—that the Other is sister/brother is not necessarily to be connected to the truth existentially: To believe that the Other is sister/brother is not necessarily to experience any love for the Other; indeed, thanks to weakness of will or some pathology, one can believe that the Other is sister/brother *while standing on the Other's neck.*)

However, as the Polish philosopher Leszek Kolakowski has written: "When Pierre Bayle argued that morality does not depend on religion, he was speaking mainly of psychological independence; he pointed out that atheists are capable of achieving the highest moral standards . . . and of putting to shame most of the faithful Christians. That is obviously true as far as it goes, *but this matter-of-fact argument leaves the question of validity intact; neither does it solve the question of the effective sources of the moral strength and moral convictions of those 'virtuous pagans.'*"[117] That Camus achieved the highest moral standards, that he loved the Other, even that in doing so he understood himself to be engaged in a profound act of resistance and rebellion—resisting and rebelling against what he believed to be the ultimate absurdity, or meaninglessness, of the universe[118]—"leaves the question of validity intact." In particular, and as Nietzsche saw clearly, it leaves intact the question: Why should we give a damn about the well-being of all human beings, including the weak and the powerless—those whom Matthew's Gospel calls "the least of these brothers of mine"?[119]

Now, "the question of validity" (as Kolakowski calls it) is not always at issue, it is not always on the table. As I said, one can, like Camus, love the Other without being religious.[120] If two citizens, one of them religious, the other not, happen to agree that the Other is sacred, or at least that the well-being of the Other is of fundamental importance, the question of validity does not arise *between them.*[121] But that the question does not arise between them does not mean that it does not arise between or among others. After all, not everyone in the United States does, like Camus, love the Other; not everyone does agree that the well-being of all human beings—including the weak and the powerless—is of fundamental importance; not everyone agrees that he or she owes every human being respect or concern. The question of validity is often on the table—though often not explicitly—in the public square, as, for example, when redistributive issues are being debated.[122] ("Why should *we* be taxed to support *them*? Frankly, I don't give a damn about them. And even if I did, I've worked hard for my money and it's all I can do to take care of my own.") The mere fact that one can love the Other without being religious does not begin to respond to the question of validity when the question does arise, when it is at issue.[123]

There is not only the question of validity. There is also, as Kolakowski said, "the question of the effective sources of the moral strength and moral convictions of those 'virtuous pagans'." Habermas is frank in acknowledging the problem—and bleak in what he has to say about it: "Who or what gives us the courage for such a total engagement that in situations of degradation and deprivation is already being expressed when the destitute and deprived summon the energy each morning to carry on anew? The question about the meaning of life is not meaningless. Nevertheless, the circumstance that penultimate arguments inspire no great confidence is not enough for the grounding of a hope that can be kept alive only in a religious language. The thoughts and expectations directed toward the common good have, after metaphysics has collapsed, only an unstable status."[124] Consider, with respect to the problem of the adequacy of any nonreligious response to the "effective sources" question, the relevance of what Timothy Jackson has said about antirealism: "[L]etting go of realism will in all probability leave a society without the wherewithal to found or sustain a commitment to liberty, equality, or fraternity—much less sorority. Such a society may live for a time on past cultural capital embodied in liberal institutions and traditions, but a purely conventional virtue will not last long. The issue is one of motivation and consistency."[125] The bleakness of Habermas's statement—about the "unstable status" that "thoughts and expectations directed toward the common good have after metaphysics has collapsed"—lends weight to Jackson's.

Many persons will have an understandable incentive to reject the possibility that the idea of human rights is ineliminably religious: persons who do not count themselves religious, including some who count themselves antireligious, but who embrace the idea of human rights—who embrace, in particular, the conviction that every human being is sacred. They will think: "The conviction that every human being is sacred cannot be inescapably religious, for if it were, how could *we*—we who are not religious, and who may even look at religion as always and everywhere little more than a childish superstition—defend the idea of human rights?" How indeed?

Richard Rorty has recommended that we simply stop trying to defend the idea of human rights; in particular, he has recommended that we abandon what he calls our "human rights foundationalism",[126] which, in Rorty's view, has proven a futile project. For example, "Kant's account of the respect due to rational agents tells you that you should extend the respect you feel for people like yourself to all featherless bipeds. That is an excellent suggestion, a good formula for secularizing the Christian doctrine of the brotherhood of man. But it has never been backed up by an argument based on neutral premises, and it never will be."[127] Human rights foundationalism is not merely futile; it is, according to Rorty, "outmoded".[128] There is, says Rorty, a better project for us (i.e., for those of us who embrace the cause of human rights): "We see our task as a matter of making our own culture—the human rights culture—more self-conscious and more powerful, rather than demonstrating its superiority to other cultures by an appeal to something transcultural" (like the putative sacredness/ inviolability/etc. of every human being).[129]

But is it really enough, when confronted by intellectual or, worse, existential repudiations of human rights, to retreat, *pace* Rorty, into a kind of ethnocentrism—at one point Rorty refers to "our Eurocentric human rights culture"[130]—proclaiming proudly and loudly that although among us late-twentieth-century North Americans and Western Europeans (and perhaps a few others), a great fondness for human rights, or for "the moral point of view", is nothing more a culturally acquired taste, it is *our* acquired taste[131] and we are willing, if necessary, to fight and even die for it? Not even among all of us late-twentieth-century North Americans, and our like, has the taste—the cultural preference—for human rights been acquired. Recall, for example, Gauthier's Nietzschean "morality".[132] Moreover, why shouldn't those of us who have acquired a fondness for human rights try to disabuse ourselves of that fondness (if it is only an acquired taste)—at least, why shouldn't we try to moderate that fondness—once it becomes clear that indulging a fondness for human rights can be, politically, economically, militarily, and so forth, a rather costly proposition? (I commented earlier on the imitations of a self-regarding strategy for supporting human rights claims.) Most importantly, if the fondness for human rights some of us have is, at bottom, nothing more than an acquired taste, what is there to say to those who have not acquired the taste—and who might even have acquired a taste for violating (what we call) human rights—other than, perhaps, "Try it, you'll like it (maybe)"?

"Fraternity is an inclination of the heart," writes Rorty, "one that produces a sense of shame at having much when others have little. It is not the sort of thing that anyone can have a theory about or that people can be argued into having."[133] Rorty suggests that we try to convert others to our human rights culture—that we try to change their hearts—partly through a process of "manipulating sentiments, [of] sentimental education",[134] a process in which we tell "sad and sentimental stories".[135] (Rorty refers to Aeschylus's *The Persians* and Harriet Beecher Stowe's *Uncle Tom's Cabin*.[136]) I do not mean to deny the importance of such stories in effecting "a progress of sentiments", as Rorty calls it.[137] (Jesus, too, told stories: parables.) But in what sense is it a *progress*, and not merely a *change*, of sentiments, if the new sentiments don't more accurately reflect a *truth* about the Other, namely, that the Other is—*really* is—sacred, that the Other is, somehow, sister/brother? In any event, in the view of most of us who embrace the cause of human rights, the fundamental wrong done, when human rights are violated, is not that our sentiments—the sentiments of "our Eurocentric human rights culture"—are offended. The fundamental wrong done is much deeper than that: It is that, somehow, the very order of the world—the *normative* order of the world—is transgressed.

We might be quite wrong to believe—it might be false to believe—that the world has a normative order that is transgressed by violations of human rights. Relatedly, the belief might be false that "fraternity" is not *just* "an inclination of the heart" but an inclination of the heart that reflects—that is rooted in and animated by—perhaps the deepest truth about the normative order of the world, a truth that yields Jesus' "new commandment: love one another; you must love one another just as I have loved you."[138] However, Rorty does not argue that it is a false belief that the normative order of the world is transgressed by violations of human rights and that fraternity is *just* an inclination of the heart. Whether or not it is a false belief is not the sort of issue the "pragmatist" Rorty finds it useful to address; indeed, it is the sort of issue he finds it useful to marginalize.[139] (If the idea of human rights is ineliminably religious, then human rights foundationalism is, finally, a theological project. In Rorty's view, however, theology is not a useful conversation.[140])

I am skeptical, however, that we can, without serious costs, marginalize the issue. There is not only the question I have already posed: In what sense is it a progress of sentiments, and not merely a change? There are other important problems. For example: If we have no reason to believe that the world has a normative order that is transgressed by violations of human rights—at least, if we have no reason to be other than agnostic about the issue—and if we nonetheless coerce others, and perhaps even, at the limit, kill others, in the name of protecting human rights, then are we coercing and killing in the name of nothing but our sentiments, our preferences, our "inclination of the heart"? Does Rorty want to deny that it would be deeply problematic for us to coerce and kill in the name of nothing but our sentiments/preferences? (Tim Jackson has asked, in connection with Rorty's views: "Can one imagine dying for irony's sake?"[141] I want to ask: Can one imagine killing for irony's sake?) Does Rorty want to say something like this: "It's a brutal world out there. It's either them or us. It's either their culture or ours, either their sentiments/preferences or ours. It's not that might makes right. It's just that there is no right, only might. May our might, not theirs, prevail!" Rorty did once say something fully congruent with that position: "[W]hen the secret police come, when the torturers violate the innocent, there is nothing to be said to them of the form 'There is something within you which you are betraying. Though you embody the practices of a totalitarian society which will endure forever, there is something beyond those practices which condemns you.'"[142]

Although in my view, then, we should be wary about following Rorty's recommendation to abandon "human rights foundationalism," my aim in this chapter has not been to defend the (general) claim that the world has a normative order, much less the (particular) claim that every human being is sacred and therefore one attacks the normative order of the world—including one's own deepest nature—when one violates human rights. (The latter is the claim that, contra Rorty, there *is* "something within you which you are betraying.") My aim here—a much less ambitious and certainly more manageable aim—has been only to inquire whether there is an intelligible secular version of the claim, the *foundational* claim, that every human being is sacred, or whether, instead, the claim is inescapably religious.

For many religious persons, certainly, the idea of human rights simply does not make sense, it does not exert a claim, apart from, cut off from, the Gospel vision of the world and of our place in it—or from some equivalent religious vision.[143] (Simone Weil wrote: "The Gospel makes no distinction between the love of our neighbor and justice. . . . The supernatural virtue of justice consists in behaving exactly as though there were equality when one is stronger in an unequal relationship."[144]) Some even fear that the only conception of justice likely to flourish apart from the Gospel (or some equivalent) vision, once we have exhausted our "past cultural capital",[145] is the dispiriting conception implicit in Nietzsche's genealogy of justice—his genealogy, that is, of a kind of justice (a Gauthierian kind[146]):

> My dear Sir Long-Ears-and-Virtuous, we have no desire whatever to be better, we are very contented with ourselves, all we desire is not to harm one another—and therefore we forbid certain actions when they are directed in a certain way, namely against us, while we cannot sufficiently honor these same actions provided they are directed against enemies of the community—against you, for instance. We educate our children in them; we cultivate them— If we shared that "God-pleasing" radicalism that your holy madness recommends, if we were fools enough to condemn together with those actions the source of them, the "heart," the "disposition," that would mean condemning our own existence and with it its supreme prerequisite—a disposition, a heart, a passion we honor with the highest honors. By our decrees, we prevent this disposition from breaking out and expressing itself in an inexpedient way— we are prudent when we make such law for ourselves, we are also moral— Have you no suspicion, however faint, what sacrifice it is costing us, how much taming, self-overcoming, severity toward ourselves it requires? We are vehement in our desires, there are times when we would like to devour each other— But the "sense of community" masters us: please note that this is almost a definition of morality.[147]

VII

Let me emphasize that nothing in this chapter—nothing at all—is meant to defend, as credible or even as appealing, any religious-cosmological beliefs or any religious-moral beliefs, much less to commend any such beliefs to anyone. (As I said at the outset, to claim that no secular version of the conviction that every human being is sacred is intelligible is not to claim that any religious version of the conviction is plausible.[148]) One certainly need not count oneself a religious person in order to wonder—indeed, one can be one of those "good many professors and other intellectuals [who] display a hostility or skeptical indifference to religion that amounts to a thinly disguised contempt for belief in any reality beyond that discoverable by scientific inquiry and ordinary human experience"[149] and *nonetheless* wonder—whether the idea of human rights isn't ineliminably religious. One need not count oneself religious in order to wonder whether much secular moral-philosophizing hasn't been, for a very long time now, a kind of whistling in the dark.[150] (Recall, in that regard, Rorty's claim that the Kantian project has failed.[151] Recall, too, R.H. Tawney's statement, quoted at the beginning of this chapter.[152]) Jeffrie Murphy, for example, insists that it is, for him, "very difficult—perhaps impossible—to embrace religious convictions", but he nonetheless claims that "the liberal theory of rights requires a doctrine of human dignity, preciousness and sacredness that cannot be utterly detached from a belief in God or at least from a world view that would be properly called religious in some metaphysically profound sense." Murphy continues: "[T]he idea that fundamental moral values may require [religious] convictions is not one to be welcomed with joy [by nonreligious enthusiasts of the liberal theory of rights]. This idea generates tensions and appears to force choices that some of us would prefer not to make. *But it still might be true for all of that.*"[153]

Nietzsche asked: "Now suppose that belief in God has vanished: the question presents itself anew: 'who speaks?' "[154] Echoing Nietzsche's question a brutal century later, Art Leff wrote:

Napalming babies is bad.
Starving the poor is wicked.
Buying and selling each other is depraved.
Those who stood up to and died resisting Hitler, Stalin, Amin,
    and Pol Pot—and General Custer too—have earned salvation.
Those who acquiesced deserve to be damned.
There is in the world such a thing as evil.
[All together now:] Sez who?
God help us.[155]

CHAPTER 2

✦

Rights Talk

What Does It Mean? And Is It Problematic?

The heart of the idea of human rights, as I explained in chapter 1, is this: Every human being, simply as a human being, is sacred (is "inviolable", has "inherent dignity", is "an end in himself", or the like); therefore, certain choices should be made and certain other choices rejected; in particular, certain things ought not to be done to any human being and certain other things ought to be done for every human being. In chapter 1, I focused on the first part of the idea: the premise that every human being is sacred. In chapter 3, I will begin to focus on the second part: the claim that (because every human being is sacred) certain things ought not to be done to any human being and certain other things ought to be done for every human being.

In this brief chapter, I want to pause to focus on the language or vocabulary of "rights", on talk about "rights". The language of rights is the principal language in which, in this century, claims about what ought not to be done to any human being and claims about what ought to be done for every human being have come to be expressed. Yet, as I later explain, the language of rights—"rights talk"—has recently been quite controversial.

In particular, I want to address two basic questions:

- What is a human right; in particular, what does it mean to say that one has a human right? Put another way, what does the language of "rights" mean—how does the rhetoric of rights function—in discourse about what ought not to be done to human beings or about what ought to be done for them or about both? The particular discourse in which I am interested here is twofold: the discourse of the international law of human rights and the moral, especially the political-moral, discourse that underlies and shapes the international-legal discourse. I want to clarify the meaning or function of talk about rights in that twofold discourse discourse.
- Second, as it functions in such discourse, is rights talk problematic?

I

In the idea of human rights, the "should", the "ought", and the "ought not" are quite strong. First, there are certain choices it is wrong to make—that is, "morally" wrong, wrong *because* every human being is sacred (and given all other relevant information); in particular, there are certain things it is wrong do to any human being; these are choices and things, therefore, it is right ("morally" right, *because* every human being is sacred) *not* to do. Second, there are certain other choices it is wrong not to make; in particular, there are certain other things it is wrong not to do for every human being; these are choices and things it is right *to* do.[1] (In some cases, the "should", "ought", or "ought not"—the "right" or "wrong"—although strong, might be conditional rather than unconditional or absolute. I turn to this issue in chapter 4.)

An international human rights document represents a particular view or understanding of what the things are—or at least what some of them are—that ought or ought not to be done, that it is right or wrong to do or not to do. For example, the Universal Declaration of Human Rights—which "was born out of the experience of the war that had just ended"[2]—provides, in Article 4: "No one shall be held in slavery or servitude; slavery and the slave trade shall be prohibited in all their forms." Article 5 provides: "No one shall be subjected to torture or to cruel, inhuman or degrading punishment." Article 18: "Everyone has the right to freedom of thought, conscience and religion." Article 19: "Everyone has the right to freedom of opinion and expression." Article 26: "Everyone has the right to education. Education shall be free, at least in the elementary and fundamental stages." And so on. The International Covenant on Civil and Political Rights, the International Covenant on Economic, Social and Cultural Rights, and many other international human rights documents represent especially detailed views of what the "certain things" are that ought not to be done to any human being or that ought to be done for every human being.

The special concern of the international law of human rights is action and inaction by states. The behavior of states has traditionally been the sole concern of international law—which, significantly, is often called "the law of nations"; the behavior of others has traditionally been the concern of domestic law. Moreover, the instrumentalities of a state—the police, for example—typically have much greater power, both for good and for ill, than do other actors. However, the international law of human rights is not unconcerned with nonstate action: A state's obligations under international law typically include the obligation to outlaw, and then to take effective steps to prevent, certain practices and to punish those practices when committed in its jurisdiction by nonstate actors or others. "International law doctrine now goes beyond the state duty not to interfere with international human rights, to hold states accountable for not acting positively to ensure rights. Moreover, . . . international law now obligates states to use due diligence to prevent, investigate, and punish systemic and egregious human rights violations between private actors."[3]

Let us assume that a particular international human rights document, D, binds a state, S, as international law.[4] If according to D some act, A, is not to be done by a state (or perhaps by any actor, state or private) to any human being,[5] then, in what we can call lawspeak, every human being has a "right"—that is, a *legal* right, a right *according to*, or *"under"*, D—that S not subject him or her to A. Correlatively, S has a (legal) "duty" not to subject any human being to A. A might be, for example, torture, or incarceration on account of religion. If according to D some act, B, is to be done by a state for every human being within (or perhaps "lawfully" within[6]) its territory (or perhaps just for every human being who is a "citizen" of the state[7]), then every such person has a "right" that S do B for him or her; every such person has a "right" or "claim", against S, to B—an "entitlement" (against S) to B. Correlatively, S has a "duty" to do B for every such person. B might be, for example, the act of providing police protection, a free elementary education, or an opportunity to vote in an election.[8]

I have accounted, in the preceding paragraph, for rights in the sense of "freedoms from" (or "immunities"): rights not to have someone or some entity, like the state, do something to us—rights to be free from someone's or some entity's doing something to us. I have also accounted for rights in the sense of "claims" or "entitlements": rights to have someone or some entity do something for us—for example, to give something to us. But what about rights in the sense of "freedoms to" (or "privileges"): rights, vis-à-vis someone or some entity, to do something—for example, to practice one's religion or to speak one's mind? In the context of human rights documents, rights-as-freedoms-to are a species of rights-as-freedoms-from. The freedom—the "liberty" or "privilege"—a person has, vis-à-vis the state, to do something (e.g., practice her religion) is typically a right not to have the state act for the purpose of preventing her from doing that something, of interfering with her doing it, or of punishing or otherwise disadvantaging her because she has done it; it is typically a right to be free from such hostile action by the state. Look again at Article 18 of the Universal Declaration: "Everyone has the right to freedom of thought, conscience and religion." That means, in the context of the Universal Declaration, that everyone has a right that the state (among others) not punish or otherwise act against her on the basis of her "thought, conscience or religion".[9]

In short: In the context of discourse about the rights human beings have *under international law*, and about the correlative duties states have, talk about rights (and duties) is mainly just a particular way of talking—that is, *in lawspeak, in the legal language or vocabulary of "rights" (and "duties")*—about those choices that, according to the speaker's understanding of a provision of international law, every state governed by the provision may or may not make; it is a way of talking, in particular, about those things that every state may not do to any human being or must do for every human being (or for every human being "lawfully" within its territory, etc.). (Again, in some cases the "may not do to" or "must do for" might be conditional rather than unconditional or absolute.[10])

Not all talk about the rights human beings have—that is, about the human rights they have, the rights they have simply as human beings—is talk about the rights human beings have as a matter of international law. Some talk about the rights human beings have is talk about the rights they have simply as a matter of "morality". I have suggested how rights talk functions in *legal* (i.e., international-legal) discourse: discourse about the rights human beings have as a matter of international law. Rights talk functions in *moral* (including political-moral) discourse in an analogous way: In the context of discourse about the rights human beings have as a matter of one or another morality, rights talk (and correlative duty talk) is one way of talking about those things that, according to the speaker's understanding of the particular morality—the particular moral convictions—he or she is invoking, one may not do to, or one must do for, any human being. (Here, too, for some things one may not do or must do, the "may not do" or "must do" might be conditional rather than absolute.[11]) It perhaps bears emphasis that there is no "neutral" basis on which to rest moral claims about what one may not do to, or one must do for, any human being: Such a claim is a part of the content of one or another *particular* morality— though two or more different moralities might converge in their support for one or another such claim. In any event, "the modern vocabulary and grammar of [moral] rights is [an] instrument for reporting and asserting the requirements or other implications of a relationship of justice *from the point of view of the person(s) who benefit(s) from that relationship*. It provides a way of talking about 'what is just' from a special angle: the viewpoint of the 'other(s)' to whom something (including, inter alia, freedom of choice) is owed or due, and who would be wronged if denied that something."[12] (It might be the case that a human being has a particular right *both* as a matter of [one or another] morality *and* as a matter of law.)

⚬⚬⚬

Again, the second part of the idea of human rights is, in part, the claim that (because every human being is sacred) there are certain choices that should be made and certain other choices, rejected; in particular, certain things ought not to be done to any human being and certain other things ought to be done for every human being. In chapter 1, in a footnote,[13] I qualified the claim; I said that there are certain things that ought not to be done, if not to any human being, at least to any human being *in particular circumstances*, and certain other things that ought to be done, if not for every human being, at least for every human being *in particular circumstances*. I also said, in the footnote, that for some of the certain things that ought or ought not to be done, it might be the case that only some human beings, not all human beings, ought or ought not to do the certain things. I now want to translate both points into the language of rights and then give examples.

Not every (plausible) moral or legal human rights claim is a claim against each and every human being. Some human rights claims are claims against every human being, but some are not. Some human rights claims are claims against only some human beings: for example, the officials of one's government. Article 25 of the International Covenant of Civil and Political Rights is illustrative. It provides, in part: "Every citizen shall have the right and the opportunity . . . [t]o vote . . . at genuine periodic elections which shall be by universal and equal suffrage and shall be held by secret ballot . . . ." The right to vote protected by Article 25 is a right not against every human being; it is a right against one's own government (i.e., against the relevant officials of one's own government), but not against a government not one's own.[14]

Moreover, not every (plausible) moral or legal human rights claim is a claim by (or for) each and every human being. Some human rights claims are claims by every human being, but some are not. Some human rights claims are claims only by some human beings, namely, those in particular circumstances: those in a state of poverty, for example, or those "lawfully within the territory of the state". Article 25 of the International Covenant is again illustrative. The right to vote protected by Article 25 is a right not of every human being but only of human beings in particular circumstances, namely, circumstances such that the human beings are citizens (of the state against whose government the right exists). Nonetheless, the right to vote is substantially a "human" right, and not merely a "citizen" right, because, under the International Covenant, no human being "lawfully within the territory of the state" may be denied citizenship on the basis of "race, colour, sex, language, religion, political or other opinion, national or social origin, property, birth or other status."[15]

Article 25 is not unique. However, any claim about what one is due as a human being only in particular circumstances, including the circumstance of being "lawfully within the territory of the state", is essentially just a specification of a more general claim about what one is due simply as a human being—at the limit, a specification of a claim about the basic or minimum respect and concern due one simply as a human being. Put another way, any claim about what one is due as a human being in particular circumstances is essentially just a claim about the contextual implications or requirements—the implications or requirements "in the circumstances"—of a norm concerning what anyone and everyone is due simply as a human being. In that sense, human rights claims—including claims about what one is due as a human being in particular circumstances—are invariably about what one is due simply as a human being. Hence, it is not merely common to understand claims to be *human* rights claims when their terms are about what one is due as a human being in particular circumstances; it makes perfect sense—it is correct—to understand them that way.

Again, some rights claims commonly understood to be human rights claims are, by their terms, claims not by (or for) every human being but only by some human beings: those in particular circumstances. It bears emphasis that this can include the circumstance of being a woman, or that of being a child. For the reason indicated in the preceding paragraph, it makes perfect sense to understand both "women's" rights and "children's" rights as "human" rights. For example, *a woman's* right not to be subjected to rape is a specification of *any human being's* right not to be subjected to violent, degrading treatment and is, therefore, a human right. In commenting on the Convention on the Rights of the Child, Cynthia Cohen has noted that "existing treaties were too general to protect adequately the special needs of children.... Rights which were previously protected only as general concepts were clearly spelled out as to their applicability to children."[16] Much the same may be said of the Convention on the Elimination of All Forms of Discrimination Against Women and the Declaration on the Elimination of Violence Against Women: "Rights which were previously protected only as general concepts were clearly spelled out in their applicability to" women. Commenting on Articles 6–16 of the Convention on the Elimination of All Forms of Discrimination Against Women, Henry J. Steiner and Philip Alston have observed: "These articles evidence how a treaty devoted to one set of problems—here, ending discrimination against women and achieving equality—makes possible discrete, disaggregated treatment of the different issues relevant to these problems. Clearly the variety and detail in these articles would have been out of place, indeed impossible, in a treaty of general scope like the [International Covenant on Civil and Political Rights]."[17]

II

So much for the meaning or function of rights talk in the discourse of the international law of human rights and in the moral, especially the political-moral, discourse that underlies and shapes the international-legal discourse. Let us now turn to the question whether rights talk is problematic—either moral rights talk or legal rights talk.

One or another understanding of the (moral or legal) rights human beings have might be quite controversial.[18] One or another conception of what moral rights are might be controversial.[19] One or another view of the role moral rights play, or should play, in moral decisionmaking[20] or in legal decisionmaking might be controversial. But is rights talk itself problematic? Even if moral rights talk is derivative and dispensable,[21] is there anything problematic about the way talk about *human rights* functions either in international-legal discourse or in the moral discourse that shapes it?

In addressing that question, it might be helpful to consider Mary Ann Glendon's thoughtful and provocative book *Rights Talk: The Impoverishment of Political Discourse*. Given the title of Glendon's book, those inclined to suspect that rights talk is somehow problematic can be expected to turn to the book for confirmation. In her book, however, Professor Glendon insists that not all rights talk is problematic. She takes aim only at "a certain kind of rights talk[,] ... a new version of rights discourse that has achieved dominance over the past thirty years."[22] (Glendon is concerned both with legal rights talk and, especially, with the moral rights talk that shapes legal rights talk.) She identifies the object of her critique as "[o]ur current American rights talk", which "is but one dialect in a universal language that has developed during the extraordinary era of attention to civil and human rights in the wake of World War II."[23] Lest she be misunderstood, Glendon declares: "The problem is not, ... as some contend, with the very notion of rights, or with our strong rights tradition. ... [W]hat is needed is not the abandonment, but the renewal, of our strong rights tradition."[24]

What is wrong (in Glendon's view) with "our current American rights talk"? It is, she says, "set apart by the way that rights, in our standard formulations, tend to be presented as absolute, individual, and independent of any necessary relation to responsibilities."[25] Glendon decries "[t]he most distinctive features of our American rights dialect . . .: its penchant for absolute, extravagant formulations, its near-aphasia concerning responsibility, its excessive homage to individual independence and self-sufficiency, [and] its habitual concentration on the individual and the state at the expense of the intermediate groups of civil society."[26] Glendon then goes on to explain how, in consequence of those distinctive features, American rights talk impoverishes American political discourse:

> Our rights talk, in its absoluteness, promotes unrealistic expectations, heightens social conflict, and inhibits dialogue that might lead towards consensus, accommodation, or at least the discovery of common ground. In its silence concerning responsibilities, it seems to condone acceptance of the benefits of living in a democratic social welfare state, without accepting the corresponding personal and civic obligations. In its relentless individualism, it fosters a climate that is inhospitable to society's losers, and that systematically disadvantages caretakers and dependents, young and old. In its neglect of civil society, it undermines the principal seedbeds of personal and civic virtue.[27]

I am not interested here in evaluating Glendon's claim that there is an "American rights dialect" or her arguments about the ways in which that dialect is problematic and impoverishes American political discourse. Others have subjected Glendon's provocative arguments to critical scrutiny.[28] I want only to suggest that Glendon's bill of particulars would fail as an indictment of talk about human rights as that talk functions both in international discourse about human rights (i.e., in international-legal discourse and in the moral discourse that shapes it). Again, Glendon does not mean her book to be an indictment of such rights talk; to the contrary, she often favorably compares such rights talk to "American rights talk". Nonetheless, I want to consider—briefly—whether, despite her limited intentions, Glendon's critique of what she describes as "our current American rights talk" applies as well to international human rights talk. Is it far-fetched to believe that someone hostile not merely to American rights talk but to rights talk generally might try to use Glendon's critique as a weapon against rights talk generally, including international human rights talk? In any event, American rights talk, *as portrayed by Glendon*, is a convenient counterpoint to international human rights talk: We can learn something useful about the general character of international discourse about human rights if we compare it to Glendon's portrayal of American rights talk.

First, does international human rights talk have a "penchant for absolute, extravagant formulations"? Many persons, including Mary Ann Glendon, believe that certain things ought *never* to be done to any human being and certain other things ought *always* to be done for every human being. They believe, that is, that some human rights are absolute or unconditional—and that they should be protected as such by international law. And, indeed, international law does protect some human rights as absolute. But it does not protect all the human rights it protects as absolute. Nor should it, because not all human rights are absolute. As Glendon herself notes approvingly,[29] the rights and freedoms articulated by the Universal Declaration of Human Rights are subject to "such limitations" (but "only" to such limitations) "as are determined by law solely for the purpose of securing due recognition and respect for the rights and freedoms of others and of meeting the just requirements of morality, public order and the general welfare in a democratic society."[30] Similar provisos inhabit the other principal international human rights documents.[31] (I discuss the matter of "absolute" or "unconditional" vs. "conditional" human rights in chapter 4.) It is difficult to see how, given such provisos—provisos that make many of the protected human rights nonabsolute—international human rights talk "promotes unrealistic expectations, heightens social conflict, and inhibits dialogue that might lead towards consensus, accommodation, or at least the discovery of common ground."

Second, does international human rights talk suffer from "near-aphasia concerning responsibility"? To believe in human rights—and to insist that they be adequately protected by international as well as by domestic law—is not to disbelieve in or otherwise minimize a human being's responsibilities to other human beings, in particular to the community to which she belongs. Quite the reverse is true. At the very foundation of human rights claims is the conviction that because every one of us human beings is sacred (inviolable, etc.), every one of us bears certain responsibilities to every other one of us. In the religious version presented in the preceding chapter, the conviction is that every one of us human beings is bound or connected to every other one of us as members of the same family, as brothers/sisters, and that we therefore bear certain responsibilities to one another. The conviction that there are certain things that no one ought to do to any human being and certain other things that are owed to every human being is essentially the conviction that we human beings bear certain responsibilities to one another. The International Covenant on Economic, Social and Cultural Rights and the International Covenant on Civil and Political Rights, in the preamble common to the covenants, are explicit on the point: "*Realizing* that the individual, having duties to other individuals and to the community to which he belongs, is under a responsibility to strive for the promotion and observance of the rights recognized in the present Covenant, *[a]gree* upon the following articles . . . ." Moreover, the international law of human rights is explicit (if often general) about what some of those responsibilities are. For example, and as Glendon notes approvingly,[32] the Universal Declaration of Human Rights states, in Article 29: "Everyone has duties to the community in which alone the free and full development of his personality is possible." Specifying something that is, whatever else it is, a duty to the community, the International Covenant on Civil and Political Rights states, in Article 20: "Any advocacy of national, racial, or religious hatred that constitutes incitement to discrimination, hostility or violence shall be prohibited by law."[33] According to the view represented by the International Covenant, everyone has a responsibility, which the law should enforce, to refrain from advocating the kind of hatred addressed by Article 20.

Although the principal emphasis of international human rights documents is understandably on human rights (and on correlative state duties), it would be a mistake to conclude that human responsibilities are only a marginal concern of such documents. In addition to the provisions quoted in the preceding paragraph, consider, for example, the European Convention for the Protection of Human Rights and Fundamental Freedoms, which states, in Article 10: "The exercise of [the right to freedom of expression], since it carries with it duties and responsibilities, may be subject to such formalities, conditions, restrictions or penalties as are prescribed by law and are necessary in a democratic society in the interests of national security, territorial integrity, or public safety, for the prevention of disorder or crime, for the protection of health or morals, for the protection of the reputation or rights of others, for preventing the disclosure of information received in confidence, or for maintaining the authority and impartiality of the judiciary." The American Declaration of the Rights and Duties of Man, in Articles 29–38, articulates several human responsibilities, including duties to children and parents and even "the duty of every person to vote in the popular elections of the country of which he is a national, when he is legally capable of doing so." The African [Banjul] Charter on Human and Peoples' Rights states in the preamble that "the enjoyment of rights and freedoms also implies the performance of duties on the part of everyone." The African Charter then lists, in Article 29, several human responsibilities, including "the duty to preserve the harmonious development of the family and to work for the cohesion and respect of the family, to respect his parents at all times, to maintain them in case of need" and "the duty to preserve and strengthen positive African cultural values in his relations with other members of the society, in the spirit of tolerance, dialogue and consultation and, in general, to contribute to the promotion of the moral well-being of society."[34] It is difficult to see how, given provisions like those quoted or referred to in the preceding paragraph and in this one[35]—provisions anything but "silent concerning responsibilities"—international human rights talk "condones acceptance of the benefits of living in a democratic social welfare state, without accepting the corresponding personal and civic obligations." Plainly, international human rights talk does not suffer from "near-aphasia concerning responsibility".

Finally, is international human rights talk characterized by "excessive homage to individual independence and self-sufficiency [and] habitual concentration on the individual and the state at the expense of the intermediate groups of civil society"? There are two points to be made here. First, the fact that many Western-style human rights provisions—in particular, those protecting freedom of speech and religious liberty—are often defended on an excessively individualistic basis does not mean that they need be, or that they should be, defended on that basis; it does not mean that the moral presuppositions of such rights are in fact individualistic. A more attractive and indeed firmer basis of support for such rights might well be nonindividualistic. In his essay "A Communitarian Reconstruction of Human Rights: Contributions from Catholic Tradition," David Hollenbach suggests an alternative "way of interpreting freedom of speech and religion"—one that "views immunity from interference in these domains as in the service of active participation in the public life of society. People should be free to express their political and religious beliefs in public in order that the true nature of the common good of the community might be more adequately understood and pursued."[36] It is one thing, and fair, to attack the excessively individualistic cast of much American discourse about rights like the right to freedom of speech and the right to religious liberty. It is another thing, and deeply mistaken, to discount the value of such rights. The much more sensible strategy, for one who (like Glendon) objects to the individualistic cast of much American discourse about human rights, is to do what Hollenbach is doing: construct, or reconstruct, a nonindividualistic basis for such rights.

The second point concerns the "the intermediate groups" to which Glendon refers, especially those she calls "the seedbeds of civic virtue ... families, religious communities, and other primary social groups." They are not, says Glendon, "in peak condition."[37] The Universal Declaration of Human Rights, in Article 16, the International Covenant on Civil and Political Rights, in Article 23, and the American Convention on Human Rights, in Article 17, all state: "The family is the natural and fundamental group unit of society and is entitled to protection by society and the State." The International Covenant on Economic, Social and Cultural Rights, in Article 10, states: "The widest possible protection and assistance should be accorded to the family, which is the natural and fundamental group unit of society, particularly for its establishment and while it is responsible for the care and education of dependent children." The American Declaration of the Rights and Duties of Man states, in Article 7: "Every person has the right to establish a family, and to receive protection therefor." The Universal Declaration of Human Rights states, in Article 18: "Everyone has the right to freedom of thought, conscience and religion; this right includes the ... freedom, either alone or in community with others and in public or private, to manifest his religion or belief in teaching, practice, worship and observance." The International Covenant on Civil and Political Rights states, in Article 27: "In those States in which ethnic, religious or linguistic minorities exist, persons belonging to such minorities shall not be denied the right, in community with other members of their group, to enjoy their own culture, to profess and practice their own religion, or to use their own language." In light of these and similar provisions that appear in various international human rights documents, it would be difficult to maintain that international human rights talk is exclusively or even excessively individualistic. Such talk is characterized, not by "excessive homage to individual independence and self-sufficiency and habitual concentration on the individual and the state at the expense of the intermediate groups of civil society," but by an acute awareness both of human interdependence and, especially, of human vulnerability, including the vulnerability of the family and of minority religious, ethnic, and linguistic communities—an awareness painfully heightened by the genocidal horrors of the twentieth century. International human rights talk cannot fairly be said to "foster a climate that is inhospitable to society's losers, systematically disadvantages caretakers and dependents, young and old, undermines the principal seedbeds of personal and civic virtue," and so on.

None of this is to deny that even in the context of international discourse about human rights, particular instances of talk about human rights might be problematic in one or more of the ways Glendon claims American rights talk is problematic. But an extension of Glendon's critique beyond American rights talk to international human rights talk is implausible: The documentary record simply will not support the claim that international human rights talk generally proceeds in a dialect that is individualistic or absolutist or that impedes talk about human responsibilities. (An extension of the critique to all rights talk is therefore implausible.) In the period since the end of the Second World War, our experience with international discourse about human rights demonstrates that, in contrast to "our current American rights talk" (as portrayed by Glendon), international human rights talk is *not* "set apart by the way that rights, in our standard formulations, tend to be presented as absolute, individual, and independent of any necessary relation to responsibilities."

In his recent critique of rights talk, Allan Hutchinson has generalized across all rights talk. According to Hutchinson's bill of particulars—his list of "the vices of rights talk"—rights talk is "abstract", "individualistic", "legalistic", "myopic", "anemic", "absolute", "exclusionary", "narrow", and "blunt".[38] The response to Hutchinson's indictment—and to all similar indictments of rights talk—is both obvious and compelling. Rights talk is not inherently absolutist, individualistic, and so on. It all depends on the particular claims—claims about about what ought or ought not to be done—that are being advanced (in the language of rights). I concur in Nancy Fraser's judgment: "[U]nlike some communitarian, socialist, and feminist critics, I do not believe that rights talk is inherently individualistic, bourgeois-liberal, and androcentric [etc.]—rights talk takes on those properties only when societies establish the *wrong* rights, for example, when the (putative) right to private property is permitted to trump other, social rights."[39] As this chapter illustrates, it is simply not credible, in critiquing rights talk, to generalize across all rights talk the way Hutchinson does.[40] (Again, and in contrast to Hutchinson, Glendon does *not* generalize across all rights talk in her critique.)

III

Anyone tempted to use Glendon's critique as a weapon against all rights talk, including international human rights talk, is in the grip of two misconceptions. First, as I have just demonstrated, if Glendon's critique has force,[41] it has force only against—and, indeed, was meant by Glendon to have force only against—American rights talk. A particular human right, as defined by international law or by the morality (or moralities) that shapes it, might protect the individual human being in his or her individuality; it might do so absolutely (unconditionally); and in doing so it might be silent about any question of human responsibility (other than, implicitly, the question of the responsibility—the duty—not to violate the right). Nonetheless, as a general matter neither the international law of human rights—as represented by various international human rights documents—nor the moral claims about human rights that shape the international law of human rights can fairly be said to be excessively individualistic or absolutist or insensitive to basic human responsibilities.

The second misconception is more fundamental—and is arguably invited by the title of Glendon's book, which is *Rights Talk: The Impoverishment of Political Discourse*: Glendon's critique of American rights talk, as we can now see, is not really a critique of rights talk at all. That is, Glendon's critique is not a critique of the language or vocabulary of rights. It is, instead, a critique of particular claims about rights: claims that, in Glendon's view, are too individualistic or absolutist or that ignore or marginalize human responsibilities. Moreover, the force of Glendon's critique does not depend on whether the claims are expressed in the language of rights or in some other language.[42] Thus, despite its title, Glendon's book is not really about "rights talk" but about (some) "rights claims".

However one evaluates one or another claim about what ought not to be done to any human being or about what ought to be done for every human being—and, indeed, even if one believes that one or another such claim is excessively individualistic or absolutist or insensitive to basic human responsibilities—there is nothing discernibly problematic about the language of rights in which such claims are often cast. To the contrary: As John Finnis has said, "The modern language of rights provides . . . a supple and potentially precise instrument for sorting out and expressing the demands of justice."[43] At least, it provides a supple and potentially precise instrument for sorting out and expressing what one perceives to be the demands of morality. Thus, it is most unlikely—and in any event international human rights discourse powerfully disconfirms—that "[r]ights-talk has had its day."[44]

The serious challenges to the idea of human rights do not include a challenge to rights talk; they do not include a challenge to the language or vocabulary of rights in which, in this century, claims about what ought not to be done to human beings and claims about what ought to be done for human beings have come to be expressed. Except for challenges to the premise that every human being is sacred, the serious challenges to the idea of human rights are not to the *language* of human rights claims but to their *content*—their *substance*. One of the most serious such challenges is to what we can call the "universalism" of the idea of human rights: the notion that (because every human being is sacred) there are things that ought not to be done to *any* human being, *no matter what his or her situation or culture or society*, and other things that ought to be done for *every* human being, *no matter what his or her situation or culture or society*. Moreover, the force of this challenge to the idea of human rights—which I call the relativist challenge—does not depend on whether or not a claim about what ought not to be done to or about what ought to be done for human beings happens to be cast in the language of rights. (I address the relativist challenge, and related challenges, in the next chapter.)

Note, too, that the force of a claim about what ought not to be done to or about what ought to be done for human beings does not depend on whether the claim is expressed in the language of rights. Even though the language of moral rights is, as Finnis has indicated, useful, it is not essential. Indeed, properly understood, rights talk is a derivative and even dispensable feature of modern moral discourse. "[I]t is salutary to bear in mind that the modern emphasis on the powers of the right-holder, and the consequent systematic bifurcation between 'right' (including 'liberty') and 'duty', is something that sophisticated lawyers were able to do without for the whole life of classical Roman law. . . . And in this, the vocabulary of Roman law resembles more than one pre-modern legal vocabulary."[45] What really matters—what we should take seriously—is not human rights talk but the claims such talk is meant to express: the claims about what ought not to be done to or about what ought to be done for human beings. We can take rights seriously (so to speak) without taking rights talk too seriously.

⁂

In the course of reflecting on the idea of human rights, it was important to do what we did here:

- Because the language of rights—"rights talk"—is ubiquitous in international discourse about what ought not to be done to and what ought to be done for human beings, it was important to clarify the meaning or function of rights talk.
- There have recently been indictments of rights talk (actually, of rights claims), both of rights talk generally (e.g., Hutchinson) and of a particular "dialect" of rights talk (Glendon). It was also important, therefore, to inquire whether, as it functions in international discourse about what ought not to be done to and what ought to be done for human beings, rights talk is problematic in one or more respects.

With this work done, however, it is now important, it is now time, to put all the talk about rights talk behind us and move on to other questions—questions that are, in my view, both more serious and more difficult.

CHAPTER 3

Are Human Rights Universal?

The Relativist Challenge and Related Matters

A vision of future social order is . . . based on a concept of human nature. If in fact man is an indefinitely malleable, completely plastic being, with no innate structures of mind and no intrinsic needs of a cultural or social character, then he is a fit subject for the "shaping behavior" by the state authority, the corporate manager, the technocrat, or the central committee. Those with some confidence in the human species . . . will try to determine the intrinsic human characteristics that provide the framework for intellectual development, the growth of moral consciousness, cultural achievement, and participation in a free community.

—Noam Chomsky[1]

The great concern of our contemporaries for historicity and for culture has led some to call into question . . . the existence of "objective norms of morality" valid for all peoples of the present and the future, as for those of the past. . . . It must certainly be admitted that man always exists in a particular culture, but it must also be admitted that man is not exhaustively defined by the same culture. . . . [T]he very progress of cultures demonstrates that there is something in man which transcends those cultures. This "something" is precisely human nature: This nature is itself the measure of culture and the condition ensuring that man does not become the prisoner of any of his cultures, but asserts his personal dignity by living in accordance with the profound truth of his being.

—John Paul II[2]

The idea of human rights consists of two parts: the premise or claim that every human being is sacred (inviolable, etc.), and the further claim that *because* every human being is sacred (and given all other relevant information), certain choices should be made and certain other choices rejected; in particular, certain things ought not to be done to any human being and certain other things ought to be done for every human being. (As I explain in chapter 4, in some cases

the "should", "ought", or "ought not" might be conditional rather than unconditional or absolute.) One fundamental challenge to the idea of human
rights addresses the first part of the idea; it contests the claim that every human
being is sacred. Another fundamental challenge, the one with which I am prin-
cipally concerned in this chapter, addresses the second part of the idea. According to this latter challenge, whether or not every human being is sacred—and,
so, even if every human being *is* sacred—there are no things that ought not to
be done (not even any things that *conditionally rather than unconditionally* ought
not to be done) to *any* human being and no things that ought to be done (not
even any things that *conditionally rather than unconditionally* ought to be done) for
every human being.[3] That is, no putatively "human" right is truly a *human* right:
no such right is the right of *every* human being; in that sense, no such right—
no such "ought" or "ought not"—is truly universal. Before addressing this
challenge, which I shall call the relativist challenge to the idea of human rights,
I want to comment on the other fundamental challenge, which contests the
claim that every human being is sacred.

I

One can contest the claim that every human being is sacred by making either
of two distinct arguments:

First, one can contend that no argument for the claim that *any* human
being, much less *every* human being, is sacred—neither any religious argument
nor any secular argument—is persuasive. (Indeed, one can contend that no secular version of the claim is even intelligible. I inquired, in chapter 1, whether
there is any intelligible secular version of the claim.) In particular, one can insist
that after the death of God (Nietzsche)[4]—or "after metaphysics has collapsed"
(Habermas)[5]—sacredness (inviolability, etc.) cannot plausibly be predicated of
human beings.

Second, one can contend that not every human being is sacred, but only
some human beings—the members of one's tribe, for example, or of one's nation.

Typically, the claim that only some human beings are sacred takes the form,
not that only some human beings are sacred, but that only some persons are
really human beings; in particular, it takes the form that some (other) persons—
women, for example, or persons of African ancestry, or Jews, or Bosnian Muslims, and so on—are not truly human or, at least, that they are not fully human
and that therefore they lack the sacredness characteristic of those who are truly
and fully human. But to accept that every human being is sacred while insisting that women, or persons of African ancestry, or Jews, or Bosnian Muslims,
and so on, are not really human beings—that they are not truly human or that
they are not fully human—is to reject the claim that every human being is sacred and to accept instead the competing claim that only some human beings

are sacred. This is because the first part of the idea of human rights—the claim that every human being is sacred—is the claim that every member of the species Homo sapiens is sacred (or at least every *born* member[6]); it is the claim that the sacredness of a human being (Homo sapiens) does not depend on his or her "race, colour, sex, language, religion, political or other opinion, national or social origin, property, birth or other status." (This language appears in Article 2 of the Universal Declaration of Human Rights and is repeated in the International Covenant on Economic, Social and Cultural Rights and in the International Covenant on Civil and Political Rights.) To insist that women, or persons of African ancestry, or Jews, or Bosnian Muslims, and so on, are not truly human—that, instead, they are pseudohumans—and, unlike true humans, are not sacred, is to say that only some human beings (Homo sapiens) are sacred.

Cast as the claim that only some persons are human beings, the claim that only some human beings are sacred has been, and remains, quite common. According to Nazi ideology, for example, the Jews were pseudohumans.[7] There are countless other examples, past and present:

> Serbian murderers and rapists do not think of themselves as violating human rights. For they are not doing these things to fellow human beings, but to *Muslims*. They are not being inhuman, but rather are discriminating between the true humans and the pseudohumans. They are making the same sort of distinction as the Crusaders made between the humans and the infidel dogs, and the Black Muslims make between humans and blue-eyed devils. [Thomas Jefferson] was able both to own slaves and to think it self-evident that all men are endowed by their creator with certain inalienable rights. He had convinced himself that the consciousness of Blacks, like that of animals, "participates more of sensation than reflection." Like the Serbs, Mr. Jefferson did not think of himself as violating *human* rights.
>
> The Serbs take themselves to be acting in the interests of true humanity by purifying the world of pseudohumanity.[8]

As I emphasize later in this chapter, Martha Nussbaum's important work is quite helpful in responding to the second basic challenge to the idea of human rights, the relativist challenge, which is the principal subject of this chapter. The relativist challenge is addressed to the second part of the idea of human rights; therefore, Nussbaum's work is quite helpful in defending the second part of the idea. Her work is not helpful, however, in defending the first part of the idea, the claim that every human being is sacred. My point here is a general one: Nussbaum's work illustrates that even the most persuasive rebuttals of relativist arguments (I look at several such arguments in the course of this chapter) typically fail to address challenges to the fundamental claim that all human beings are sacred.

In a recent essay critiquing "skepticism about practical reason in literature and in the law", Nussbaum asserts that "the good of other human beings is an end worth pursuing in its own right, apart from its effect on [one's] own pleasure or happiness."[9] (It is clear, in her essay, that by "other human beings" Nussbaum is referring not just to *some* other human beings but to *all* other human beings.) But *why* is the good of every human being an end worth pursuing in its own right? Nussbaum does not say. She merely reports, in the final paragraph of her essay, that "it seems to be a mark of the human being to care for others and feel disturbance when bad things happen to them."[10] Now, few will deny that it seems to be a mark of the human being to care for *some* other human beings—the members of one's family, say, or even of one's tribe or nation or race or religion. But it is not a mark of all human beings—it is not a mark of "the human being" as such—to care for *all* other human beings. Recall, from chapter 1, Primo Levi's comments about "us-ism".[11] Recall, too, Rorty's comparison of "the rather rare figure of the psychopath, the person who has no concern for any human being other than himself[,]" to "the much more common case: the person whose treatment of a rather narrow range of featherless bipeds is morally impeccable, but who remains indifferent to the suffering of those outside this range, the ones he or she thinks of as pseudohumans."[12] (According to Rorty, moral philosophy, to its detriment, has "systematically neglected" the latter in favor of the former.[13]) Rorty's "much more common case" is also much more common than the person at the other extreme from the psychopath: someone who cares deeply about the authentic well-being of every human being. We sometimes mark just how *uncommon* such persons are, in the real world, by calling them "saints".

If it were a mark of every human being to care for every other human being (and to feel disturbance when bad things happen to any other human being), the "why" question would be merely academic. But because very many human beings—indeed, perhaps most human beings—have not in the past cared for, nor do they today care for, every human being, the question is both practical and urgent: Why is the good of every human being an end worth pursuing in its own right? In her essay, Nussbaum stands mute before that question. One answer—the answer that informs the international law of human rights— is that the good of every human being is an end worth pursuing in its own right *because every human being is sacred*. I suggested, in chapter 1, that there might be no intelligible secular version of that answer—no intelligible secular version of the conviction that every human being is sacred.

⚜

Again, two arguments against the idea of human rights address the first part of the idea. According to one of the arguments, neither any religious nor any secular support for the claim that any human being (much less every human being) is sacred is persuasive; according to the other argument, only some human beings are sacred (or, equivalently, only some persons are human beings). I do not want to address either argument here. (If the conviction that every human being is sacred is, as I suggested in chapter 1, inescapably religious, then meeting either argument would require a *religious* counterargument.) The principal argument I want to address in this chapter challenges the second part of the idea of human rights. According to the argument, even if *arguendo* every human being is sacred, it does not follow and in fact is not true that there are things that ought not to be done to *any* human being or things that ought to be done for *every* human being.

II

Why might one who believes—or, at least, who accepts *arguendo*—that every human being is sacred also believe that there is nothing that ought not to be done to *any* human being and nothing that ought to be done for *every* human being? Imagine that you reject the proposition that human beings are all alike in some respects such that there are things that are good and things that are bad for every human being: things that serve—that enhance, that are friendly to— the well-being (or some aspect of the well-being) of every human being and things that disserve—that diminish, that are hostile to—the well-being of every human being.[14] ("Good" and "bad" obviously admit of degrees: Some things serve our well-being, and some things disserve it, much more radically than some other things do.) You believe that although some things are good and some things are bad for some human beings, nothing is good and nothing is bad for every human being.[15] In particular, you believe that even if every human being is sacred, there is nothing—there is no practice—that ought not to be done to any human being, because while a practice might be bad for some, even many, human beings, no practice is bad for every human being. Similarly, you believe that there is no practice that ought to be done for every human being, because while a practice might be good for some, even many, human beings, no practice is good for every human being.[16]

This, then, is the heart of the relativist challenge to the idea of human rights: the claim that nothing is good and nothing is bad for every human being —nothing serves and nothing disserves the well-being of every human being— because human beings are not all alike in any respect that supports generalizations either about what is good or about what is bad, not just for some human beings, but for every human being.[17] This position—nothing is good and nothing is bad for every human being—is "relativist" in the sense that, according to the position, what is good and what is bad for a particular human being are never good and bad for her in virtue of anything she has in common with every other human being—in particular, what is good and what is bad for her are not good and bad for her in virtue of a common nature, a *human* nature. Rather, what is good and what is bad for a particular human being always depend on—

they are always relative to—some thing about her or about her context or situation, some thing that is never true about every human being or about the situation of every human being.

Is the relativist challenge to the idea of human rights plausible? Should we take it seriously? A few fragments from the real world might help to focus the mind. On January 20, 1993, the *New York Times* reported:

> In its final global human rights report, the Bush Administration said today that Serbian forces in Bosnia and Herzegovina were conducting a campaign of "cruelty, brutality, and killing" unrivaled since Nazi times.
>
> The survey of 189 countries issued by the State Department described a Serbian policy of terror against civilians that made "a mockery" of the Geneva Convention. The Serbs' "ethnic cleansing" campaign includes widespread and systematic rape and murder and the systematic shelling and starvation by siege of large cities, the report said.
>
> Non-Serbs were subjected to "almost every conceivable form of torture, humiliation and killing," it said, including the deliberate disfigurement and the excision of body parts of prisoners in Serb-run camps.[18]

The following three reports add some detail to what the *Times* story only sketched in broad outline:

> On the basis of . . . statements of witnesses and actual raped people, one can confirm that . . . occupying Serbian forces formed special concentration camps for women and children. . . .
>
> [W]ar crimes are being committed in special women's concentration camps where little girls, girls and women are being raped in the presence of their parents, brothers and sisters, husbands or children. After that, according to witnesses' statements, the raped persons are further brutalized and even massacred, their breasts are sliced off and their wombs are ripped out. . . . The young girls couldn't physically survive the rapes and quickly died. . . . [O]ver 300 young girls in The Home for Retarded Children were raped.[19]

⚔

> Once a young woman with a baby was taken in the middle of the hall. . . . They ordered her to take off her clothes. She put the baby on the floor next to her. Four Chetniks raped her; she was silent, looking at her crying child.
>
> When she was left alone she asked if she could breast-feed the baby. Then a Chetnik cut the child's head off with a knife. He gave the bloody head to the mother. The poor woman screamed. They took her outside and she never came back.[20]

⚔

> A Muslim man in Bosani Petrovac . . . [was] forced to bite off the penis of a fellow-Muslim. . . . If you say that a man is not human, but the man looks

like you and the only way to identify this devil is to make him drop his trousers—Muslim men are circumcised and Serb men are not—it is probably only a very short step, psychologically, to cutting off his prick. . . . There has never been a campaign of ethnic cleansing from which sexual sadism has gone missing.[21]

The following report, which adds more detail, was broadcast on *World News Tonight with Peter Jennings* on February 18, 1994:

> [Richard Gizbert, ABC News:] An investigation by German TV led to the arrest [in Germany] of Dusko Tadic, a Serb guard at the notorious Omarska prison camp. He's charged with aiding and abetting genocide. The only pictures the Serbs allowed at Omarska don't tell the real story. Human rights groups say that at least a thousand Bosnians were killed there, many tortured. Tesma Elezovic was a prisoner at Omarska. She says she was forced to wipe up the blood of Dusko Tadic's victims.
>
> [Tesma Elezovic, through interpreter:] I saw with my own eyes Tadic beat the prisoners, throw them into hot oil, force them to castrate each other, beating them so badly they died.
>
> [Richard Gizbert:] Another former prisoner afraid of identification says prisoners were forced to listen to others being tortured.
>
> [Former prisoner, through interpreter:] I never heard such terrible screams, not even in horror films.[22]

These reports all concern the situation in the early 1990s in the former Yugoslavia.[23] One could reproduce—one could fill volumes with—similar reports of horror that concern countless other situations at countless other times in countless other places, reports of cruelty so calculated that simply to hear of it tears the soul.[24] But the reports I have reproduced here are more than adequate—even reports of cruelty less calculated, or of acts less cruel, would be more than adequate—to illustrate and clarify the fundamental point: Some things are bad, indeed some things are horrible—conspicuously horrible, undeniably horrible—for *any* human being to whom the thing is done.

But can we also say that some things are *good* for every human being for whom the thing is done? We can identify concrete ways of life that would be bad, or horrific, for any human being. We cannot identify, however, concrete ways of life that would be good, much less best, for every human being. (More about that below.) But just as we can confidently identify some things, indeed many things, that are bad for any human being, we can confidently identify some things that are good for every human being: for example, "affection, the cooperation of others, a place in a community, and help in trouble."[25]

The relativist challenge to the idea of human rights is not plausible. (It only appears plausible, to some, because some confuse it with a different position that is not only plausible, but correct. More about that below.) It cannot seriously be denied—or perhaps I should say, we should not take seriously the denial—

that human beings *are* all alike in at least some respects such that there *are* some things that are good and some things that are bad for every human being— some things that serve and some things that disserve the well-being of every human being (or, at least, of every human being who is not in a persistent vegetative state). Some things are good and some things are bad, not merely for some human beings, but for every human being. If every human being is sacred, some things—some practices—ought not to be done to any human being, because the practice is bad for every human being; some practices ought to be done for every human being, because (i.e., in part because) the practice is good for every human being. Human beings are all alike in some respects that support generalizations both about what is good and about what is bad, not just for some human beings, but for every human being.

All this seems so obvious that we can fairly wonder who, if anyone, denies it—and why?

III

I said that the relativist challenge to the idea of human rights, though not plausible, appears plausible to some persons: those who confuse the relativist position with a different position. That different position, which is not only plausible but correct, is pluralism about human good.

To say that human beings *are* all alike in at least some respects such that some things are good and some things are bad for *every* human being is not to deny that human beings are *not* all alike in many other respects; it is not to deny that some things are good and some things are bad for *some* human beings *but not for others*. Even though some needs, social as well as biological, are common to all human beings, other needs are not common to all human beings; even though some wants ("preferences") are common to many human beings, many wants are not common to all human beings.[26] That which serves the well-being of—that which is congenial to the flourishing of—one or more human beings is not, therefore, necessarily congenial to the flourishing of every human being, and that which disserves the well-being of—that which is hostile to the flourishing of—one or more human beings is not necessarily hostile to the flourishing of every human being. In particular, a concrete way of life good for one or more human beings might not be good for every human being, and a way of life bad for one or more human beings might not be bad for every human being. Moreover, a way of life good for one or more human beings—or even for every human being—might not be the only way of life good for those human beings; even for a particular human being, there might be two (or more) ways of life that, as a practical matter, are mutually exclusive but each of which would be good for her (albeit in different ways). As David Wong has put it, "[T]here is no [determinate] feature or set of features [of human nature] that eliminates all but one ideal [of the good for man] as valid. . . . [I]nsofar as there is such a thing as a fixed human nature, remaining invariant from social environment to social environment, it is not sufficiently determinate to justify the claim that there is a determinate good for man, a complex of activities arranged in an ideal balance, which any rational and informed person would find the most rewarding."[27] Stuart Hampshire has made the same point: To acknowledge that "[t]here are obvious limits set by common human needs to the conditions under which human beings flourish and human societies flourish" is not to deny that "human nature, conceived in terms of common human needs and capacities, always underdetermines a way of life, and underdetermines an order of priority among virtues, and therefore underdetermines the moral prohibitions and injunctions that support a way of life."[28]

None of this seems particularly controversial. Universalism about human good is correct: Human beings are all alike in some respects, such that some things good for some human beings are good for every human being and some things bad for some human beings are bad for every human being. But pluralism about human good is correct, too: There are many important respects in which human beings are not all alike; some things good for some human beings, including a concrete way of life, might not be good for every human being, and some things bad for some human beings might not be bad for every human being.[29] (This is true intraculturally as well as interculturally.) Indeed, some things good for some human beings, or even for every human being, might not be compatible with every other thing good for them; two or more mutually exclusive things might both be good for a human being.[30] Undeniably, then, any plausible conception of human good must be pluralist. A conception of human good, however, can be, and should be, universalist as well as pluralist: It can acknowledge sameness as well as difference, commonality as well as variety.[31]

There are often differences about how universalist and how pluralist a conception of human good should be. (There are often differences, too, about which universalist position is most credible.[32]) But is a radically antiuniversalist position reasonable? I have in mind here the anthropological view according to which nothing of consequence is good for every human being because, beyond some biological needs, there are no significant needs (much less wants) common to all human beings, no needs, therefore, such that what satisfies them is good, not just for this person or that, or for this group or that, but for any and every person, *for human beings generally.* Is it plausible to insist that human beings do not have significant needs in common, especially *social* needs, needs beyond the merely biological needs all human beings obviously share? Is it plausible to deny that there are significant needs common to all human beings, needs such that what satisfies them is good for every human being?

Why would anyone doubt that there are significant needs common to all human beings? (Stuart Hampshire has written that "[m]oral relativism has always rested on an under-estimate of universal human needs . . .".[33]) After all, some significant senses and appetites—social senses and appetites no less than biological—certainly seem to be shared across the human species. Shared senses and appetites can be and often are shaped in different ways by different cultures *and* by different individual histories within a single culture. Not that all differences are due merely to differences in how common senses and appetites have been shaped: Some significant senses and appetites are not shared across the human species. Nonetheless, some senses and appetites *are* shared. Therefore, some significant needs, some social needs as well as biological, are shared across the human species: the needs that are the correlates of the shared appetites and senses. Some needs are universal and not merely local in character. Some needs are *human*. Philippa Foot has made the point succinctly but eloquently:

> Granted that it is wrong to assume an identity of aim between peoples of different cultures; nevertheless there is a great deal that all men have in common. All need affection, the cooperation of others, a place in a community, and help in trouble. It isn't true to suppose that human beings can flourish without these things—being isolated, despised or embattled, or without courage or hope. We are not, therefore, simply expressing values that we happen to have if we think of some moral systems as good moral systems and others as bad. Communities as well as individuals can live wisely or unwisely, and this is largely the result of their values and the codes of behavior that they teach. Looking at these societies, and critically also at our own, we surely have some idea of how things work out and why they work out as they do. We do not have to suppose it is just as good to promote pride of place and the desire to get an advantage over other men as it is to have an ideal of affection and respect. These things have different harvests, and unmistakably different connections with human good.[34]

Just as some needs (and wants) are human—just as there are significant needs common to all human beings—there are, correspondingly, some things of value to every human being: whatever satisfies, or somehow conduces to the satisfaction of, a common, human need. There are, in that sense, goods common to every human being. Some goods are universal and not merely local in character. Some goods are *human*. They include include various human capacities or capabilities or virtues, namely, those that enable human beings to struggle *against* those forces, inside them as well as outside, that periodically threaten the well-being of any human being and *for* those things, those states of affairs or those states of being, congenial to the flourishing of any human being.

In a series of related essays over the last several years, Martha Nussbaum has developed all this so well that the burden, a heavy burden, is now squarely on those who would press the relativist—the antiuniversalist or, as it is sometimes called, anti-"essentialist"—position.[35] Given the seemingly obvious truth of the basic claim—that there are significant needs and corresponding goods common to every human being—we can fairly wonder what in the world might tempt one to doubt or even to deny it. Why would anyone deny what according to Richard Rorty "historicist thinkers [ever since Hegel] have denied[:] that there is such a thing as 'human nature' or the 'deepest level of the self.' Their strategy has been to insist that socialization, and thus historical circumstance, goes all the way down, that there is nothing 'beneath' socialization or prior to history which is definatory of the human. Such writers tell us that the question 'What is it to be a human being?' should be replaced by questions like 'What is it to inhabit a rich twentieth-century democratic society?' "[36]

There is a revealing passage in his essay "Solidarity or Objectivity?" in which Rorty, *even* Rorty, seems to retreat, albeit perhaps unwittingly, from the extremity of his "historicism"—his antiuniversalism. He writes: "The pragmatists' justification of toleration, free inquiry, and the quest for undistorted communication can only take the form of a comparison between societies which exemplify these habits and those which do not, leading up to the suggestion that *nobody who has experienced both would prefer the latter*."[37] If Rorty is right that no one—no human being, no member of the species—who has experienced both would prefer the latter, what might explain such a preference: a *universal* preference? Moreover, even if Rorty is mistaken in thinking that nobody who has experienced both would prefer the latter, why would he suggest that nobody who has experienced both would prefer the latter *unless he believed that there are interests—there are senses and appetites, there are needs—common to every human being, interests the frustration of which is antithetical to the well-being of any human being?* Rorty's statement that nobody who has experienced both would prefer the latter is certainly in tension, if not inconsistent, with his insistence that (in Bernard Williams's paraphrase) "we cannot, in philosophy, simply be talking about human beings, as opposed to human beings at a given time. ... Rorty ... contrasts the approach of taking some philosophical problem and asking ... 'What does it show us about *being human?*' and asking, on the other hand, 'What does the persistence of such problems show us about *being twentieth-century Europeans?*"[38]

As the passage from his encyclical *Veritatis Splendor* that I have put at the beginning of this chapter might suggest, John Paul II has been one of the most prominent critics of what, according to Rorty, "historicist thinkers ever since Hegel" (including Rorty himself) have claimed: "that there is nothing 'beneath' socialization or prior to history which is definatory of the human." In their rejection of Rorty's historicist claim, John Paul II and Martha Nussbaum are allied. According to Nussbaum, a conception of human good, of human flourishing, can at least aspire "to be objective in the sense that it is justifiable by reference to reasons that do not derive merely from local traditions and practices, but rather from *features of humanness that lie beneath all local traditions and are there to be seen whether or not they are in fact recognized in local traditions.*"[39] The historicist insistence that it's socialization all the way down is not merely some innocuous position in a far corner of academic philosophy. As Rorty's statement about "historicist thinkers since Hegel" suggests, the denial of *human* good or well-being, of *human* needs—the denial, in that sense, of "the human", of "human nature"—has not been uncommon among contemporary thinkers. More importantly, the denial is clearly subversive of human rights claims—as Noam Chomsky emphasizes in the passage I have reproduced at the beginning of this chapter.

Because the historicist denial of human nature is subversive of human rights claims, the question is all the more urgent: What might lead to, what might explain, a denial of the human? What might lead to/explain nihilism (as distinct from pluralism) about human good? I do not have a confident answer. Perhaps a partial explanation is that some such denials confuse conceptions of human nature with human nature itself. It is one thing to insist that conceptions of human nature are irreducibly contingent, that they—like the languages, the vocabularies, in which the conceptions are expressed—bear the traces of particular times and places, of particular histories and cultures; it is another thing altogether to insist that there is no such thing as human nature. Moreover, it is one thing to insist that conceptions of human nature are socially constructed and that there are good reasons to be wary—or at least methodologically skeptical—about any such conception; it is another thing altogether to insist that we can get along quite nicely, thank you, without any conception of human nature, or to insist that putative human nature itself is, through and through, socially constructed ("there's no *there* there, it's socialization all the way down").[40]

Not everyone means the same thing by "natural law", but the position shared by John Paul II, Martha Nussbaum, and Noam Chomsky seems to me to be the principal modern natural law position. ("In so far as any common core can be found to the principal versions of the natural law theory, it seems to amount to the statement that the basic principles of morals and legislation are, *in some sense or other*, objective, accessible to reason and based on human nature."[41]) It is, in any event, the position presupposed by the idea of human rights. According to this position, the fundamental subject matter of morality is human well-being; according to the natural-law conception of the subject matter of moral knowledge, moral knowledge is knowledge of or about the constituents and conditions of human flourishing or well-being.[42] The "natural law" that the idea of human rights presupposes is simply that all (or virtually all) human beings share some significant characteristics, in that sense they share a "nature", in virtue of which some things are good for every human being—some things are valuable for (and, so, should be valued by) every human being—and some things are bad for every human being—some things are harmful to (and, so, should be disvalued by) every human being.[43] In Nussbaum's words, there are "features of humanness that lie beneath all local traditions and are there to be seen whether or not they are in fact recognized in local traditions", and these "features of humanness" constitute, in the words of John Paul II, "the measure of culture and the condition ensuring that man does not become the prisoner of any of his cultures."[44]

Moreover, as Chomsky puts it, "[t]hose with some confidence in the human species . . . will try to determine the intrinsic human characteristics that provide the framework for intellectual development, the growth of moral consciousness, cultural achievement, and participation in a free community."[45] Questions about *human* good—about what is good, or bad, not just for this or that human being, but for every human being, for human beings generally—including questions about *human* rights, are not misconceived.[46] Contra Rorty, the question "What is it to be a human being?" should not be replaced by other questions. This is not to deny that there are other important, and sometimes complementary, questions, such as "What is it to inhabit a rich twentieth-century democratic society?" Nor is it to deny "the very poignant sense in which we may be unable to choose between cultures" or between (or among) ways of life within a single culture: "We may indeed be able to understand the transition [from one culture or way of life to another] in terms of gain and loss, but there may be some of both, and an overall judgement may be hard to make."[47] It bears emphasis, however, that this inability to adjudicate between or among cultures or ways of life, as Charles Taylor explains,

> presupposes that we can, in principle, understand and recognize the goods of another society [or of another way of life] as goods-for-everyone (and hence for ourselves). That these are not combinable with our own home-grown goods-for-everyone may indeed be tragic but is no different in principle from any of the other dilemmas we may be in through facing incombinable goods, even within our own way of life. There is no guarantee that universally valid goods should be perfectly combinable, and certainly not in all situations.
>
> . . . It may be that our contact with certain cultures will force us to recognize incommensurability, as against simply a balance of goods- and bads-for-everyone that we cannot definitively weigh up. But we certainly shouldn't assume this is so *a priori*.
>
> Until we meet this limit, there is no reason not to think of the goods we are trying to define and criticize as universal, provided we afford the same status to those of other societies we are trying to understand. This does *not* mean of course that all our, or all their, supposed goods will turn out at the end of the day to be defensible as such; just that we don't start with a preshrunk moral universe in which we take as given that their goods have nothing to say to us or perhaps ours to them.[48]

✣

The relativist challenge to the idea of human rights is not, then, a plausible challenge. At least, it seems deeply contrary to experience to suggest that there are no significant respects in which human beings are all alike, and that no things, therefore—no practices, no acts or failures to act—are good and no things are bad for every human being. Moreover, as I explained, a healthy pluralism about human good is consistent with a realistic universalism about human good and does not support, and should not be confused with, the relativist challenge. In June 1993, at the UN-sponsored World Conference on Human Rights, the representatives of 172 states adopted by consensus the Vienna Declaration and Programme of Action. They were right to reject the relativist challenge. In the first of its one hundred declarations, the Vienna Declaration states of "all human rights and fundamental freedoms for all" articulated in the Universal Declaration of Human Rights and elsewhere: "The universal nature of these rights and freedoms is beyond question. . . . Human rights and fundamental freedoms are the birthright of all human beings; their protection and promotion is the first responsibility of Governments." I concur in Jack Donnelly's judgment that "[o]ne of the more heartening results of the Vienna Conference was the repudiation of . . . the relativist position. Despite lingering fears of Western neocolonialism, and a continuing preoccupation with the task of development in the former Soviet bloc and the Third World, the resolutions adopted at Vienna generally reflect a commitment to the true universality . . . of internationally recognized human rights."[49]

To reject the relativist challenge to the idea of human rights—to the idea that (because every human being is sacred) there are things that ought not to be done to any human being and things that ought to be done for every human being—is not to deny that there can be, and are, deep differences about human good. (As I have already said, there are often differences about how universalist and how pluralist a conception of human good should be—and differences, too, about which universalist position is most credible.) Different people, different cultures, different traditions have different views about the way or ways of life that are good or fitting, not merely for themselves, but for any human being and for any human community. There are "deep conflicts over what human flourishing and well-being . . . consist in . . . . Aristotle and Nietzsche, Hume and the New Testament are names which represent polar oppositions."[50] Embedded in such differences are differences both about what is bad and about what is good for every human being—and, therefore, differences about what ought not to be done to any human being and about what ought to be done for every human being. There might be radical differences, too, about who is a human being, or, equivalently, about whether every human being—every Homo sapiens—is sacred/inviolable/and so on. But even among those who agree that every human being is sacred, there can be, and are, differences about what way (or ways) of life is fitting for human beings and, in particular, about what ought not to be done to any human being and about what ought to be done for every human being.

But to acknowledge those differences—even to understand that some such differences are reasonable ones—is a far cry from claiming that nothing, that no act or failure to act, is bad and nothing is good for every human being. Indeed, that there are widespread differences about whether one or another practice is bad for every human being does not entail that the practice is not bad for every human being. ("[T]he mere fact of disagreement among the judgments of people hardly shows that there is no fact of the matter to be agreed upon. People within a culture, and people in different cultures, may disagree about all sorts of things, such as whether the winds are influenced by the earth's rotation, or whether the moon is made of rock."[51]) Moreover, whatever such differences might be, they are not typically differences between universalists on the one side and antiuniversalists (or "relativists") on the other. They are typically differences among universalists: Again, the Vienna Declaration, which repudiates the antiuniversalist position, was adopted by consensus by the representatives of 172 states at the World Conference.

Finally, whatever such differences might be, they are differences among universalists who agree, as well as disagree, about what some of the things are—indeed, about what many of the things are—that ought not to be done to, or that ought to be done for, human beings. Many beliefs about what is good for every human being and, especially, many beliefs about what is bad for every human being are widely shared across cultures. "There is nothing . . . culture-bound in the great evils of human experience, re-affirmed in every age and in every written history and in every tragedy and fiction: murder and the destruction of life, imprisonment, enslavement, starvation, poverty, physical pain and torture, homelessness, friendlessness."[52] Addressing the World Conference on Human Rights in June 1993, U.S. Secretary of State Warren Christopher observed that "[t]orture, rape, racism, anti-Semitism, arbitrary detention, ethnic cleansing, and politically motivated disappearances—none of these is tolerated by any faith, creed, or culture that respects humanity."[53] No one believes that rape, or slicing off breasts, or ripping out wombs, or decapitating a child in front of its mother (who has just been raped), or castrating a prisoner (or forcing another prisoner to do so), or throwing a prisoner into hot oil—no one believes that such acts are or might be good for them on whom the horror is inflicted.[54]

IV

Although many beliefs about what is bad for every human being and many beliefs, too, about what is good for every human being are widely shared among cultures, obviously not every such belief is shared among cultures—or even within a single culture. For example, although the proposition that raping a person attacks her (or his) well-being is not controversial, the proposition that sur-gically removing a girl's clitoris (clitoridectomy) attacks her well-being *is* con-troversial. (Clitoridectomy is one of a collection of practices often subsumed under the name "female circumcision"—or, more accurately, "female genital mutilation".[55]) Many persons in some cultures or subcultures believe that ex-cising a girl's clitoris serves her well-being.[56] Again, even among those who agree that every human being is sacred, there can be, and are, differences either about what ought not to be done to any human being or about what ought to be done for every human being, or about both. Here we encounter the basis of a second relativist challenge. This relativist challenge, however, unlike the first one, is not to the idea of human rights itself; it is not to the premise that some things are bad and some things are good for every human being. Rather, it is a challenge to the possibility of overcoming, to any significant extent, transcul-tural disagreement about what things are bad and what things are good for every human being. More precisely, it is a challenge to the possibility of over-coming transcultural disagreement—of diminishing transcultural dissensus—about whether a particular practice, like clitoridectomy, violates one or another human right, or more than one, that it is transculturally agreed that people have.

It bears emphasis that in the second half of the twentieth century—in the period since the end of World War II—significant transcultural agreement has been achieved about what many of the human rights are that people have. In-ternational human rights documents like the Universal Declaration of Human Rights, the International Covenant on Civil and Political Rights, and the In-ternational Covenant on Economic, Social and Cultural Rights are widely en-dorsed by the states of the world.[57] It is true that "[m]ost African and Asian countries did not participate in the formulation of the Universal Declaration of Human Rights because, as victims of colonization, they were not members of the United Nations."[58] But the same cannot be said about many later docu-ments, which not merely affirm but elaborate and add to the rights of the Uni-versal Declaration. For example, both the International Covenant on Civil and Political Rights (ICCPR) and the International Covenant on Economic, Social and Cultural Rights (ICESCR) were adopted in 1966; each covenant entered into force a decade later, in 1976, when the requisite number of states became signatories. As of 1994, there were 122 state parties to the ICCPR and 124 state parties to the ICESCR.[59] (The United States finally ratified the ICCPR in 1992;[60] it has yet to ratify ICESCR.[61]) The Vienna Declaration and Programme of Action was adopted (by consensus by the representatives of 172 states) even more recently, in June 1993. Thus, there is significant transcultural agreement—significant agreement across cultures—first, that people have human rights and, second, about what some, even many, of those rights are. That is, there is significant transcultural agreement: first, that because every human being is sa-cred, certain things ought not to be done to any human being and certain other things ought to be done for every human being; and, second, about what many of those things are.[62]

Though there is significant transcultural agreement both that people have human rights and about what many of those rights are, there can be, and sometimes is, significant transcultural disagreement about whether a particular practice violates one or another human right, or more than one, that it is transculturally agreed—and transculturally established, by international law—that people have.[63] Not every such disagreement is a reasonable one. Some practices undeniably violate an established human right: practices explicitly proscribed by the provision articulating the right. (Practices transculturally agreed to be moral abominations—slavery and genocide, for example—are, typically, explicitly proscribed by the international law of human rights.) But not every practice that might violate an established human right is explicitly proscribed. A practice not explicitly proscribed might nonetheless violate an established human right even if not everyone agrees that it does.

The particular relativist challenge I now want to address is a challenge to the possibility of overcoming, to any significant extent, transcultural disagreement, not so much about what human rights people have—again, there is much transcultural agreement about *that*—but about whether some practice, a practice not explicitly proscribed, violates one or more established human rights. Let's stay with the example of female circumcision, which has recently been much discussed in the human rights literature.[64]

Assume you believe that female circumcision violates a woman's human rights[65]—that subjecting a girl to the practice is unacceptable given that she is sacred (inviolable) and should therefore be treated with respect and concern rather than as an object of domination and exploitation. (In the fall of 1996, "Congress outlawed the rite of female genital cutting in the United States ... and directed federal authorities to inform new immigrants from countries where it is commonly practiced that parents who arrange for their children to be cut here, as well as people who perform the cutting, face up to five years in prison."[66]) Assume you believe that the practice violates, *inter alia*, the Universal Declaration of Human Rights, according to which every human being—including, therefore, every woman—has inherent dignity and worth and, moreover, is equal in dignity and worth to every other human being. You believe that the principal though latent function of the practice, in the cultures (or subcultures) whose practice it is, is to help maintain a social system in which men dominate and exploit women, and that a culture in which men did not dominate and exploit women would not support such a practice.[67] Perhaps you would choose to feature, in defending your position, the Convention on the Elimination of All Forms of Discrimination Against Women and, especially, the Declaration on the Elimination of Violence Against Women.[68] The Declaration, a nonbinding resolution of the United Nations General Assembly adopted in 1993, goes so far as to state, in Article 2(a). that "[v]iolence against women shall be understood to encompass ... female genital mutilation ...".

Although widely accepted in your culture and elsewhere, your evaluation of female circumcision is alien to the cultures that practice female circumcision (which is not to say that in those cultures no one opposes female circumcision). In the view of the cultures whose practice it is, and in particular in the view of many of the mothers who persist in subjecting their often willing daughters to the practice, female circumcision is morally proper—even, for the girl subjected to the practice, ennobling.[69] Someone might suggest to you that it's just a matter of conflicting "cultural preferences",[70] and that you shouldn't seek to impose your cultural preferences on the members of other cultures. You believe that there is more to it than that, that the practice is a violation of human rights. But you might be wrong. Perhaps it *is* just a matter of conflicting cultural preferences; perhaps female circumcision, however distasteful to you, does not violate any human right. Committed to the ideal of self-critical rationality,[71] you do what you can to test your position. Perhaps you accept, as Charles Taylor has suggested we should, "a 'presumption of equal worth' of cultures as an appropriate opening moral stance."[72] Taylor explains: "[I]t is reasonable to suppose that cultures that have provided the horizon of meaning for large numbers of human beings, of diverse characters and temperaments, over a long period of time—that have, in other words, articulated their sense of the good, the holy, the admirable—are almost certain to have something that deserves our admiration and respect, even if it is accompanied by much that we have to abhor and reject."[73] As Taylor then insists, "[I]t would take a supreme arrogance to discount this possibility *a priori*."[74]

In the end, however, after due deliberation, you persist in believing that female circumcision is not merely something "we have to abhor and reject", but a violation of a woman's (girl's) human rights. In this, you are supported not only by the Declaration on the Elimination of Violence Against Women, but by the UN Sub-Commission for the Prevention of Discrimination and the Protection of Minorities, which in 1988 adopted a resolution declaring that female circumcision violates the human rights of women and children.[75] The particular problem that engages you now, therefore, is this: You want the members of the cultures that practice female circumcision to come to accept the view that the practice transgresses the inviolability of a woman. (One human rights scholar has written that "[t]he goal is cross-cultural consensus not because it ... somehow validates the norms but because consensus eases implementation ...".[76] However, that there is a "cross-cultural consensus" about a norm is at least some evidence that what the norm presupposes about *human* well-being is accurate, even if the absence of such a consensus does not entail that what the norm presupposes is false.) You wonder, however, if and to what extent transcultural disagreement about the practice can be overcome. You wonder if it is realistic to think that a critical mass of the members of the cultures that practice female circumcision can be brought to share your evaluation of the practice— and if so, how? (Or if it is realistic to think that *you* might be brought to share *their* view?) You wonder whether it isn't the case, after all, that east is east and west is west—or, in the post–Cold War world, north is north and south is south—and never the twain shall meet?

However difficult it might be to achieve, productive moral discourse *is* possible interculturally as well as intraculturally. "[O]ne can maintain that truth is framework-relative, while conceding for a large range of propositions nearly all frameworks coincide."[77] Indeed, as Richard Rorty has sensibly observed, "everything which we can identify as a human being or as a culture will be something which shares an enormous number of beliefs with us. (If it did not, we would simply not be able to recognize that it was speaking a language, and thus that it had any beliefs at all.)"[78] Thus, "[a] fully individuable culture is at best a rare thing."[79] Moreover, "[c]ultures, subcultures, fragments of cultures, constantly meet one another and exchange or modify practices and attitudes."[80] Indeed, moral discourse among members of different cultures, if conducted in good faith and with an ecumenical openness to the beliefs and experiences of one's interlocutors, can be a principal medium through which different moral communities "meet one another and exchange or modify practices and attitudes." That in the period since World War II there has emerged such widespread transcultural agreement about what many of the rights are that all human beings have (because they are inviolable) disconfirms, powerfully and dramatically, that "never the twain shall meet."

Indeed, productive moral discourse might sometimes be easier to achieve interculturally than intraculturally. For example, productive moral discourse might be easier to achieve among some women from several different cultures, if and to the extent they share an experience of domination and exploitation, than between some men and some women from the same culture. It is simply a mistake to think that there is invariably a radical discontinuity of significant experiences and values between or among persons from different cultures. "Sometimes there is unexpectedly subtle and refined communication across radically different cultures," Amelie Rorty has observed; "sometimes there is insurmountable bafflement and systematic misunderstanding between relatively close cultures. For the most part, however, we live in the interesting intermediate grey area of partial success and partial failure of interpretation and communication. The grey area is to be found at home among neighbors as well as abroad among strangers . . .".[81]

A further, often related premise is also mistaken: that cultures are, or tend to be, morally monistic rather than pluralistic. We must be careful not to fall prey to the mistake of seeing a culture, one's own or another's, as much more cohesive or monistic than it really is.[82] As Nancy Kim has emphasized, with particular reference to the situation and experience of women, even "traditional" cultures are morally pluralistic:

> The label "culture" has obscured the power-play involved in the evolution of "traditional" practices that affect women. . . . "[C]ulture" is often composed of different "subcultures" that may or may not conform to the expectations and norms of the broader society. . . . The culture of which anthropologists speak is the dominant culture within society—the culture of society's power elite. Culture, thus distilled, leaves out rebels, misfits, and the disempowered. . . . In almost every society, the power elite is comprised overwhelmingly of men. Because most cultures are male dominated, how and what women choose to accept or reject as part of their culture is often ignored or suppressed.[83]

So: If it is not unrealistic to think that the members, or some members, of the cultures that practice female circumcision might be brought to share your view that the practice ought not to be performed—*morally* ought not, ought not *because every human being, including every woman, is sacred*—how might they be brought to share it? How else but by means of an *internal* critique of the practice. A critique is external if and to the extent it is based on premises and experiences that, though they have authority for the person or persons whose critique it is, happen not to have authority for persons in the culture (or cultures) to whom the critique is addressed. An internal critique draws on, it works with, premises and experiences authoritative not just for those whose critique it is, *but also for those in the culture to whom the critique is addressed*. Locating such premises and experiences—*relevant premises and experiences shared across the interlocutor cultures*—is not as difficult as some seem to believe. (Again, "[a] fully individuable culture is at best a rare thing."[84]) Commenting on "the strategy of finding within the tradition those resources that express the aspirations of suffering and oppressed people", Lee Yearley has written:

> Persuasion is much more like to be effective if it draws on a listener's own tradition, and such resources are often available. Indeed, these resources are often dramatic and powerful—for example, Aquinas's validation of theft if the need is great or Mencius's seeming acceptance of regicide to ease people's suffering. Moreover, great religious traditions are always more complex and variegated, and more defined by deep tensions and even oppositions, than is reflected in any single, contemporary vision. (Adherents also are often more concerned with proper and improper developments of their tradition than is apparent, particularly when they are forced into defensive positions.) Finally, a tradition's most sophisticated intellectual and spiritual representatives often have positions that can be helpful.[85]

There is a further, more practical sense in which a critique can be internal: The critique can be advanced primarily not by those outside the culture(s) to whom the critique is addressed, least of all by those who are citizens of a state that, when a colonial power, exercised imperial political dominion over the members of that culture. Rather, the critique can be advanced primarily by those inside the culture to whom the critique is addressed, those who have begun to object to the practice in question—perhaps, though not necessarily, because they themselves, or those dear to them, have been victimized by the practice. Indeed, a critique internal in this more practical sense might be necessary if anything is to be done about a practice. The Association of African Women for Research and Development has stated that "[f]eminists from developed countries . . . must accept that [female genital mutilation] is a problem for *African women,* and that no change is possible without the conscious participation of African women."[86] (A study by Katherine Brennan helps us to see how those outside the cultures that practice female circumcision can provide— and, under the auspices of the United Nations, have provided—fruitful opportunities for those inside the cultures, especially women, to develop and then to advance, on the basis of premises and experiences authoritative for (many) persons in those cultures, a critique, partly rooted in human rights norms, of the practice of female circumcision.[87]) Moreover, a critique internal in this more practical sense is at least somewhat less vulnerable to an effort by insiders to deflect the critique by arguing that the critique is little more than a morally imperialist attempt by outsiders to impose their values on the insiders, to make the insiders more like the outsiders. Such an effort at deflection is often conspicuously self-serving. It is often little more than an effort by some in the culture— perhaps even by a relatively few in the culture, who have the upper hand in relation to others in the culture—to maintain the status quo: men in relation to women, for example, or those with political power in relation to those those without it, or those with great wealth in relation to whose without it, and so on. Such an effort at deflection is a prime example of what Secretary Christopher has called "the last refuge of repression."[88]

One of the most insistent proponents of internal critique—internal critique in both senses of the term, but especially in the first, or substantive, sense—has been Abdullahi Ahmed An-Na'im, a prominent Islamic human rights scholar and advocate. In An-Na'im's view, "[H]uman rights advocates in the Muslim world must work within the framework of Islam to be effective."[89] He then explains, in a way that illustrates and confirms Yearley's point, that human rights advocates in the Muslim world "need not be confined, however, to the particular historical interpretations of Islam known as Shari'a. Muslims are obliged, as a matter of faith, to conduct their private and public affairs in accordance with the dictates of Islam, but there is room for legitimate disagreement over the precise nature of these dictates in the modern context. Religious texts, like all other texts, are open to a variety of interpretations. Human rights advocates in the Muslim world should struggle to have their interpretations of the relevant texts adopted as the new Islamic scriptural imperatives for the contemporary world."[90] That Islamic texts can and do support many human rights of the sort established by the international law of human rights is confirmed by the Universal Islamic Declaration of Human Rights, which was "compiled by eminent Muslim scholars, jurists and representatives of Islamic movements and thought" in 1981.[91]

The situation of women in Islam is especially problematic from a human rights perspective. Citing Islamic scholars, Chandran Kukathas writes: "Muslims may insist on the subordinate position of women as a fundamental tenet of Islamic practice. Yet the Quran's strictures on the family display a concern to ameliorate the status of women by abolishing pre-Islamic practices such as female infanticide, and according women rights of divorce, property ownership, and inheritance. Arguably, many practices which weakened women's status were the result of local customs which were often antithetical to the spirit of emancipation envisaged in the Quran."[92] Kukathas concludes that "[c]onflict between differing cultural standards on such issues might best be explained, then, not by appealing to incommensurability of values or fundamental cultural incomparabilities, but by pointing to the fact that not only outsiders but also insiders often misunderstand the traditions."[93]

Indeed, the arguments advanced in feminist Islamic theology[94]—and analogous arguments advanced in feminist Christian theology and in feminist Jewish thought—are compelling arguments to the effect that dominant insiders do misunderstand the tradition, that they marginalize or deny the deepest truths of the tradition. "There is hardly any doubt that women have been discriminated against by patriarchal Christianity as by patriarchal Islam. However, the rereading and re-interpretation of significant women-related Biblical and Qur'anic texts by feminists theologians has shown that it is possible to understand these texts in more than one way, and that—in fact—understanding them in egalitarian rather than in hierarchical terms is more in keeping with the belief, fundamental in both religious traditions, that God, the universal creator and sustainer, is just to all creation."[95] By exemplifying, powerfully, the very sort of revisionist project urged by An-Na'im, feminist theological arguments serve to illustrate that the strategy of internal critique, far from being just a naive fantasy, is an already existing practice. Moreover, recent developments in some Islamic political communities suggest that internal critique is emerging as a significant phenomenon even beyond the domain of feminist discourse; it is emerging as a relatively broadly focused practice.

> After a millenium of inertia . . . Islamic thought is on the move. From Morocco to Malaysia, Muslim intellectuals are reinterpreting the ancient dictates of Islam to fit the modern age, spearheading an extraordinary Islamic revival. In Jordan, professors at a new Islamic university are assigning student papers on the human rights implications of Islamic law's treatment of women

and non-Muslims. In Egypt, Islamic writers are condemning both the use of violence by Muslim extremists and the state's brutal response. Activists in Algeria, Turkey and even Iran are crusading for democracy based on an idea seldom heard in the Muslim world: that Islam forbids all forms of coercion.[96]

✦✦✦

Enough has been said, I think, to make us wary about assuming a priori that moral discourse between or among cultures, especially between or among very different cultures, is a futile project, a dead end. The discourse with which I have been concerned in this section is discourse about whether a particular practice violates one or another human right that it is transculturally agreed—and transculturally established, by international law—that people have. But the point applies as well to discourse about a more fundamental matter: whether a particular claim that people have this or that human right—a particular claim that this or that thing ought not to be done to any human being, or that this or that thing ought to be done for every human being—should be accepted (and, so, whether the right at issue should be established by international law, if it is not already). Recall, in that regard, that in the period since World War II there has emerged, in transcultural dialogue nurtured by the United Nations and other institutions, widespread transcultural agreement about what many of the rights are that all human beings have. (The Universal Islamic Declaration of Human Rights, though not a part of the international law of human rights or of any domestic law, is nonetheless probative of the extent of transcultural agreement about what many of the human rights are that people have.) That bit of history disconfirms that moral discourse between or among even very different cultures—including moral discourse about so fundamental a matter as whether people have such-and-such a human right—is a futile project. The emergence, in the second half of the twentieth century, of widespread transcultural agreement about what many of the rights are that all human beings have—about what many of the things are that ought not to be done to any human being and also about what many of the things are that ought to be done for every human being—teaches us that we cannot know how far moral discourse can go in resolving particular disagreements between or among particular persons from different cultures *until it is tried*. Here, too, Philippa Foot gets to the heart of the matter: "One wonders . . . why people who say this kind of thing [that moral discourse can go only a little way, at best, in resolving disagreements] are so sure that they know where discussions will lead and therefore where they will end. It is, I think, a fault on the part of relativists, and subjectivists generally, that they are ready to make pronouncements about the later part of moral arguments . . . without being able to trace the intermediate steps."[97]

V

In his address, in 1993, to the World Conference on Human Rights, Secretary Christopher said: "We respect the religious, social, and cultural characteristics that make each country unique. But we cannot let cultural relativism become the last refuge of repression."[98] What is this "cultural relativism" of which Christopher spoke? The phrase, notwithstanding the frequency of its use, has no single, canonical meaning.[99] Some positions that sometimes go by the name "cultural relativism" are so confused that they barely merit mention, much less discussion. Three, in particular, come to mind, each of which purports to support tolerance of every culture. Nothing I am about to say in criticism of the three positions entails rejection of Charles Taylor's position that "a 'presumption of equal worth' of cultures [is] an appropriate opening moral stance."[100] But Taylor's sensible presumption is, after all, a *rebuttable* presumption: We must not confuse the moral stance that is or might be appropriate at the opening with the stance appropriate at the close.

1. "No culture is better than any other. (Therefore, no culture is worse than any other.) Every culture is as good as every other." From *what* or *whose* evaluative standpoint—on the basis of what or whose norms or criteria—is every culture supposed to be as good as every other? Yours? Mine? Theirs? God's? From any particular evaluative standpoint, every culture is obviously *not* as good as every other. "[T]here is a difference between saying that every community is as good as every other and saying that we have to work out from the networks we are, from the communities with which we presently identify. . . . The view that every tradition is as rational or as moral as every other could be held only by a god, someone who had no need to use (but only to mention) the terms 'rational' or 'moral,' because she had no need to inquire or deliberate. Such a being would have escaped from history and conversation into contemplation and metanarrative."[101] (To say that from any particular evaluative standpoint every culture is not as good as every other is not to deny that there might be one or another evaluative standpoint from which one or another culture is as good as one or another other culture, in this sense: "We may indeed be able to understand the transition [from a particular culture or way of life to another] in terms of gain and loss, but there may be some of both, and an overall judgement may be hard to make."[102])

2. "No evaluative standpoint is better than any other. In particular, the evaluative standpoint of no culture is better than that of any other. Every evaluative standpoint is as good as every other." Same problem: From *what* or *whose* evaluative standpoint is every evaluative standpoint supposed to be as good as every other? From any particular evaluative standpoint, every evaluative standpoint is not as good as every other.

3. "No culture is, *from its own evaluative standpoint*, inferior to any other

culture. *From its own evaluative standpoint*, every culture is at least as good as every other." The confusion here consists in thinking that the claim somehow supports tolerance of every culture. Even if it were sound, the claim would not support tolerance: Even if by the standards of *his* culture the person standing on my neck, or on my neighbor's neck, or on the neck of a member of his own culture, has a right to do so, that does not mean that by the standards of *our* culture—by the standards *we* accept as correct—we ought to tolerate his doing so; to the contrary, we might be obligated, by our standards, to do what we can to remove his foot even from the neck of a member of his own culture.[103] In any event, the claim is not sound: It makes the mistake, discussed in the preceding section, of treating a culture as much more monistic than any large culture really is—the mistake of treating the norms that have authority for many in a culture as much more coherent overall than they really are.[104] Some aspect (or aspects) of a culture might be deeply problematic—and, indeed, quite inferior to some aspect of another culture—on the basis of some of the norms authoritative in the culture.[105] Put another way, some aspect of a culture might be deeply problematic from the particular evaluative standpoint of those in the culture, or of some of them, who are victimized by the aspect at issue (e.g., women).[106]

By contrast with the three relativist positions I have just now criticized, neither of the two relativist challenges I have addressed in the preceding sections of this chapter is confused. Both of them are, however, as I have explained, problematic.

- The first challenge, directed against the idea of human rights (i.e., against the second part of the idea), claims that human beings do not have a common nature, a *human* nature; it claims, in other words, that there is no *human* being, only *cultural* being. "I have seen in my time Frenchmen, Italians, and Russians. I even know, thanks to Montesquieu, that one may be a Persian, but as for Man, I declare that I have never met him in my life; if he exists it is without my knowledge."[107] Because it makes a claim in "the science of man", that is, a claim about human nature—namely, the claim that there is no human nature or being, only cultural being—we can call this position "anthropological" relativism.

- The second challenge claims that because the beliefs human beings accept vary so much from one culture to another, there is little possibility, if any, for productive dialogue between or among cultures about whether a particular practice violates one or another human right it is agreed and established that people have—or, more fundamentally, about what human rights people have. On the basis of a (correct) presupposition about the nature of justification or legitimation—that successful justification is always "coherentist" or "holist"[108]—this relativism makes an

(exaggerated) claim about the (im)possibility of transcultural justification; thus, we can call this position "epistemological" relativism.

I now want to consider yet a third relativist position, which we can aptly
call "cultural" relativism. Unlike anthropological relativism and epistemological
relativism, cultural relativism, as I present it here, is quite sound—though, as I
will explain, it is a position that, as a defense to a critique of one or another cultural practice, can be, and has been, invoked implausibly or even in bad faith.

The rights and freedoms articulated both in many national constitutions
and in various international documents, like the Universal Declaration of
Human Rights, represent values—that is, *valued states of affairs*—to be achieved
(or they represent disvalues to be avoided). A perusal of international human
rights documents will disclose many examples of such values—for instance,
"the best interests of the child" standard in the Convention on the Rights of
the Child.[109] Examples from the Bill of Rights of the Constitution of the
United States include "the free exercise of religion" (First Amendment), "the
freedom of speech" (same), "the freedom of the press" (same), and "due process
of law" (Fifth Amendment). (An example of a disvalue to be avoided is "cruel
or unusual punishment" [Eighth Amendment].) The Constitution of Japan
speaks of "freedom of thought and conscience" (Article 19), "freedom of religion" (Article 20), "freedom of assembly and association as well as speech, press
and all other forms of expression" (Article 21); such values are "not to be violated" (Article 19) or are "guaranteed to all" (Article 21). The Basic Law of Israel states that "[t]he ... dignity of any person shall not be violated."[110]

With respect to values like those just mentioned, it cannot plausibly be said
that there is always—that is, in *every* context—only one concrete embodiment
(instantiation) of a value that is right or correct *no matter what the particularities of
the context in which the value is to be achieved*. The embodiment of the value that
makes the most sense in any context inevitably depends on the particularities of
the context in which the value is to be achieved.[111] The embodiment that
makes the most sense in one context, given the other legitimate values or interests that compete with the value *in that context*, might not make the most
sense in a different context, where the nature of the competing values or interests is different.[112]

We can refer to the process of embodying or shaping a value on the basis of
the particularities of the context in which the value is to be achieved as the
process of "specifying" the value. A specification "of a principle for a specific
class of cases is not a deduction from it, nor a discovery of some implicit meaning; it is the act of setting a more concrete and categorical requirement in the
spirit of the principle, and guided both by a sense of what is practically realizable (or enforceable), and by a recognition of the risk of conflict with other
principles or values."[113] What Anthony Kronman has said of the process of

"judgment" accurately describes the process of specifying a value. Such specification is a species of judgment.

> Good judgment, and its opposite, are in fact most clearly revealed in just those situations where the method of deduction is least applicable, where the ambiguities are greatest and the demand for proof most obviously misplaced. To show good judgment in such situations is to do something more than merely apply a general rule with special care and thoroughness, or follow out its consequences to a greater level of detail. Judgment often requires such analytic refinement but does not consist in it alone. That this is so is to be explained by the fact that we are most dependent on our judgment, most in need of *good* judgment, in just those situations that pose genuine dilemmas by forcing us to choose between, or otherwise accommodate, conflicting interests and obligations whose conflict is not itself amenable to resolution by the application of some higher-order rule. It is here that the quality of a person's judgment comes most clearly into view and here, too, that his or her deductive powers alone are least likely to prove adequate to the task.[114]

If the embodiment or specification that makes the most sense in any context inevitably depends on the particularities of the context in which the value is to be achieved, then the embodiment that makes the most sense in the context of one culture might well not make the most sense in the context of a different culture. Moreover, there might be room for a reasonable difference of judgment about what embodiment makes the most sense in a particular cultural context. The embodiment that makes the most sense, in a particular cultural context, to those charged, or to a majority of those charged, with achieving the value in that context might not make the most sense to others, whether inside or outside the culture, and yet the position of those charged with achieving the value might nonetheless be a reasonable one.[115] Philip Alston is right to emphasize that "in spite of its undoubted importance in terms of rejecting what might be termed crude relativist attacks, the diplomatic/legal vindication of the principle of universality cannot be taken to have resolved the deeper, more enduring challenge of ensuring greater openness and sensitivity to different cultural contexts in the implementation of human rights standards. . . . [N]o amount of universalist aspirations can cancel out the inevitable influence of cultural values and perceptions."[116] Focusing in particular on "the best interests of the child" standard under the Convention on the Rights of the Child, Alston suggests that "it might be argued that, in some highly industrialized countries, the child's best interests are 'obviously' best served by policies that emphasize autonomy and individuality to the greatest possible extent. In more traditional societies, the links to family and the local community might be considered to be of paramount importance and the principle that 'the best interests of the child' shall prevail will therefore be interpreted as requiring the sublimation of the individual child's preferences to the interests of the family or even the extended family."[117]

Add to the stew provisions like the following one, which are not uncommon in the international law of human rights, and the point I am making here becomes overwhelming: Article 19 of the International Covenant on Civil and Political Rights states that "the right to freedom of expression" (which Article 19 protects) "may . . . be subject to certain restrictions, . . . [and that] these shall only be such as . . . are necessary . . . *[f]or the protection of national security or of public order, or of public health or morals*" (emphasis added). There is obviously room for a reasonable difference of judgment, intraculturally and even more so interculturally, about what the requirements of the "public morals" are—and room, too, therefore, for a reasonable difference of judgment about when it is necessary to compromise the value of free expression in the interest of the public morals. "[I]dentical norms can lead to very different results, but results that may well be, in the light of the prevailing and other cultural circumstances, largely compatible with the international norms."[118] A society that is highly individualistic (like the United States?) will tend to see the requirements of the public morals one way; a society that is more communitarian (like Canada or Ireland?) will tend to see them at least somewhat differently, maybe a lot differently. (I collect and discuss provisions like Article 19 in chapter 4, where I comment on the nonabsolute character, in international law, of many human rights.) As Alston points out, "In contrast to criticisms which tend to portray international human rights norms as being not only hostile, but also impervious, to non-Western cultural influences, [it is clear] that there is enormous scope for such differences to be taken into account in the implementation of those norms at the domestic level."[119]

Here, then, is a "cultural relativism" difficult to dispute: The best, or optimal, specification of some of the values represented in an international human rights document like the Universal Declaration cannot be determined acontextually; it depends on, *it is relative to*, particularities of context. Most importantly for present purposes, the optimal specification might be relative to cultural particularities. And, indeed, the Vienna Declaration acknowledges that "the significance of national and regional particularities and various historical, cultural and religious backgrounds must be borne in mind . . .". Jack Donnelly's cautionary note is sound: "Political histories, cultural legacies, economic conditions, and human rights problems do differ not only among the First, Second, and Third Worlds, but within each world as well. In the practical world of implementing universal human rights, this needs to be kept in mind. Internationally recognized human rights provide general direction. They do not provide a plan of implementation that can be applied mechanically, irrespective of political, economic, and cultural diversity."[120] No less an opponent of "moral relativism" than John Paul II supports the point: "Certainly there is a need to seek out and to discover the most adequate formulation for universal and permanent moral norms *in the light of different cultural contexts* . . .".[121]

We must not overstate (or overread) the point, however: In the very same sentence in which it acknowledges that the differences among nations and regions "must be borne in mind", the Vienna Declaration goes on to insist that, *nonetheless*, "it is the duty of States, regardless of their political, economic or cultural systems, to promote and protect all human rights and fundamental freedoms." Similarly, Secretary Christopher, in his address to the conference that produced the Vienna Declaration, stated: "That *each* of us comes from different cultures absolves *none* of us from our obligation to comply with the Universal Declaration [on Human Rights]."[122] Obviously we cannot exclude *a priori* the possibility that one or another controversial specification of a human rights value is—even allowing for all the relevant particularities of context, including cultural particularities—unreasonable. "Footbinding in pre-World War II China, child slavery or bondage, and female infanticide in various societies are examples of practices in relation to which culture-based arguments have already had to yield (in theory, if not always in practice) in favour of human rights norms."[123] In particular, we cannot exclude the possibility that one or another ungenerous specification of a human rights value is not really an honest effort to take the value seriously in the context at hand but is, instead, an effort to marginalize the value while paying it lip service. Indeed, there might not even be a plausible culturally based justification for one or another ungenerous specification of a human rights value. It is always important, therefore, to undertake a careful scrutiny of "claims of relativism in terms of their foundations within the cultural, philosophical, or religious traditions of societies. Many claims made have no foundation whatsoever in such traditions."[124]

The position that female circumcision does not violate any established human right constitutes a controversial specification of the right or rights in question. Allowing for all the relevant cultural particularities, is that specification reasonable? The same inquiry might be pursued with respect to many other "cultural" practices. "[T]here are . . . many . . . cases in which cultural arguments continue to be used today to justify the denial of children's rights. They include arguments designed to defend the full range of practices relating to female circumcision, to justify the non-education of lower class or caste children, or to justify the exclusion of girls from educational and other opportunities which would make them less sought after in marriage."[125] The question whether a particular specification isn't, finally, unreasonable is different from the question whether those whose specification it is could be brought, in transcultural discourse, to see that it is unreasonable. The latter question—the possibility of productive transcultural discourse about human rights—is one of the issues I have addressed in this chapter.

VI

My principal aim in this chapter has been to address the three "relativisms" that challenge discourse about human rights. (That is, I have addressed the three relativisms worth addressing. As I noted earlier, not every position that goes by the name "cultural relativism" merits much consideration.) In the human rights literature, different relativist positions are not always distinguished from one another with due care. Each of the three positions I have discussed here is distinct from the other two. Recognizing them as distinct positions—positions that say different things, that make different claims, and thus that merit different responses—is a step in the direction of clarity. Let me summarize.

1. *Anthropological relativism.* I have claimed that, and explained why, the first and principal relativism—the relativist challenge to the (second part of the) idea of human rights—is simply not plausible. However fashionable this relativism (antiuniversalism, antiessentialism, etc.) might be in some quarters today, some things are bad and some things are good, not just for some human beings, but for every human being.

That some things are bad and some things are good for every human being—even that there is widespread transcultural agreement to that effect—does not entail that there is widespread transcultural agreement either about what, precisely, is bad or about what, precisely, is good for every human being. As it happens, however, there *is* widespread transcultural agreement about what many of the things are that are bad for every human being and also about what many of the things are that are good for every human being. That widespread agreement is evidenced by the widespread support the major international human rights documents enjoy among the states of the world today.

2. *Epistemological relativism.* The second relativism is skeptical about the possibility of overcoming, to any significant extent, transcultural disagreement about whether a particular practice, like female circumcision, violates one or another established human right; it is skeptical about the possibility of productive transcultural moral dialogue. This relativism derives whatever plausibility it has mainly from the mistaken presupposition that there is, often if not always, a radical discontinuity of significant premises and experiences between or among different cultures—which presupposition is often aided and abetted by a further presupposition, also mistaken: that cultures are, or tend to be, morally monistic rather than pluralistic.

3. *Cultural relativism.* The third relativism insists that particularities of context, especially cultural particularities, do and should play a role in determining the specific shape—for example, the specific institutional embodiment—one or another culture gives to a value (e.g., freedom of the press) represented by a human rights provision. This relativism, unlike the other two, is not merely plausible, but correct.

CHAPTER 4

✦❀✦

Are Human Rights Absolute?

The Incommensurability Thesis and Related Matters

We can imagine extreme cases where killing an innocent person may save a whole nation. In such cases it seems fanatical to maintain the absoluteness of the judgment, to do right even if the heavens will in fact fall.

—Charles Fried[1]

There are hard cases, as everybody knows. The prospect . . . of damage apparently avertable by violating the moral absolutes, can seem indubitable and be felt as overwhelming. But these are cases in which we do not see the relevant parts of the scheme of providence—a scheme of which we never, in this life, see the whole or even much. . . . To deny the truth of moral absolutes . . . is incoherent with faith in divine providence. . . . [T]o respect the moral absolutes which are made known to us by God through reason and faith is to cooperate with God, who has practical knowledge of everything without limit.

—John Finnis[2]

Now we come to the final of our four inquiries. Let us pause to survey the ground we have covered thus far.

Again, the idea of human rights consists of two parts: the premise or claim that every human being is sacred (inviolable, etc.), and the further claim that *because* every human being is sacred (and given all other relevant information), certain choices should be made and certain other choices rejected; in particular, certain things ought not to be done to any human being and certain other things ought to be done for every human being.

In chapter 1, I addressed a question about the first part of the idea of human rights: Is there any intelligible secular version of the claim that every human being is sacred—or, instead, is the claim inescapably religious and the idea of human rights, therefore, ineliminably religious?

In chapter 2, I addressed two questions about the language or vocabulary

87

of "rights", which is the principal language in which, in this century, claims about what ought not to be done to any human being and claims about what ought to be done for every human being have come to be expressed: What does "rights talk" mean—how does the rhetoric of rights function—both in the discourse of the international law of human rights and in the moral, especially the political-moral, discourse that underlies and shapes the international-legal discourse? And, as it functions in that twofold discourse, is rights talk problematic?

In chapter 3, I turned to the second part of the idea of human rights. The central question in chapter 3: Are human rights truly universal? The principal position I examined in chapter 3, which I called "the relativist challenge", holds that whether or not every human being is sacred—and, so, even if every human being *is* sacred—there are no things that ought not to be done (not even any things that *conditionally rather than unconditionally* ought not to be done) to any human being and no things that ought to be done (not even any things that *conditionally* ought to be done) for every human being. That is, no putatively "human" right is truly a *human* right: no such right is the right of *every* human being; in that sense, no such right—no such "ought" or "ought not"—is truly universal. In chapter 3, I contended against this relativist challenge to the (second part of the) idea of human rights; I also identified and addressed various other "relativisms" that are relevant to the idea of human rights or are implicated by debates about what human rights, if any, human beings have.

In this, the final chapter, I continue to focus on the second part of the idea of human rights. The central question: Are human rights are absolute? Assuming that every human being is sacred, are there some things that ought *never* (i.e., under any circumstances or conditions) to be done to any human being or some things that ought *always* (under all conditions) to be done for every human being? Or, instead, are there only things that *conditionally* ought not to be done to any human being and things that *conditionally* ought to be done for every human being—things that ought not to be done, and things that ought to be done, under some, even most, conditions, but not under every imaginable condition?

I

No one argues that every human right—every "ought" and "ought not"—established by the international law of human rights is or even should be absolute. Indeed, some human rights established by international law are explicitly conditional rather than unconditional—and appropriately so. Consider, for example, Article 2(1) of the International Covenant on Economic, Social, and Cultural Rights (ICESCR): "Each State Party to the present Covenant undertakes to take steps, individually and through international assistance and co-operation, especially economic and technical, to the maximum of its available resources, with a view to achieving progressively the full realization of rights recognized in the Covenant by all appropriate means, including particularly the adoption of legislative measures." Consider, too, Article 11(2): "The State Parties to the present Covenant recognize the right of everyone to an adequate standard of living for himself and his family, including adequate food, clothing and housing, and to the continuous improvement of living conditions. The State Parties will take appropriate steps to ensure the realization of this right . . .". As these and several other, comparable provisions in the ICESCR and in other human rights documents[3] make clear, some of the human rights claims articulated in international law—claims about what a state ought to do, about the "welfare" it ought to secure, for every one of its citizens—are too conditional to be considered absolute in any meaningful sense of the term. According to Article 2(1), what a state ought to do for its citizens under Article 11(1) depends on—it is conditional on—the extent of "its available resources". Moreover, such claims are not merely conditional, they are conspicuously indeterminate (more precisely, underdeterminate) in many of the contexts in which they are implicated. There are many contexts in which there can be reasonable disagreement about whether, given its available resources, the "food, clothing and housing" a state is acting to secure for its citizens rise to the level of "adequate"—or about whether the state is doing enough, whether it is taking sufficient steps, legislatively or otherwise, to secure adequate welfare for its citizens.[4]

Even some rights that many members of liberal democratic societies consider to be "fundamental" or "core" human rights—for example, the rights to freedom of expression and to freedom of religion—are, as established by international law, conditional rather than unconditional. For example, Article 19(2) of the International Covenant on Civil and Political Rights (ICCPR) states: "Everyone shall have the right to freedom of expression; this right shall include freedom to seek, receive and impart information and ideas of all kinds, regardless of frontiers, either orally, in writing or in print, in the form of art, or through any other media of his choice." But then Article 19(3) states: "The exercise of the rights provided for in paragraph 2 of this article carries with it special duties and responsibilities. It may therefore be subject to certain restrictions, but these shall only be as are provided by law and are necessary: (a) For respect of the rights or reputations of others; (b) For the protection of national security or of public order (*ordre public*), or of public health or morals." Thus, according to Article 19 of the ICCPR, one's right to freedom of expression is not absolute but conditional: One has the right only on condition that—only if and to the extent that—one's having the right does not conflict with certain competing values, in the interest of which the right may be limited or restricted. Moreover, restrictions on the right—and, in that sense, the overall right itself—are somewhat indeterminate in some contexts in which it is implicated: There are some contexts, perhaps many, in which there can be reasonable disagreement about whether, all things considered, a limitation on the right—in the interest, for example, of "the public morals"—is necessary or otherwise appropriate.[5] Article 19 is not unique; other provisions of the ICCPR—Article 18 (protecting "the right to freedom of thought, conscience, and religion"), Article 21 ("the right of peaceful assembly"), and Article 22 ("the right to freedom of association with others")—provide that the protected right is "subject ... to such limitations as are prescribed by law and are necessary to protect public safety, order, health, or morals of the fundamental rights and freedoms of others." (This language is from Article 18, but Articles 21 and 22 contain virtually identical language.)

Moreover, the same observations, about conditionality and indeterminacy, apply to many other "fundamental" human rights provisions in other human rights documents. (Indeed, the Universal Declaration on Human Rights contains a provision, Article 29(2), that on its face is not limited to particular human rights: "In the exercise of his rights and freedoms, everyone shall be subject only to such limitations as are determined by law solely for the purpose of securing due recognition and respect for the rights and freedoms of others and of meeting the just requirements of morality, public order and the general welfare in a democratic society.") Consider, for example, Article 1(3) of the Declaration on the Elimination of All Forms of Intolerance and of Discrimination Based on Religion or Belief, which states that the "[f]reedom to manifest one's religion or belief [in worship, observance, practice and teaching] may be subject only to such limitations as are prescribed by law and are necessary to protect public safety, order, health or morals or the fundamental rights and freedoms of others."[6] Consider, too, the European Convention for the Protection of Human Rights and Fundamental Freedoms, which contains several similar provisions: One's "right to respect for his private and family life, his home and his correspondence" (Article 8), one's "right to freedom of thought, conscience, and religion" (Article 9), one's "right to freedom of expression" (Article 10), and one's "right to freedom of peaceful assembly and to freedom of association with others" (Article 11) may all be restricted so long as the restrictions "are prescribed by law and are necessary in a democratic society in the interests of public safety, for the protection of public order, health, or morals, or for the protection of the rights and freedoms of others." (This language is from Article 9, but Articles 8, 10, and 11 all contain virtually identical language.)[7]

Now let us consider a different and more dramatic way in which international law makes some human rights—including some quite fundamental ones—conditional. Article 4 of the International Covenant on Civil and Political Rights states:

> 1. In times of public emergency which threaten the life of the nation and the existence of which is officially proclaimed, the State Parties to the pre-

sent Covenant may take measures derogating from their obligations under the present Covenant to the extent strictly required by the exigencies of the situation, provided that such measures are not inconsistent with their other obligations under international law and do not involve discrimination solely on the ground of race, colour, sex, language, religion or social origin.

2. No derogation from Articles 6, 7, 8 (paragraphs 1 and 2), 11, 15, 16 and 18 may made be made under this provision.

Let's put aside for the moment those rights that are "nonderogable" under Article 4(2). According to Article 4(1), some human rights are, as established by the ICCPR, "derogable": for example, the right not to "be subjected to arbitrary arrest or detention" (Article 9(1)); the right of "[e]veryone lawfully within the territory of a State" to, "within that territory, . . . liberty of movement and freedom to choose his residence" (Article 12(1)); the right not to "be subjected to arbitrary or unlawful interference with his privacy, family, home or correspondence" (Article 17); "the right to freedom of expression (Article 19); "[t]he right of peaceful assembly" (Article 21); and "the right of freedom of association with others" (Article 22). None of these rights, as established by the ICCPR, is absolute; all are conditional; they may each be curtailed, "to the extent strictly required by the exigencies of the situation," so as to meet a "public emergency which threatens the life of the nation".

Similarly, Article 15 of the European Convention on Human Rights provides:

1. In time of war or other public emergency threatening the life of the nation any High Contracting Party may take measures derogating from its obligations under this convention to the extent strictly required by the exigencies of the situation, provided that such measures are not inconsistent with its other obligations under international law.

2. No derogation from Article 2, except in respect of deaths resulting from lawful acts of war, or from Articles 3, 4 (paragraph 1) and 7 shall be made under this provision.

According to Article 15(1), some human rights are, as established by the Convention, derogable, including "the right to freedom of thought, conscience and religion" (Article 9), "the right to freedom of expression" (Article 10), and "the right to freedom of peaceful assembly and to freedom of association with others" (Article 11).

It makes good sense that some human rights are, as established by international law, not absolute but only conditional, because some human rights—like the right to freedom of expression—are, as a moral matter, nonabsolute. It is one thing to say that something, A, conditionally ought not to be done to any human being—that it ought not to be done to any human being *unless certain conditions exist*. It is another thing to say that A ought not to be done to any human being *no matter what conditions exist*, that it may not be done to any human being *under any conditions*. But whether A ought not to be done to a *particular* human being, or to *particular* human beings, might well depend on various particularities of context, such that it would be mistaken to say that A absolutely—unconditionally—ought not to be done to any human being, that it may not be done no matter what the particularities of context. If so, a human being's right that A not be done to her is conditional rather than absolute. It is a good thing that the international law of human rights provides substantial guidance both about what ought not to be done to any human being and about what ought to be done for every human being. But because it would be impossible to know in advance all the relevant particularities of all the relevant contexts that exist or might come to exist, international law, in providing such guidance, must as a practical matter do what provisions like those presented here do: make some human rights conditional rather than absolute or unconditional by indicating the conditions the existence of which defeats the rights-claim.

Moreover, it makes sense that the international law of human rights indicates what those conditions are in somewhat general outline. This makes some provisions of the international law of human rights at least somewhat indeterminate in some contexts in which the provisions are implicated—that is, in some contexts this leaves room for a reasonable difference of judgment about whether, given all the relevant particularities, the necessary conditions exist. But as a practical matter, this is as it must be. In a part of *The Concept of Law* relevant here, H.L.A. Hart emphasized that "a feature of the human predicament . . . that we labour under . . . whenever we seek to regulate, unambiguously and in advance, some sphere of conduct by means of general standards to be used without further official directions on particular occasions . . . is our relative ignorance of fact . . . [and] our relative indeterminacy of aim."[8] Given that "feature of the human predicament", it makes sense that many legal (and other) norms are somewhat open-ended. "If the world in which we live were characterized only by a finite number of features, and these together with all the modes in which they could combine were known to us, then provision could be made in advance for every possibility. We could make rules, the application of which to particular cases never called for a further choice. Everything could be known, and for everything, since it could be known, something could be done and specified in advance by rule. . . . Plainly this world is not our world. . . . This inability to anticipate brings with it a relative indeterminacy of aim."[9] The point is not that determinate norms cannot be achieved.[10] The point, rather, is that such norms ought not always to be a goal, for then we will have "secure[d] a measure of certainty or predictability at the cost of blindly prejudging what is to be done in a range of future cases, about whose composition we are ignorant. We shall thus succeed in settling in advance, but also in the dark, issues which can only reasonably be settled when they arise and are identified."[11] (In chapter 3, I pointed out that some human rights provisions are indeterminate in some contexts in which they are implicated, in the sense that in some contexts there can be a reasonable difference of judgments, both in-traculturally and interculturally, about what a human rights provision forbids or about what it requires.[12])

Not every human rights provision or other legal norm need be made in-determinate, however, or indeterminate to the same degree. As Hart himself ac-knowledged, "[We] need to remind ourselves that human inability to anticipate the future, which is at the root of this indeterminacy, varies in degree in different fields of conduct ...".[13] One might be tempted to think that, similarly, not every human rights provision need be made conditional—that some human rights provisions have been made, and some should be made, absolute. The question arises, therefore, whether there are at least some things such that whether a state (or other actor) ought not to do them to any human being, or whether a state ought to do them for every human being, should not be thought to depend on the existence or nonexistence of any conditions, it should not be thought to depend on any particularities of context? International law establishes some human rights not as conditional but as absolute or unconditional. Does this make sense? As a moral matter, are some human rights absolute? Is it the case that some things ought not to be done to any human being not merely conditionally but unconditionally—that some things ought not to be done to any human being *no matter what*, that they ought *never* to be done? Is it the case that some things ought to be done for every human being *no matter what*?

Consider, in that regard, some of the rights that Article 4(2) of the ICCPR makes nonderogable: "the inherent right to life" (Article 6);[14] the right not to "be subjected to torture or to cruel, inhuman or degrading treatment or pun-ishment" (Article 7); and the right not to "be held in slavery ... [or] in servi-tude" (Article 8(1) & 8(2)). Article 15(2) of the European Convention makes substantially the same rights nonderogable.[15] It bears emphasis that even *if* these rights are not, as *moral* rights, absolute, it might make sense, all things consid-ered, for international law to do what it does: make such rights, as *legal* rights, nonderogable. (In my view, it *does* make sense for international law to make some rights nonderogable even if the rights are not, as moral rights, absolute. I explain why at the end of this chapter.) But it would make even more sense that international law makes such rights nonderogable if the rights are, as moral rights, absolute. Are they?

For example, is the human right not to be subjected to torture an absolute moral right? Article 1 of the Declaration on Protection from Torture defines "torture" as "any act by which severe pain or suffering, whether physical or mental, is intentionally inflicted by or at the instigation of a public official on a person for such purposes as obtaining from him or a third person information or confession, punishing him for an act he has committed or is suspected of having committed, or intimidating him or other persons." (The definition in

Article 1 of the Convention Against Torture and Other Cruel, Inhuman or Degrading Treatment or Punishment is substantially the same.) Article 3 of the Declaration states: "No State may permit or tolerate torture or other cruel, inhuman or degrading punishment. Exceptional circumstances such as a state of war or a threat of war, internal political instability or any other public emergency may not be invoked as a justification for torture or other cruel, inhuman or degrading punishment or treatment." (Article 2(2) of the Convention against Torture is substantially the same.) Is it really the case that there are no imaginable conditions under which it would be morally permissible to subject a person to torture? An affirmative answer is counterintuitive. Imagine that the person, a terrorist, has placed a nuclear bomb in the middle of a large city, that the bomb has been set to go off within a few hours, and that the terrorist, just captured in another city, will disclose the location of the bomb, which can be defused, only if he is tortured. Indeed, imagine that the terrorist will disclose the location of the bomb only if an innocent person dear to him is tortured (an innocent person, let us imagine, who either does not consent to being tortured or is incompetent to do so). The point of this thought experiment is not to induce skepticism about the wisdom of making the human right not to be subjected to torture nonderogable under international law. The point is only to suggest why the claim that the *moral* right not to be subjected to torture is absolute or unconditional is, for many persons, deeply counterintuitive.

Consider, for example, a case recently before the Supreme Court of Israel, involving the use of physical force in the interrogation of a Palestinian detainee believed to have "extremely vital information whose immediate extraction would help save lives and prevent severe terror attacks in Israel." The attorney for the government argued that the physical force in question was "moderate" but that in any event "[n]o enlightened nation would agree that hundreds of people should lose their lives because of a rule saying torture is forbidden under any circumstances."

> Justices Aharon Barak, Mishael Cheshin and Eliahu Mazza joined the debate, pressing [the Israeli human-rights lawyer, Andre] Rosenthal to declare whether he agreed that torture was justifiable if it could lead investigators to a bomb about to explode. When Mr. Rosenthal demurred from full agreement, Justice Cheshin turned angrily on him: "That's the most immoral and extreme position I've ever heard in my life," he said. "A thousand people are about to be killed, and you propose that we don't do anything."

Later, after the court granted the government's request to lift an injunction on the use of the physical force in question, Mr. Rosenthal explained "that what he and other human-rights lawyers had been seeking was not so much a ban on force, but a review by the court of the limits of the law, and making public the criteria for using force."[16]

That a claim is counterintuitive—including that claim that the moral right not to be subjected to torture is absolute—does not mean that the claim is wrong. Perhaps, after due reflection, we should judge our intuition about some matter to be mistaken. ("It is astonishing . . . to hear philosophers talking about their 'intuitions' as something to be trusted and left unscrutinized, unless they come into conflict with one another. 'My intuitions are that . . .' is a common way to begin a philosophical discussion, as if one represented the eternal voice of mankind."[17]) Again, are any human rights, as moral rights, absolute? Let's move beyond the human right not to be subjected to torture and consider what many believe to be the most fundamental of all human rights—or certainly one of them: a human being's right to life. Let us return to our hypothetical about the urban terrorist, who, let us imagine, will disclose the location of the bomb to the authorities only if they kill an innocent person, P, dear to the terrorist and then threaten to continue the process of killing innocent persons dear to him until he discloses the location of the bomb. (As before, P either does not or is incompetent to consent to this strategy.) Let's put aside the question whether, in the circumstances, the authorities are morally obligated to kill P. The question at hand is simply whether killing P is a choice the authorities are morally permitted to make—or whether that choice is morally impermissible, morally wrong, no matter what the circumstances and no matter what the consequences of their not killing P. According to John Finnis, the authorities are not morally permitted (much less morally obligated) to choose to kill P even if doing so is the only way to save the lives of millions of person in the city where the nuclear bomb is set to go off; it would be morally wrong for them to make that choice.[18] (Indeed, choosing to kill P would be wrong, in Finnis's view, even if the life of every human being on earth hung in the balance.) Finnis's position will seem, to many persons, not merely counterintuitive, but incredible. "We can imagine extreme cases where killing an innocent person may save a whole nation. In such cases it seems fanatical to maintain the absoluteness of the judgment, to do right even if the heavens will in fact fall."[19] What is Finnis's reasoning?

II

Even though the well-being of a human being can be an instrumental good—even though it can have instrumental value (value as a "means" to an "end")—for another human being, let us assume that the well-being of every human being is a basic good, an intrinsic (noninstrumental) good, not just for herself but for every other human being. Certainly one who believes that all human beings are truly sisters/brothers to one another will accept some such proposition.[20] ("Never send to know for whom the bell tolls; it tolls for thee.") Let us assume, too, that the "life"—the "being alive"—of every human being is an aspect of her well-being and, as such, is a basic good or value for every human being.

Now, Finnis's argument. It would be morally wrong for the authorities to kill P, says Finnis, because

> one should not choose to do any act which *of itself does nothing but* damage or impede a realization or participation of any one or more of the basic forms of human good . . . . [K]ill[ing] some innocent person to save the lives of some hostages . . . is an act which of itself does nothing but damage the basic value of life. The goods that are expected to be secured in and through the consequential release of the hostages (if it takes place) would be secured not in or as an aspect of the killing of the innocent man but in or as an aspect of a distinct, subsequent act, an act which would be one "consequence" amongst the innumerable multitude of incommensurable consequences of the act of killing.[21]

What does Finnis mean by an act that "of itself does nothing but" damage a basic human value? And why does he put so much weight on the fact that an act "of itself does nothing but" damage a basic human value?[22]

> Perhaps the consequences of one's act seem likely to be very good and would themselves directly promote further basic human good. Still, these expected goods will be realized (if at all) not as aspects of one-and-the-same act, but as aspects or consequences of other acts (by another person, at another time and place, as the upshot of another free decision . . .). So, however "certainly foreseeable" they may be, they cannot be used to characterize the act as, *in and of itself*, anything other than an intentional act of, say, man-killing. This is especially obvious when a blackmailer's price for sparing his hostages is "killing that man"; the person who complies with the demand, in order to save the lives of many, cannot deny that he is choosing an act which of itself does nothing but kill.[23]

Let us assume that, in our hypothetical, killing P does nothing "of itself" but damage a basic human value: P's life. No choice of an act that of itself does nothing but damage a basic human good or value (in Finnis's example, "life"— the life of an innocent person) can ever be justified on consequentialist grounds, argues Finnis—it can never be justified on the basis of the act's overall consequences, its consequences "on the whole and in the long run"—because different basic human values are incommensurable, and so damage to one such value can never be weighed against benefit to another. (On his list of basic human values, Finnis includes, inter alia, life, knowledge, and friendship.[24]) According to Finnis, it is never the case that consequences in the form of damage to one or more basic value or values can be outweighed by consequences in the form of benefit to one or more other basic value or values. Because each of the basic human values is "primary, incommensurable with the others in point of objective importance . . . consequences, even to the extent that they can be 'foreseen as certain,' cannot be commensurably *evaluated*, which means that 'net beneficial consequences' is a literally absurd general objective or criterion."[25]

Is Finnis right that different basic human values—including, for example, P's life and the millions of lives that will be lost if the nuclear bomb explodes—are incommensurable? What does it mean to say that two or more things are not commensurable? According to the *Oxford English Dictionary*, "commensurable" means "measurable by the same standard or scale of values."[26] Two things are commensurable, therefore, if they can be put on the same scale, if they can be measured against, compared to, one another in terms of a single standard. (For example, one human life can be compared to two human lives, or to two million, in terms of, e.g., number of lives.) Two things would be incommensurable, then, if there were no single standard of comparison in terms of which they could be measured.

But it is not meaningful to assess the commensurability *vel non* of any two (or more) things apart from one or another standard of comparison, because commensurability and incommensurability are relative. Two things that are not commensurable relative to one standard might be commensurable relative to a different standard. Indeed, there are no two things that are not commensurable relative to at least some standard of comparison. Think of any two things—any two things *at all*—and then consider this standard: which of the two things, A or B, if either; you need to talk about, or need more to talk about, right now. You might need to talk about A but not B; or, about B but not A; or, about neither A nor B; or, about both A and B (and about one more than the other or about one the same as the other).

In any event, it is simply not true that values—including Finnis's basic human values—are incommensurable relative to every standard of comparison. Any two (or more) values can be measured in terms of some standard. Consider, for example, this standard: which of the two values, if either, is more important to you, *given your most fundamental commitments and projects and the hierarchy among them*. So, if in saying that basic human values are incommensurable it is meant that no two basic human values can be compared in terms of a single standard, the incommensurability thesis is plainly wrong. Indeed, Finnis seems understand that the thesis is mistaken, for he seems to acknowledge that any two basic human values *can* be compared in terms of a single standard, namely, the standard derived from the requirements of my (or your or her or anyone's) most fundamental commitments and projects. In *Natural Law and Natural Rights*, Finnis acknowledges that "[w]here a person or a society has created a personal or social hierarchy of practical norms and orientations, through reasonable choice of commitments, one can in many cases reasonably measure the benefits and disadvantages of alternatives. (Consider a man who has decided to become a scholar, or a society that has decided to go to war.)"[27] Later, in *Fundamentals of Ethics*, Finnis writes: "Just as we adopt systems of weights and measures in terms

of which we can *then* carry out commensurations, comparisons and computa-
tions of quantities, so we as individuals and societies adopt sets of commitments
that *bring* the basic human values into relation with each other sufficient to enable us to choose projects and, in some cases, to undertake a cost-benefit analysis to identify better and worse (and even, sometimes best) solutions."[28]

What, then, is Finnis's incommensurability point? We can infer an answer
from this passage: "[T]he adopting of . . . a basic set of commitments is . . . *nothing like* carrying out a computation of commensurable goods. . . . My point is
simply that those commitments cannot be justified, even in principle, by [a con-
sequentialist] method."[29] Finnis is right. We cannot justify, on a consequentialist basis, those of our commitments and projects that supply us with our
fundamental standards of comparison, because we need those standards of comparison before we can undertake any consequentialist weighing. Any effort to
justify, on consequentialist grounds, such commitments and projects would end
up being circular, in that the consequentialist justification would have to presuppose the authority of the very commitments/projects/standards to be
justified. Thus, Finnis's actual thesis (one of them, at least) is not really that no
two basic human values can be compared, but that no two such values can be
compared except in terms of a standard given by commitments and projects
that cannot themselves be justified on a consequentialist basis.

The problem for Finnis is that *that* thesis does not support his position that
a choice of an act that of itself does nothing but damage a basic human value
can never be justified on consequentialist grounds because different basic
human values are incommensurable. As I've just explained, different basic
human values *are* commensurable; they *can* be compared in terms of a single
standard. Now, one might object—either on nonconsequentialist grounds or
on consequentialist grounds that employ a different standard—to the standard
being employed. Or, one might conclude that the standard is altogether unob-
jectionable. But the question of the merits or demerits of the standard (or of any
standard) is different from the question whether, *given* the standard, different
basic human values are commensurable.

And so when faced with a choice whether to commit an act that of itself
does nothing but damage a basic human value, V, one *can* make a judgment
about whether, on the whole and in the long run, the act would have consequences in the form of benefit to one or more basic human values that out-
weigh (in terms of the standard being applied) the consequences in the form
of damage to V. This is not to say that if the answer seems to be yes, one is
morally obligated to commit the act. After all, the constitutive moral commitments of the authorities—or of the political community they represent—
might preclude them choosing to kill P. Or, the authorities might reasonably
doubt their ability, especially when caught in the grip of a tragic situation, to
foresee accurately all the relevant consequences of their killing P. (Finnis puts

some weight on this possibility, but Finnis's basic argument is not that it might be impossible to foresee accurately all the relevant consequences, but that even if it were possible to do so, the choice of killing P could never be justified on the basis of those consequences, no matter what they might be.) Indeed, at this point I do not mean to suggest even that killing P is a morally permissible choice. My point is simply that Finnis's argument that the choice of killing P would be morally wrong—morally wrong no matter what the circumstances and no matter what the consequences—is inadequate.

One might try to argue that any person's most fundamental commitments and projects are necessarily "arbitrary" and so whatever standards of comparison they supply are necessarily "arbitrary," too, and so any consequentialist justification is ultimately—at its root—"arbitrary". But, to his credit, Finnis does not make that argument. To the contrary. That "the adopting of . . . a basic set of commitments" cannot be justified on consequentialist grounds, writes Finnis,

> is not to say that the adopting of basic commitments is that "choosing of basic values" which some contemporary sceptics make the basis of all practical reasoning and "ethics." On the contrary, basic values can be identified by intelligence, and as thus identified provide the basis of all choices however basic. Basic commitments shape our response to, our participation in, basic values— in the form of choices of career, of marriage, of forms of education, of preference for wealth as against leisure or liturgy, or for speed of communication as against safety.
>
> The making of basic commitments is not arbitrary, directionless or indiscriminate. It is mere technocratic illusion to suppose that a choice not guided by cost-benefit computations must be arbitrary.[30]

If our commitments and projects and the standards of comparison they supply us with are not necessarily arbitrary—if, as Finnis insists, they can be reasonable—then why isn't it open to us to use those standards when we must decide whether to commit an act that of itself does nothing but damage a basic human value, just as it is open to us (as Finnis acknowledges[31]) to use them in other situations of choice? Again, one might object to a particular standard for any number of reasons—for example, because the standard mistakenly presupposes that the world is flat, or, worse, that some human beings (e.g., Bosnian Muslims) are *not* sacred. But the possibility that a particular standard is objectionable does not depend on whether the act we are thinking about committing—the act whose consequences we are evaluating in terms of the standard—does nothing of itself but damage a basic human value. Moreover, and more importantly for present purposes, that the act we are thinking about committing does nothing of itself but damage a basic human value (e.g., P's life) does not itself entail, it does not necessarily mean, that the standard of comparison we are bringing to bear is "arbitrary" or otherwise objectionable. There might be moral norms or standards that "trump" any standard supplied by reasonable commitments and projects. Many (myself included) believe that "Always treat another human being lovingly, for she is like yourself" is one such norm.[32] The question at hand is whether "never choose an act that of itself does nothing but damage a basic human value" is such a norm, or, put another way, whether we should believe that it is such a norm. Finnis's argument that it is such a norm—an argument based on the supposed "incommensurability of basic human values"—is, as I have explained here, not persuasive.

This is not to deny that some other argument, even one not yet developed, might be persuasive. Is it the case, for example, that choosing an act that does nothing of itself (and that the person choosing the act understands to do nothing of itself) but damage a basic human value necessarily denies that each and every human being is sacred? At least, is it the case that choosing an act that does nothing of itself but destroy a human life necessarily denies the sacredness of the human being whose life is destroyed? Or, relatedly, that such a choice necessarily contravenes the norm "Always treat another human being lovingly"? (If choosing an act that does nothing of itself but destroy a human life does not necessarily deny the sacredness of the human being whose life is destroyed, then, on the assumption that no basic human value should be regarded as more important than a human life, choosing an act that does nothing of itself but damage a basic human value *other than a human life* does not necessarily deny the sacredness of any human being.[33]) If so, then the idea of human rights—according to which each and every human being is sacred—forbids choosing an act that does nothing of itself but destroy the life of a human being.

That possibility brings us back to the central question of this chapter: Are any human rights absolute or unconditional? (Again, no one argues that *all* human rights are absolute. The serious question is whether *some* are.) Assuming that every human being is sacred, are there at least some things that ought *never* to be done to any human being? Are there at least some things that ought *always* to be done for every human being? Or, instead, are there only things that *conditionally* ought not to be done to any human being and things that *conditionally* ought to be done for every human being—things that ought not to be done, and things that ought to be done, under some, even most, conditions, but not under all conditions?

III

Why might one think that choosing an act that does nothing of itself but destroy the life of a human being necessarily denies the sacredness of the human being whose life is destroyed? Let us consider three scenarios.

In Scenario 1 (S1), the authorities chose an act that of itself did one thing: destroyed the life of N. N was someone whom authorities regarded as subhuman and chose to kill as part of an "ethnic cleansing" campaign in which the world without N (and his ethnic kin) was regarded as intrinsically better than a world with him. In S2, the authorities chose an act that of itself did two things: destroyed the life of a human being, O, *and* saved the lives of five other human beings. The authorities correctly believed that the act in question — diverting a runaway trolley car from a track where, like a bomb thrown at them, it was virtually certain to kill the five to a track where, like a bomb thrown at him at him, it was virtually certain to kill (only) O — was the only way to save the lives of the five; they chose as they did in order, and only in order, to save the five; and they had no special obligation to O, no obligation above and beyond their obligation to each of the five. In S3, the authorities chose an act that of itself did one thing: destroyed the life of P. P was the innocent person in the hypothetical I have been using in this chapter; the authorities chose to kill him because, and only because, they correctly determined that this was the only sure way to save the lives of the millions of persons in the city where the nuclear bomb was set to go off.

The authorities' choice in S1 represented a conspicuous denial of the sacredness of N. In S2, most persons would agree that the authorities' choice did not deny that O was sacred. Although the authorities chose an act that caused the death of O, they did not desire his death even partly as an end in itself and indeed devoutly wished that O did not have to die in order that the five be saved. They devoutly wished that there had been some alternative not involving the death of O. Why, then, should we conclude that in S3, the authorities' choice denied — indeed, necessarily denied — that P was sacred? In S3, no less than in S2, the authorities did not desire the death of the person they chose to kill even partly as an end in itself; true, the authorities chose an act that did nothing of itself but cause the death of P, but, as in S2, the authorities devoutly wished that their victim did not have to die in order that millions be saved. They devoutly wished that there had been some alternative not involving the death of P. Given the morally relevant similarities between S2 and S3, it is far from clear why we should conclude that in S3, the authorities' choice denied (much less, *necessarily* denied) that P was sacred.

Are there any morally relevant dissimilarities between S2 and S3, such that it makes sense to conclude that in S3, but not in S2, the authorities' choice denied the sacredness of the person whose life was sacrificed? One might say that in S3, the authorities "intended" to kill P, whereas in S2, the authorities did not "intend" to kill O, but merely accepted the death of O as an inevitable but unintended consequence of the chosen act.[34] But the presence in S3 of an "intention" to kill does not *entail* that the authorities' choice denied — it does not mean that their choice *necessarily* denied — the sacredness of the person who was killed. It is one thing to insist that killing a human being "intentionally" — in the sense of choosing an act that does nothing of itself (and that is understood to do nothing of itself) but destroy the life of a human being—is almost always a morally reprehensible act. It is quite another thing to insist that killing a human being "intentionally" is invariably, because necessarily, a morally reprehensible act. In order to know whether a particular instance of killing a human being "intentionally" is morally reprehensible, one needs to know more than that the instance of killing was "intentional". (Recall Abraham, poised to slay his son.) In particular, one needs to know whether the "intentional" killing was at least partly an act of hate for, or even just of indifference toward, the victim, or perhaps an act of excessive self-regard. Or was the act, instead, an expression of love for the victim? One example should suffice here both to make and to illustrate the point:[35] What if my child and I are captives who are about to be tortured unto death, and I sieze a momentary opportunity to suffocate my child before the torturers return to begin their work? It is patent nonsense to suggest that in "intending" to kill my child, thereby mercifully sparing him the horrors that await him a few moments later—torture unto death—I thereby deny that my child is sacred. Most parents would recognize my act as one of parental love—as an affirmation, not a denial, of the sacredness of my child. In many cases, one's "intention" about means says little if anything, by itself, about one's desires or character.[36]

The similarities between S2 and S3 are morally relevant, not the dissimilarity that in S3, but not in S2, the authorities "intended" to kill their victim: The presence in S3 of an "intention" to kill does not mean that the authorities' choice in S3, unlike the authorities' choice in S2, necessarily denied the sacredness of the person who was killed. There is, finally, no good reason to conclude that in S3, unlike in S2, the authorities' choice denied the sacredness of the innocent person whose life was sacrificed. More broadly, there is no good reason to conclude that choosing an act that of itself does nothing but destroy the life of a human being (e.g., my choosing to suffocate my child to spare him the horrors of torture unto death) *necessarily* denies the sacredness of the human being whose life is destroyed.[37] (Indeed, there is no good reason to conclude that choosing an act that of itself does nothing but damage a basic human value is *necessarily* morally wrong. Why judge such an act to be necessarily—because invariably or unconditionally—morally wrong if the project of which the act is merely a constituent is otherwise morally worthy?[38])

Am I committed, by the argument I have been making here, to the unsavory proposition that it is always morally permissible to choose an act that does nothing of itself but destroy the life of a human being if the act saves, and is done solely in order to save, the lives of two or more human beings? Certainly not. My argument is only that such a choice does not *necessarily* deny the sacredness of the human being whose life is destroyed. But, still, it might be the case that a particular instance of such a choice denies the sacredness of the human being whose life is destroyed. What we need are criteria for deciding if a particular instance of such a choice denies the sacredness of the human being whose life is destroyed and thereby contravenes the idea of human rights.

I have already intimated one criterion: Is the act at least partly an expression of love, or of "deserved reverence", for the victim—as it might be if the two or more human beings whose lives are saved by the act are the victim's own children, for whom she would have gladly given her own life?[39] Another criterion—actually, a set of related criteria—has been suggested by Eric Rakowski in an important essay, *Taking and Saving Lives*:

> [P]eople may . . . be killed to save a larger number of others if several conditions are met: (1) a majority of those affected by a life-saving decision either endorsed a policy maximizing the number of lives saved or would have welcomed that policy in the circumstances in which they found themselves were they aware of their moral and religious beliefs, their desires and aversion to risk, and their personal abilities and history, but ignorant of whether they would be killed or saved under the policy; (2) those who dissent or would have dissented for either moral or religious reasons (and not so that they could ride free) under the counterfactual condition just described, and who would be killed if the greater number were saved, could not fairly have been excluded from the benefits of a maximizing scheme; and (3) the dissenters' chances of staying alive would have been boosted by the prior adoption of a maximizing policy.[40]

Rakowski acknowledges that "[d]etermining when these conditions are met might at times be difficult. Life-saving choices are frequently pressured and unexpected; rescuers often lack pertinent information." But, says Rakowksi, "this difficult determination may not be shirked. For unless these preconditions are met, killing somebody to save others is morally intolerable." Why? "[B]ecause it takes from someone what he probably values most, without his consent, indeed without even the possibility of his having benefited, and for the sake of someone else who, as his moral peer, is entitled to no preference. To conform killing to a less demanding standard is to blink our moral equality and the value of human life."[41]

Perhaps Rakowski is wrong to suggest that satisfaction of his criteria is not merely sufficient, but necessary, if choosing to kill somebody to save others is to be morally tolerable. It might be the case that virtually every instance of choosing to kill somebody to save others is morally intolerable unless Rakowski's criteria (or some such criteria) are satisfied. Still, perhaps choosing to kill somebody to save others does not *necessarily* deny the sacredness of every human being even if Rakowski's critera are not satisfied.[42] In any event, in the context of many societies, including the United States, Rakowski's criteria are satisfied both in S2 and in S3; at least, it seems much more likely that they are satisfied than that they are not. According to Rakowski's criteria, it is not morally intolerable that, in S2, the one was allowed to die so that the five could live or that, in S3, P was killed so that millions could live.

My present interest, however, is neither in passing judgment on the details of Rakowski's thoughtful, careful argument nor in applying his criteria to hypothetical cases, but only in emphasizing this: Although a particular instance of "choosing an act that does nothing of itself (and that is understood to do nothing of itself) but destroy the life of a human being, where the act saves, and is done solely in order to save, the lives of two or more human beings" might deny the sacredness of the human being whose life is destroyed, not every such choice necessarily denies the sacredness of the human being whose life is destroyed. Where I talk about denying the "sacredness" of a human being, Rakowski would talk, equivalently, about denying the "moral equality" of a human being. Others would talk still differently, though still equivalently—for example, about not respecting every human being as a "rational creature".[43]

⚜

Again, "[W]e can imagine extreme cases where killing an innocent person may save a whole nation. In such cases it seems fanatical to maintain the absoluteness of the judgment, to do right even if the heavens will in fact fall."[44] In the end, Finnis relies on his theology to resist the charge of fanaticism:

> There are hard cases, as everybody knows. The prospect of loss of human good (of persons), of damage apparently avertable by violating the moral absolutes, can seem indubitable and be felt as overwhelming. But these are cases in which we do not see the relevant parts of the scheme of providence—a scheme of which we never, in this life, see the whole or even much. . . . In these cases, then, the moral absolutes call for a refusal to dishonor the basic human good at stake in our choice; they call us to leave providence to settle the "balance" of human goods, a balance which we would merely deceive ourselves if we supposed we could truly see and settle for ourselves.
>
> . . .
>
> In short: To deny the truth of moral absolutes by arguing that they block the reasonable and responsible pursuit of greater amounts of premoral human good is incoherent with faith in divine providence. . . . [T]o respect the moral absolutes which are made known to us by God through reason and faith is to cooperate with God, who has practical knowledge of everything without limit. And to cooperate thus with God is to *take into account everything . . . in the only way we can*.[45]

Consider, for a moment, Finnis's claim that "the moral absolutes [that he defends] are made known to us by God through reason and faith". If by "reason" Finnis means his argument for "moral absolutes", then God does not make known to us through "reason" (not yet, anyhow) what Finnis imagines God to make known, for Finnis's argument simply does not work. Although Finnis is a Roman Catholic, it is not clear what Finnis means here by "faith". Perhaps

Finnis thinks that his "moral absolutes" are supported by the correct interpretation of the sacred texts of Christianity.[46] Or that the will of God is infallibly represented by the *ex cathedra* pronouncements of the pope on matters of faith and morals. Or both.

In any event, it is difficult to see how one who accepts Finnis's "moral absolutes"[47] but who does not accept Finnis's "faith" or the theology implicit in his "faith" can resist the charge of fanaticism. It bears mention that it is not only religious nonbelievers who do not accept Finnis's comforting theology, with its trust that divine "providence" will somehow prevent the heavens from falling and its conviction that if, alas, the heavens *do* fall, then, because divine providence allowed them to fall, their falling cannot really be the cataclysmic event it appears to us myopic, and often deluded, human beings to be. Very many religious believers, too, cannot bring themselves to accept such a theology, especially in this post-Holocaust age of innocence lost.

IV

Does it follow from the fact that "[w]e can imagine extreme cases where killing an innocent person may save a whole nation" and that "[i]n such cases it seems fanatical to maintain the absoluteness of the judgment, to do right even if the heavens will in fact fall" that international law should not establish any human rights as unconditional or absolute? Does it necessarily follow from the fact that, as *moral* rights, no human rights are unconditional that, as *legal* rights—in particular, as international legal rights—no human rights should be unconditional? For one who does not agree with my conclusion that, as moral rights, no human rights are unconditional, the question can be put hypothetically: If, as moral rights, no human rights were unconditional, would it necessarily follow that, as legal rights, no human rights should be unconditional?

Whether or not any human rights are, as moral rights, unconditional, some human rights should be established, by law, as unconditional rights. In particular, it makes good sense for international law to do what it does: make some human rights "nonderogable". (I listed several nonderogable rights earlier in this chapter.[48]) Three related considerations support this conclusion.

- If there are some imaginable conditions under which it would be morally permissible to violate the human rights that international law makes nonderogable—conditions where a failure to violate such a right would mean that "the heavens will in fact fall"—the possibility that those conditions exist or will come to exist is so unlikely as to be negligible. At least, the possibility that such conditions will often exist is negligible.
- If, in anticipation of such imaginable-but-extremely-unlikely conditions, international law rights were to make such rights derogable, if it were to

establish them as merely conditional legal rights—if it were, in that sense, to create an "escape clause" for the political authorities—there might well be at least some more, and perhaps many more, morally unjustified violations of the underlying moral rights by states than if international law rights were to do what it already does: establish and protect the rights as nonderogable.

- But what if one of those imaginable-but-extremely-unlikely conditions occurs—as in the third scenario (S3) above? It is politically unrealistic, wildly so, to believe that the fact that a human right is nonderogable under international law rights would keep political authorities from violating the right if they really did believe it necessary to do so in order to keep the heavens from falling. In many situations, and certainly *in extremis*, the international "law" of human rights is more a moral force than a legal one. In any event, why should political authorities worry about the possibility of sanctions under international law when they are struggling desperately to keep the heavens in place (as they would surely be doing if they were trying to prevent a nuclear explosion that would take the lives of millions)?[49]

Therefore, it makes very good sense, as a practical matter, that international law establishes some moral rights as unconditional (nonderogable) legal rights.[50]

❦

The question that is the title of this chapter states the fourth, and final, inquiry of this book: Are human rights absolute? The answer is mixed. No one claims that *all* human rights are, either as moral rights or as legal rights, absolute. Many human rights are, both as moral rights and as legal rights, conditional, not unconditional. The serious claim is that *some* human rights are, as moral rights, absolute. I have argued in this chapter to the contrary. But that argument is perhaps mainly of theoretical interest. The much more important point is practical, not theoretical: Even if *no* human rights are, as moral rights, absolute, *some* human rights, as international legal rights, should be—and, happily, are—absolute.[51]

Notes

INTRODUCTION

1. Leszek Kolakowski, Modernity on Endless Trial 214 (1990).

2. See United Nations Commission on the Truth for El Salvador, From Madness to Hope: The Twelve-Year War in El Salvador (1993).

3. Christopher Lehmann-Haupt, "The Nature of One Particular War," New York Times, May 9, 1994, at C15.

4. In parts of two earlier books—*Morality, Politics, and Law* (1988) and *Love and Power: The Role of Religion and Morality in American Politics* (1991)—I first addressed several questions that are the principal subject matter of this book. Although published in 1988, *Morality, Politics, and Law* was finished in 1986.

5. Another book of mine, *Love and Power*, note 4, also bears traces of that journey.

6. For an explanation, see Darcy O'Brien, A Dark and Bloody Ground 1 (1993).

7. See, e.g., Louis B. Sohn, "The New International Law: Protection of the Rights of Individuals Rather Than States," 32 American U. L. Rev. 1 (1982); Robert F. Drinan, Cry of the Oppressed: The History and Hope of the Human Rights Revolution (1987).

There are many good studies of different aspects of the international law of human rights. See, e.g., Philip Alston, ed., The United Nations and Human Rights: A Critical Appraisal (1992); 1 and 2 Theodor Meron, ed., Human Rights in International Law: Legal and Policy Issues (1984). For relatively brief overviews of the international law of human rights, see Thomas Buergenthal, International Human Rights (2nd ed. 1995); Scott Davidson, Human Rights (1993). For an excellent collection of teaching materials, see Henry J. Steiner & Philip Alston, eds., International Human Rights in Context: Law, Politics, Morals (1996). There are many excellent periodical sources of articles about international human rights—for example, the *Harvard Human Rights Journal* and the *Human Rights Quarterly*.

8. Tom J. Farer & Felice Gaer, "The UN and Human Rights: At the End of the Beginning," in United Nations, Divided World 240 (Adam Roberts & Benedict Kingsbury eds., 2nd ed. 1993).

9. Indeed, in the view of one observer:

[After 1945, the] idea of human rights quickly became perverted . . . . The reality of the idea of human rights has been degraded. Human rights . . . became a plaything of governments and lawyers. The game of human rights has been played in international statal organizations by diplomats and bureaucrats, and their appointees, in the setting and the ethos of traditional international relations.

The result has been that the potential energy of the idea has been dissipated. Alienation, corruption, tyranny, and oppression have continued wholesale in many societies all over the world. And in all societies governments have been reassured in their arrogance by the idea that, if they are not proved actually to be violating the substance of particularized human rights, if they can bring their willing and acting within the wording of this or that formula with its lawyerly qualifications and exceptions, then they are doing well enough. The idea of human rights should intimidate governments or it is worth nothing. If the idea of human rights reassures governments it is worse than nothing.

Philip Allott, Eunomia: New Order for a New World 287 (1990). Allott does allow, however, that "there is room for optimism, on two grounds. (1) The idea of human rights having been thought, it cannot be unthought. It will not be replaced, unless by some idea which contains and surpasses it. (2) There are tenacious individuals and non-statal societies whose activity on behalf of the idea of human rights is not part of international relations but is part of a new process of international reality-forming." Id.

10. See, e.g., Zarbanoo Gifford, "Slavery—A Modern Curse," [London] Tablet, Oct. 5, 1996; Human Rights Watch, Children in Bondage (1996) (reporting, inter alia, that in India more than 15 million children are in the virtual slavery of bonded labor).

11. See Amnesty International, A Glimpse of Hell: Reports on Torture Worldwide (1996).

12. What is the proper role of religious arguments—for example, a religious argument that every human being is sacred—as a basis of political choice, especially coercive political choice? (A law that makes violation of one or more human rights a criminal act is a coercive policy choice.) See Michael J. Perry, Religion in Politics: Constitutional and Moral Perspectives, ch. 3 (1997).

13. In *Life's Dominion*, Dworkin writes: "Some readers . . . will take particular exception to the term 'sacred' because it will suggest to them that the conviction I have in mind is necessarily a theistic one. I shall try to explain why it is not, and how it may be, and commonly is, interpreted in a secular as well as in a conventionally religious way. But 'sacred' does have ineliminable religious connotations for many people, and so I will sometimes use 'inviolable' instead to mean the same thing, in order to emphasize the availability of that secular interpretation." Ronald Dworkin, Life's Dominion: An Argument About Abortion, Euthanasia, and Individual Freedom 25 (1993).

14. See id.

15. See Richard Rorty, "Human Rights, Rationality, and Sentimentality," in On Human Rights: The Oxford Amnesty Lectures 1993, at 111 (Stephen Shute & Susan Hurley eds., 1993).

16. Mary Ann Glendon, Rights Talk: The Impoverishment of Political Discourse x (1991).

17. D.J. O'Connor, Aquinas and Natural Law 57 (1968).

18. Bernard Williams, "Republican and Galilean," New York Review of Books,

Nov. 8, 1990, at 45, 48 (reviewing Charles Taylor, Sources of the Self: The Making of Modern Identity (1989)).

19. Such questions—such worries—are at the heart of recent work by Charles Taylor. See Charles Taylor, Sources of the Self: The Making of Modern Identity (1989); Charles Taylor, The Ethics of Authenticity (1992).

20. And of others, too. See Amnesty International, Childhood Stolen: Grave Human Rights Violations Against Children (1995).

CHAPTER 1

1. J.M. Winter & D.M. Joslin, eds., R.H. Tawney's Commonplace Book 67 (1972). Tawney wrote the quoted passage in his diary on Aug. 13, 1913. Three days earlier, on Aug. 10, he quoted in his diary T.W. Price, Midland secretary of the Workers' Educational Association and lecturer at Birmingham University: "Unless a man believes in spiritual things—in God—altruism is absurd. What is the sense of it? Why shld a man recognize any obligation to his neighbor, unless he believes that he has been put in the world for a special purpose and has a special work to perform in it? A man's relations to his neighbors become meaningless unless there is some higher power above them both." Id.

2. Ronald Dworkin, "Life Is Sacred: That's the Easy Part," New York Times Mag., May 16, 1993, at 36.

3. Hannah Arendt, The Origins of Totalitarianism 299 (Harvest ed. 1973).

4. The representatives of 172 states adopted by consensus the Vienna Declaration and Programme of Action.

5. Or, at least, certain things ought not to be done to any human being *in particular circumstances* and certain other things ought to be done for every human being *in particular circumstances*. See chapter 2.

For some of the things that ought or ought not to be done, it might be the case that only some human beings, not all human beings, ought or ought not to do them. See chapter 2.

For some of the things that ought or ought not to be done, the "ought" or "ought not" might be conditional rather than unconditional or absolute. See chapter 4.

6. Article 2 continues: "Furthermore, no distinction shall be made on the basis of the political, jurisdictional or international status of the country or territory to which a person belongs, whether it be independent, trust, non-self-governing or under any other limitation of sovereignty."

7. Commenting, in 1944, on a phrase—"the dignity of the human person"—that would soon appear in all the three documents of the International Bill of Human Rights, Jacques Maritain wrote: "The human person possesses rights because of the very fact that it is a person, . . . which consequently is not merely a means to an end, but an end, an end which must be treated as such. The dignity of the human person? The expression means nothing if it does not signify that . . . the human person has the right to be respected, is the subject of rights, possesses rights. These are things that are owed to man because of the very fact that he is a man." Jacques Maritain, The Rights of Man 37 (1944). Cf. Maurice Cranston, What Are Human Rights? 7 (1973): "In classifying

human rights as moral rights it is important to notice something which distinguishes them from other kinds of moral rights. This is that they are *universal*."

8. But cf. Robert Ombres, O.P., "The Ethics of Human Rights," L. & Justice, No. 114/115, 140 (1992): "[R]eferences to God, Nature and even Human Nature were deleted from the drafts of the 1948 Universal Declaration of Human Rights shortly before its adoption."

9. Cf. Ronald Dworkin, Life's Dominion: An Argument About Abortion, Euthanasia, and Individual Freedom 25 (1993): "Some readers . . . will take particular exception to the term 'sacred' because it will suggest to them that the conviction I have in mind is necessarily a theistic one. I shall try to explain why it is not, and how it may be, and commonly is, interpreted in a secular as well as in a conventionally religious way. But 'sacred' does have ineliminable religious connotations for many people, and so I will sometimes use 'inviolable' instead to mean the same thing, in order to emphasize the availability of that secular interpretation."

10. Nietzsche was unrelentingly contemptuous of the conviction that every human being is sacred—as, for example, in this bleak and sobering passage from *The Will to Power*:

> In moving the doctrine of selflessness and love into the foreground, Christianity was in no way establishing the interests of the species as of higher value that the interests of the individual. Its real *historical* effect, the fateful element in its effect, remains, on the contrary, in precisely the enhancement of egoism, of the egoism of the individual, to an extreme (—to the extreme of individual immortality). Through Christianity, the individual was made so important, so absolute, that he could no longer be sacrificed: but the species endures only through human sacrifice— All "souls" became equal before God: but this is precisely the most dangerous of all possible evaluations! If one regards individuals as equal, one calls the species into question, one encourages a way of life that leads to the ruin of the species: Christianity is the counterprinciple to the principle of *selection*. If the degenerate and sick ("the Christian") is to be accorded the same value as the healthy ("the pagan"), or even more value, as in Pascal's judgment concerning sickness and health, then unnaturalness becomes law—
>
> This universal love of men is in practice the *preference* for the suffering, underprivileged, degenerate: it has in fact lowered and weakened the strength, the responsibility, the lofty duty to sacrifice men. All that remains, according to the Christian scheme of values, is to sacrifice oneself: but this residue of human sacrifice that Christianity concedes and even advises has, from the standpoint of general breeding, no meaning at all. The prosperity of the species is unaffected by the self-sacrifice of this or that individual (—whether it be in the monkish and ascetic manner or, with the aid of crosses, pyres, and scaffolds, as "martyrs" of error). The species requires that the ill-constituted, weak, degenerate, perish: but it was precisely to them that Christianity turned as a conserving force; it further enhanced that instinct in the weak, already so powerful, to take care of and preserve themselves and to sustain one another. What is "virtue" and "charity" in Christianity if not just this mutual preservation, this solidarity of weak, this hampering of selection? What is Christian altruism if not the mass-egoism of the weak, which divines that if all care for one another each individual will be preserved as long as possible?—

If one does not feel such a disposition as an extreme immorality, as a crime against life, one belongs with the company of the sick and possesses its instincts oneself—

Genuine charity demands sacrifice for the good of the species—it is hard, it is full of self-overcoming, because it needs human sacrifice. And this pseudo humaneness called Christianity wants it established that no one should be sacrificed—

Friedrich Nietzsche, The Will to Power 141–42 (Walter Kaufmann & R.J. Hollingdale trans. & Walter Kaufmann ed., 1967).

11. My discussion here is adapted from a longer discussion elsewhere. See Michael J. Perry, Love and Power: The Role of Religion and Morality in American Politics, ch. 5 (1991).

12. Charles Taylor, Sources of the Self: The Making of the Modern Identity 18 (1989). Taylor also observes that "those whose spiritual agenda is mainly defined in this way are in a fundamentally different existential predicament from that which dominated most previous cultures and still defines the lives of other people today." Id. On the "notorious vagueness" of the question "What is the Meaning of Life?", see W.D. Joske, "Philosophy and the Meaning of Life," in The Meaning of Life 248, 248 et seq. (E.D. Klemke ed., 1981). See also R.W. Hepburn, "Questions About the Meaning of Life," in id. at 209.

13. Albert Camus, The Myth of Sisyphus and Other Essays 5 (1944; Eng. trans., 1955). See Leszek Kolakowski, The Presence of Myth (1989), especially ch. 8: "The Phenomenon of the World's Indifference". Cf. Blaise Pascal, Pensées 95 (Penguin ed., 1966): "The eternal silence of these infinite spaces fills me with dread."

14. See David Tracy, Plurality and Ambiguity: Hermeneutics, Religion, Hope 87 (1987): "Like strictly metaphysical questions, religious questions must be questions on the nature of Ultimate Reality. Unlike metaphysical questions, religious questions deliberately ask the question of the meaning and truth of Ultimate Reality not only as it is in itself *but as it is existentially related to us*. The religious classics are testimonies to the responses of the religions to those questions." (Emphasis added.)

15. Abraham J. Heschel, Who Is Man? 75 (1965). Cf. Fyodor Dostoevsky, The Brothers Karamazov 235 (Norton ed., 1976): "For the secret of man's being is not only to live but to have something to live for. Without a stable conception of the object of life, man would not consent to go on living, and would rather destroy himself than remain on earth, though he had bread in abundance." (This is one of the Grand Inquisitor's statements in ch. 5 of bk. 5.)

16. Cf. "Religion," 13 Oxford English Dictionary 568 (1989).

17. See David Braybrooke, "Ideology," in 4 Encyclopedia of Philosophy 124 (Paul Edwards, ed., 1967).

18. Harvey Egan has written that "there is a sense in which all great religions are mystical at heart and that mysticism is the full-flowering of any religious tradition." Harvey Egan, What Are They Saying About Mysticism? 17 (1982). According to Wayne Proudfoot, the very ubiquity of mystical experience among the world religions suggests that mysticism may be regarded as "a *paradigm* of religious experience." Wayne Proudfoot, Religious Experience xviii (1985). Some commentators distinguish between two fundamental types of mystical experience, two kinds of experience of union with

God or the Absolute: (1) the experience of union but not identity with God (as attested to by mystics in theistic traditions such as Christianity, Judaism, and Islam), and (2) the experience of complete absorption into the divine. Cf. id. at 121: "The terms in which the subject understands what is happening to him are constitutive of the experience; consequently those in different traditions have different experiences. Jewish and Buddhist mystics [for example] bring entirely different doctrinal commitments, expectations, and rules for identifying their mental and bodily states to their experiences, and thus *devekuth* and *nirvana* cannot be the same."

19. According to William James, "transience" is a third mark of mystical experience. Commenting on James, Proudfoot writes: "The two secondary marks by which James characterizes the mystical state, transience and passivity, are also related to the noetic quality of the experience. Passivity conveys the sense of being grasped and of being subject to some power beyond oneself. Both passivity and transience reflect the perception that the experience is not under the subject's voluntary control. It cannot be manipulated or guaranteed by the subject's decision or by causes that he might set in motion. He can prepare himself for it, but the experience is finally not subject to his control. The rules for the identification of an experience as mystical include the condition that he judge it to be something other than an artifact of his own thought and actions." Proudfoot, note 19, at 147–48.

20. Milan Kundera, The Unbearable Lightness of Being 139 (1984) (emphasis added).

21. "Not the individual man nor a single generation by its own power, can erect the bridge that leads to God. Faith is the achievement of many generations, an effort accumulated over centuries. Many of its ideas are as the light of the star that left its source a long time ago. Many enigmatic songs, unfathomable today, are the resonance of voices of bygone times. There is a collective memory of God in the human spirit, and it is this memory which is the main source of our faith." From Abraham Heschel's two-part essay "Faith," first published in vol. 10 of *The Reconstructionist*, Nov. 3 & 17, 1944. For a later statement on faith, incorporating some of the original essay, see Abraham Joshua Heschel, Man Is Not Alone 159–76 (1951). On community/tradition as a principal matrix of moral beliefs, see Michael J. Perry, Morality, Politics, and Law 24–33 (1988).

22. See Robert Coles, The Spiritual Life of Children 37 (1990): "The questions Tolstoy asked, and Gauguin in, say, his great Tahiti triptych, completed just before he died ('Where Do We Come From? What Are We? Where Are We Going?'), are the eternal questions children ask more intensely, unremittingly, and subtly than we sometimes imagine." Cf. Heschel, Who Is Man?, note 15, at 28: "In an old rabbinic text three other questions are suggested: '*Whence* did you come?' '*Whither* are you going?' 'Before *whom* are you destined to give account?'"

23. Tracy, note 14, at 86.

24. David Tracy, The Analogical Imagination 4 (1981).

25. Robin W. Lovin & Frank E. Reynolds, "Focus Introduction," 14 J. Religious Ethics 48, 56–57 (1986). See id.; Robin W. Lovin & Frank E. Reynolds, "In the Beginning," in Cosmogony and Ethical Order: New Studies in Comparative Ethics 1 (Robin W. Lovin & Farnk E. Reynolds eds., 1985).

26. Cf. Nietzsche, note 10, at 184: "What is the *counterfeiting* aspect of morality?—

It pretends to *know* something, namely what 'good and evil' is. That means wanting to know why mankind is here, its goal, its destiny. That means wanting to know that mankind *has* a goal, a destiny—" What was Nietzsche's teleology? See id. at 544–50 ("The Eternal Recurrence").

27. See note 54 and accompanying text.

28. John 13:34. See John 15:12, 17. (This and the other translations in this chapter are those of *The New Jerusalem Bible* (1985).) See generally Edmund N. Santurri & William Werpehowski, eds., The Love Commandments: Essays in Christian Ethics and Moral Philosophy (1992). See also Garth L. Hallett, Christian Neighbor-Love: An Assessment of Six Rival Versions (1989). (For a recent collection of secular philosophical essays on "altruism", see 10 Social Philosophy & Policy 1–245 (1993).) On the relation between the commandment to "love God" and the commandment to "love one another", see note 46. Cf. Nietzsche, note 10, at 183: "'[L]ove': the ideal state of the herd animal that no longer wants to have enemies."

29. Matthew 5:43–48. See Luke 6:27–35. (Such a conception of the good is not confined to semitic spiritualities: For Buddhists, for example, the good life centrally involves compassion (*karuna*) for all sentient creatures and therefore for all human beings.) Cf. Nietzsche, note 10, at 120: "One drives nature out of morality when one says 'Love your enemies': for then the natural 'Thou shalt love thy neighbor and hate thy enemy' in the law (in instinct) has become meaningless; then this love of one's neighbor must also find a new basis (as a kind of love of God). Everywhere, God is inserted and utility withdrawn; everywhere the real origin of morality is denied: the veneration of nature, which lies precisely in the recognition of a natural morality, is destroyed at its roots—"

30. See Tracy, note 24.

31. In the Bible, God—Ultimate Reality—is often imaged as "parent", sometimes as "father", sometimes as "mother". Cf. Elizabeth A. Johnson, She Who Is: The Mystery of God in Feminist Theological Discourse (1992).

32. Hilary Putnam, The Many Faces of Realism 60–61 (1987).

33. National Conference of Catholic Bishops, Economic Justice for All v (1986) (emphasis added).

34. Ben Zion Bokser & Baruch M. Bokser, "Introduction: The Spirituality of the Talmud," in The Talmud: Selected Writings 7 (1989).

35. Id. at 30–31.

36. Nietzsche, note 10, at 466–68.

37. See Martha C. Nussbaum, Aristotle on Human Nature and the Foundations of Ethics 22 (1990): "[T]o find out what our nature is seems to be one and the same thing as to find out what we deeply believe to be most important and indispensable [in a human life]."

38. See Ludwig Wittgenstein, Philosophical Investigations, sec. 217 (1953) ("I have reached bedrock, and this is where my spade is turned.") (quoted in Putnam, note 32, at 85).

39. Cf. Robert Nozick, Philosophical Explanations 403 (1981):

Recall Glaucon's challenge to Socrates in Plato's *Republic*: show that being moral is better for the agent, apart from its external consequences. To isolate these consequences, Glaucon imagines a ring that makes someone invisible. With this ring he is able to act immorally with no external penalty: he can rob, murder, and rape without being caught or punished. Is there any reason why he should not do this? Glaucon sharpens the issue by imagining that the immoral man has the reputation of being moral, he is honored and praised as moral, while another man is thought to be immoral and so is condemned and shunned. Glaucon asks Socrates to show, despite this, that the second moral person is better off than the first immoral one, that we would be better off being that second than the first.

"[T]he answer that [Plato] puts into the mouth of Socrates is that the just man is happy because his soul is harmoniously ordered, because, as we would say, he has an integrated personality, whereas the unjust man's personality is disintegrated, and the man who represents the extreme of injustice is psychotic, his soul is a chaos of internal strife." J.L. Mackie, Ethics: Inventing Right and Wrong 190–91 (1977). Should we take Socrates' response seriously? See Bernard Williams, Ethics and the Limits of Philosophy 46 (1985):

> There is also the figure, rarer perhaps than Callicles supposed, but real, who is horrible enough and not miserable at all but, by any ethological standard of the bright eye and the gleaming coat, dangerously flourishing. For those who want to ground the ethical life in psychological health, it is something of a problem that there can be such people at all. But it is a significant question, how far their existence, indeed the thought of their existence, is a cultural phenomenon. They seem sleeker and finer at a distance. Some Renaissance grandee fills such a role with more style than the tawdry fascist bosses, gangsters, or tycoons who seem, even as objects of fantasy, to be their chief contemporary instances. Perhaps we deceive ourselves about the past.

40. See James Tunstead Burtchaell, "The Source of Conscience," 13 Notre Dame Mag. 20, 20–21 (Winter 1984–85):

> The Catholic tradition embraces a long effort to uncover the truth about human behavior and experience. Our judgments of good and evil focus on whether a certain course of action will make a human being grow and mature and flourish, or whether it will make a person withered, estranged and indifferent. In making our evaluations, we have little to draw on except our own and our forebears' experience, and whatever wisdom we can wring from our debate with others. . . .
>
> What we are trying to unpuzzle are things like childbearing and immigration and economic policy and infant mortality and drug use and family fidelity and so much else about which we must frame moral judgments. With our fellow communicants we share commitments and assumptions: that we are happier giving than getting, that there is no greater love than to put down your life for your neighbor, and that your neighbor always turns out to be the most unlikely person.

On our neighbor always turning out to be the most unlikely person, see note 42 and accompanying text (Parable of the Good Samaritan). (For a revised version of Burtchaell's essay, and for several other illuminating essays by Father Burtchaell, see James Tunstead Burtchaell, The Giving and Taking of Life (1989).)

41. See Matthew 22:34–40: "But when the Pharisees heard that he had silenced the Sadducees they got together and, to put him to the test, one of them put a further question, 'Master, which is the greatest commandment of the Law?' Jesus said to him, 'You must love the Lord your God with all your heart, with all your soul, and with all your mind. This is the greatest and the first commandment. The second resembles it: You must love your neighbor as yourself. On these two commandments hang the whole Law, and the Prophets too." See also Mark 12:28–34; Luke 10:25–28. (On the relation between the two commandments, see note 46.) Cf. Mackie, note 39, at 243: "D.D. Raphael, in 'The Standard of Morals', in Proc. of the Aristotelian Society 75 (1974–75) follows Edward Ullendorff in pointing out that whereas 'Thou shalt love thy neighbor as thyself' represents the Greek of the Septuagint (Leviticus 19:18) and of the New Testament, the Hebrew from which the former is derived means rather 'You shall treat your neighbor lovingly, for he is like yourself.'" (Thus, Bruce Ackerman need not worry that he is being asked to love the "stranger" as himself. *That*, protests Ackerman, "[o]nly a God could do . . .: there are too many strangers with too many strangenesses." Bruce Ackerman, The Future of Liberal Revolution 21 (1992).)

42. See Luke 10:29–37:

> But the man was anxious to justify himself and said to Jesus, "And who is my neighbour?" In answer Jesus said, "A man was once on his way down from Jerusalem to Jericho and fell into the hands of bandits; they stripped him, beat him and then made off, leaving him half dead. Now a priest happened to be travelling down the same road, but when he saw the man, he passed by on the other side. In the same way a Levite who came to the place saw him, and passed by on the other side. But a Samaritan traveller who came on him was moved with compassion when he saw him. He went up to him and bandaged his wounds, pouring oil and wine on them. He then lifted him onto his own mount and took him to an inn and looked after him. Next day, he took out two denarii and handed them to the innkeeper and said, 'Look after him, and on my way back I will make good any extra expense you have.' Which of these three, do you think, proved himself a neighbour to the man who fell into the bandits' hands?" [The man] replied, "The one who showed pity towards him." Jesus said to him, "Go, and do the same yourself."

In the annotation of *The New Jerusalem Bible*, a footnote appended to "Samaritan" says that "[t]he contrast is between the element in Israel most strictly bound to the law of love, and the heretic and stranger, . . . from whom normally only hate could be expected."

43. Richard Rorty, "Human Rights, Rationality, and Sentimentality," in On Human Rights: The Oxford Amnesty Lectures 1993 111, 123–24 (Stephen Shute & Susan Hurley eds., 1993).

44. I can love the Other even if I do not understand that the Other is my sister/brother. And I can understand that the Other is my sister/brother and yet fail to love the Other.

45. See note 41.

46. Matthew 25:31–46. In Matthew's Gospel, these are Jesus' final words to his disciples before the beginning of the passion narrative. Matthew 26:1–2 states: "Jesus had

now finished all he wanted to say, and he told his disciples, 'It will be Passover, as you know, in two days' time, and the Son of Man will be handed over to be crucified.' "

In the view of great German Catholic theologian Karl Rahner—a view consistent with the eschatology of the Last Judgment passage—not only is there no tension between the commandment to love God and the commandment to love one another, there is "a radical identity of the two loves." Karl Rahner, 6 Theological Investigations 231, 236 (1969). In his "Reflections on the Unity of the Love of Neighbor and the Love of God," Rahner wrote: "It is radically true, i.e. by an ontological and not merely 'moral' or psychological necessity, that whoever does not love the brother whom he sees, also cannot love God whom he does not see, and that one can love God whom one does not see only *by* loving one's visible brother lovingly." Id. at 247. Rahner's reference is to a passage in John's First Letter in which it is written: "Anyone who says 'I love God' and hates his brother, is a liar, since whoever does not love the brother whom he can see cannot love God whom he has not seen." 1 John 4:20. See note 42 and accompanying text (Parable of the Good Samaritan). In Rahner's view, the two great commandments are really one. See Rahner, this note, at 232. Rahner argued that if and to the extent one loves one's neighbor one has achieved the ontological/existential state of being/consciousness that constitutes "love of God" even if one does not "believe in God". See id. at 238–39. If Rahner is right, then it is a mistake, a confusion, to say that one should love the Other *because* we love, or should love, God and God wants us to— or *because* we fear, or should fear, God and God wants us to. We should say, instead, that to love the Other (who is "sister/brother") just is to love God (who is "parent")—and that we should achieve the ontological/existential state of being/consciousness that constitutes "love of the Other" (= "love of God") because that state is the highest human good; to have achieved that radically unalienated condition is to have become "truly, fully" human. "We are well aware that we have passed over from death to life because we love our brothers. Whoever does not love, remains in death." 1 John 3:14.

Has Rahner pushed a good idea—that no one can be judged to love God who fails to love his/her neighbor—too far? One can accept that idea while rejecting Rahner's identification of love of God with love of neighbor. Tim Jackson has suggested, in correspondence, that "surely there is such a thing as the *direct* love of God, as for instance in the ecstatic prayer of some mystics or in Holy Communion. Human beings are social animals, no doubt, but they are also born for a vertical relation to the Supernatural." Cf. Jean Porter, "Salvific Love and Charity: A Comparison of the Thought of Karl Rahner and Thomas Aquinas," in Santurri & Werpehowski, note 28, at 249.

47. I cannot tell whether Martha Nussbaum understands this. See Martha C. Nussbaum, "Skepticism About Practical Reason in Literature and the Law," 107 Harvard L. Rev. 714, 739–40 (1994).

48. On the death of such a "God", see Charles Larmore, "Beyond Religion and Enlightenment," 30 San Diego L. Rev. 799, 799–802 (1993).

Indeed, as my footnote references to Buddhism—whose "theological" discourse is, in the main, nontheistic—suggest, the vision is not necessarily even theistic *in any conventional sense*. Whether mainline Buddhism is theistic in an unconventional sense is a difficult question. See David Tracy, "Kenosis, Sunyata, and Trinity: A Dialogue with Masao Abe," in The Emptying God: A Buddhist-Jewish-Christian Conversation 135 (John B. Cobb, Jr., & Christopher Ives eds., 1990).

49. In Buddhism, the relevant conviction is that the Other—who, appearances (illusions) to the contrary notwithstanding, is not really other at all, not, at any rate, in any deep sense—is an object of infinite compassion. (The Buddhist greeting "namasté" means, roughly, "I greet the place within you where we are one.")

50. See Perry, note 11, at 72–73. Nor is such a vision necessarily attended by belief in an afterlife. Cf. Timothy P. Jackson, "The Disconsolation of Theology: Irony, Cruelty, and Putting Charity First," 20 J. Religious Ethics 1, 19 (1992) (arguing that "a future heaven and/or hell ought not to play much of a role in [Christian] ethics, whatever role they may play in cosmology").

51. T.D.J. Chappell, "Why Read Aquinas?," Times Literary Supp., May 1, 1992, at 25 (reviewing Brian Davies, The Thought of Thomas Aquinas (1992)).

52. See id. at 25.

David Tracy's comments about the richness, the variety, but, finally, the problematic character—the limits—of all talk about Ultimate Reality, and especially of God-talk (talk about God, "theo-logizing"), are compelling:

> In and through even the best speech for Ultimate Reality, greater obscurity eventually emerges to manifest a religious sense of that Reality as ultimate mystery. Silence may be the most appropriate kind of speech for evoking this necessary sense of the radical mystery—as mystics insist when they say, "Those who know do not speak; those who speak do not know." The most refined theological discourse of the classic theologians ranges widely but returns at last to a deepened sense of the same ultimate mystery: the amazing freedom with all traditional doctrinal formulations in Meister Eckhart; the confident portrayals of God in Genesis and Exodus become the passionate outbursts of the prophets and the painful reflections of Job, Ecclesiastes, and Lamentations; the disturbing light cast by the biblical metaphors of the "wrath of God" on all temptations to sentimentalize what love means when the believer says, "God is love"; the proclamation of the hidden and revealed God in Luther and Calvin; the *deus otiosus* vision of God in the Gnostic traditions; the repressed discourse of the witches; the startling female imagery for Ultimate Reality in both the great matriarchal traditions and the great Wisdom traditions of both Greeks and Jews; the power of the sacred dialectically divorcing itself from the profane manifested in all religions; the extraordinary subtleties of rabbinic writing on God become the uncanny paradoxes of kabbalistic thought on God's existence in the very materiality of letters and texts; the subtle debates in Hindu philosophical reflections on monism and polytheism; the many faces of the Divine in the stories of Shiva and Krishna; the puzzling sense that, despite all appearances to the contrary, there is "nothing here that is not Zeus" in Aeschylus and Sophocles; the terror caused by Dionysius in Euripides' *Bacchae*; the refusal to cling even to concepts of "God" in order to become free to experience Ultimate Reality as Emptiness in much Buddhist thought; the moving declaration of that wondrous clarifier Thomas Aquinas, "All that I have written is straw; I shall write no more"; Karl Rahner's insistence on the radical incomprehensibility of both God and ourselves understood through and in our most comprehensible philosophical and theological speech; . . . the "God beyond God" language of Paul Tillich and all theologians who acknowledge how deadening traditional God-language can

easily become; the refusal to speak God's name in classical Judaism; the insistence on speaking that name in classical Islam; the hesitant musings on the present-absent God in Buber become the courageous attempts to forge new languages for a new covenant with God in the post-*tremendum* theologies of Cohen, Fackenheim, and Greenberg. There is no classic discourse on Ultimate Reality that can be understood as mastering its own speech. If any human discourse gives true testimony to Ultimate Reality, it must necessarily prove uncontrollable and unmasterable.

Tracy, note, at 108–09. See also Martin Buber, quoted in Hans KÜng, Does God Exist? An Answer for Today 508 (1978; Eng. trans., 1980):

["God"] is the most loaded of all words used by men. None has been so soiled, so mauled. But that is the very reason I cannot give it up. Generations of men have blamed this word for the burdens of their troubled lives and crushed it to the ground; it lies in the dust, bearing all their burdens. Generations of men with their religious divisions have torn the word apart; they have killed for it and died for it; it bears all their fingerprints and is stained with all their blood. Where would I find a word to equal it, to describe supreme reality? If I were to take the purest, most sparkling term from the innermost treasury of the philosophers, I could capture in it no more than a noncommittal idea, not the presence of what I mean, of what generations of men in the vastness of their living and dying have venerated and degraded. . . . We must respect those who taboo it, since they revolt against the wrong and mischief that were so readily claimed to be authorized in the name of God; but we cannot relinquish it. It is easy to understand why there are some who propose a period of silence about the "last things," so that the misused words may be redeemed. But this is not the way to redeem them. We cannot clean up the term "God" and we cannot make it whole; but, stained and mauled as it is, we can raise it from the ground and set it above an hour of great sorrow.

Cf. David Hollenbach, S.J., "Afterword: A Community of Freedom," in Catholicism and Liberalism: Contributions to American Public Philosophy 323, 337 (R. Bruce Douglass & David Hollenbach, S.J., eds., 1994):

For Christian believers, it is a challenge to recognize that their faith in God and the way of life it entails is a historical reality—it is rooted in historically particular scriptures and symbols and it is lived and sustained in historically particular communities. This historicity means that the task of interpreting the meaning of their faith will never be done as long as history lasts. The God in whom they place their faith can never be identified with any personal relationship, social arrangement, or cultural achievement. God transcends all of these. Though Christians believe that in Jesus Christ they have been given a definitive revelation of who this God is, they cannot claim to possess or encompass God in any of their theologies or understandings of the ultimate good of human life. Thus, in the words of Avery Dulles, "The Christian is defined as a person on the way to discovery, on the way to a revelation not yet given, or at least not yet given in final form."

(Quoting Avery Dulles, S.J., "Revelation and Discovery," in Theology and Discovery: Essays in Honor of Karl Rahner 27 (William J. Kelly, S.J., ed., 1980).) Hollenbach adds:

"Because the Christian community is always on the way to the fullness of its own deepest faith, hope, and love, it must be continually open to fresh discoveries. Encounter with the other, the different, and the strange must therefore characterize the life of the church. Active participation in a community of freedom is a prerequisite to such discovery." Hollenbach, this note, at 337.

For a powerful feminist-theological reflection on God-talk, see Johnson, note 31. See also Judith Plaskow & Carol C. Christ, eds., Weaving the Visions: New Patterns in Feminist Spirituality, pt. 2 ("Naming the Sacred") (1989).

53. As was Martin Buber, and as is David Tracy. See note 52.

54. See Dan Cohn-Sherbok, ed., World Religions and Human Liberation (1992); Hans Küng & Jürgen Moltmann, eds., The Ethics of World Religions and Human Rights (1990); Leroy S. Rouner, ed., Human Rights and the World's Religions (1988); Arlene Swidler, ed., Human Rights in Religious Traditions (1982); Robert Traer, Faith in Human Rights: Support in Religious Tradtions for a Global Struggle (1991).

55. See, e.g., Patrick Collinson, "Religion and Human Rights: The Case of and for Protestantism," in Historical Change and Human Rights: The Oxford Amnesty Lectures 1994, at 21 (Olwen Hufton, ed., 1995).

56. See Sandra M. Schneiders, "Does the Bible Have a Postmodern Message?," in Postmodern Theology: Christian Faith in a Pluralist World 56, 64–65 (Frederic B. Burnham ed., 1989):

> [There are] two problems: the ideological *use* of Scripture, which is, if you will, an exterior problem; and the ideological *content* of Scripture, which is intrinsic to the text.
>
> The question of the *use* of Scripture for purposes of oppression is being focused in the third-world struggle of the poor from domination by the rich and for participation in the societies and cultures which have been, for so long, controlled by the economically powerful for their own advantage. The struggle involves wresting the sacred text from those who have used it to legitimate their oppressive regimes and strategies and delivering it into the hands of the oppressed as a resource for liberation. . . . The problem of the ideological use of scripture is soluble and is slowly being solved.
>
> The second problem . . ., that of the ideological *content* of Scripture, is much more complicated. It is being focused in the struggle of women for liberation from patriarchal oppression in family, society, and church, and in the struggle of feminists, both men and women, to destroy the patriarchal ideology which grounds not only sexism but racism, classism, clericalism, and all the other forms of dualistic hierarchy in which the powerful dominate the weak in the name of God. Here the problem is not the Scripture has been *used* to legitimate oppression (although this is a continuing problem) but that the Bible itself is both a product and a producer of oppression, that some of its *content* is oppressive.

Schneiders's elaboration of the problem and her overview of the various responses of women (especially feminist theologians) and others to it (id. at 63–71) are excellent. (Schneiders is a Catholic theologian.)

57. Arthur Schlesinger, Jr., "The Opening of the American Mind," New York Times Book Rev., July 23, 1989, at 26.

58. Tracy, note 14, at 105.

59. Id. at 100.

60. Id. at 84–85, 86, 97–98, 112.

61. Jürgen Habermas, "Transcendence from Within, Transcendence in this World," in Habermas, Modernity, and Public Theology 226, 238 (Don Browning & Francis Schüssler Fiorenza eds., 1992).

62. Glenn Tinder, "Can We Be Good Without God: The Political Meaning of Christianity," Atlantic, Dec. 1989, at 69, 80 (passages rearranged and emphasis added).

63. Nor does the point lose anything if the emphasis is put, for example, on the (Mahayana) Buddhist tradition, with its insistence on compassion for all sentient creatures as the fitting response to the true—as distict from the illusory—nature of the world.

64. See Larmore, note 48.

65. Bruce Ackerman has announced: "There is no moral meaning hidden in the bowels of the universe." Bruce A. Ackerman, Social Justice in the Liberal State 368 (1980). This brings to mind one of Nietzsche's passages:

> Man a little, eccentric species of animal, which—fortunately—has its day; all on earth a mere moment, an incident, an exception without consequences, something of no importance to the general character of the earth; the earth itself, like every star, a hiatus between two nothingnesses, an event without plan, reason, will, self-consciousness, the worst kind of necessity, *stupid* necessity— Something in us rebels against this view; the serpent vanity says to us: "all that *must* be false, *for* it arouses indignation— Could all that not be merely appearance? And man, in spite of all, as Kant says—"

Nietzsche, note 10, at 169.

66. Id. at 147.

67. Charles Taylor, The Ethics of Authenticity 68 (1991).

68. See Joske, note 12, at 250: "If, as Kurt Vonnegut speculates in *The Sirens of Titan*, the ultimate end of human activity is the delivery of a small piece of steel to a wrecked space ship wanting to continue a journey of no importance whatsoever, the end would be too trivial to justify the means." See also Nozick, note 39, at 586: "If the cosmic role of human beings was to provide a negative lesson to some others ('don't act like them') or to provide needed food to passing intergalactic travelers who *were* important, this would not suit our aspirations—not even if afterwards the intergalactic travelers smacked their lips and said that we tasted good."

69. Paul Edwards, "Life, Meaning and Value of," 4 Encyclopedia of Philosophy 467, 470 (Paul Edwards ed., 1967). Whether Clarence Darrow was in fact "one of the most compassionate men who ever lived" is open to serious question. For a revisionist view of Darrow, see Gary Wills, Under God: Religion and American Politics, chs. 8–9 (1990).

70. John Leslie, "Is It All Quite Simple? The Physicist's Search for a Theory of Everything," Times Literary Supp., Jan. 29, 1993, at 3 (reviewing, inter alia, Steven Weinberg, Dreams of a Final Theory (1992)). Cf. Paul Davies, "The Holy Grail of Physics," New York Times Book Rev., Mar. 7, 1993, at 11 (reviewing, inter alia, Weinberg's book): "Reductionism [in physics] may be a fruitful research method, but it is a bleak philosophy. . . . If the world is but a collection of inert atoms interacting through blind and

purposeless forces, what happens to ... the meaning of life?" For a controversial critique of such scientific reductionism, see Brian Appleyard, Understanding the Present: Science and the Soul of Modern Man (1992). On philosophical inquiry into cosmology, see Derek Parfit, "The Puzzle of Reality," Times Literary Supp., July 3, 1992, at 3.

Several recent papers in a fierce and ongoing debate about the consistency or inconsistency of claims made in evolutionary biology with Christian claims are relevant here. All the papers are by persons who identify themselves as Christians. In the September 1991 issue of *Christian Scholar's Review*, see Alvin Platinga, "When Faith and Reason Clash: Evolution and the Bible"; Howard J. Van Till, "When Faith and Reason Cooperate"; Ernan McMullin, "Platinga's Defense of Special Creation"; Alvin Platinga, "Evolution, Neutrality, and Antecedent Probability: A Reply to McMullin and Van Till." In the June/July 1993 issue of *First Things*, see Howard J. Van Till & Philip E. Johnson, "God and Evolution: An Exchange."

71. Dworkin, "Life Is Sacred," note 2, at 36.

72. Id. at 36.

73. Dworkin, Life's Dominion, note 9, at 195.

74. Id. at 25.

Curiously, elsewhere in his book Dworkin writes that that he "can think of no plausible account of the content that a belief must have in order to be deemed religious that would rule out convictions about why and how human life [is sacred], except the abandoned notion that religious belief must presuppose a god." Id. at 163. He also says that "why and how human life is sacred" is an "essentially religious issue". Id. at 165. It is not obvious why, if (as Dworkin insists) there is a secular interpretation or version of the idea that human life is sacred, the issue of why and how human life is sacred is *essentially* religious. If the idea that human life is sacred is *not* essentially religious, why is the issue of why and how human life is sacred essentially religious? Dworkin's principal incentive to claim that the idea that human life is sacred can be interpreted in a secular as well as in a religious way is that, for purposes of his characterization of the abortion controversy, he wants to be able to attribute the idea (in its secular version) to secular folks as well as (in its religious version) to religious ones. His principal incentive to claim that the issue of why and how human life is sacred is essentially religious is that, for purposes of his argument about the (un)constitutionality of restrictive abortion legislation, Dworkin wants to be able to rely on a constitutional premise according to which government may not take coercive action predicated on nothing more than a contested position on an essentially religious issue. See id. at 160–68. (That there is such a constitutional premise is open to question. Cf. Michael J. Perry, "Religious Morality and Political Choice: Further Thoughts—and Second Thoughts—on *Love and Power*," 30 San Diego L. Rev. 703 (1993).)

75. Dworkin, "Life Is Sacred," note 2, at 36 (emphasis added).

76. Dworkin, Life's Dominion, note 9, at 69–71.

77. A.W. Price, "Varieties of Objectivity and Values," 83 Proc. of the Aristotelian Society 103, 106 (1983). See David Hume, A Treatise of Human Nature 469 (L. Selby-Bigge ed., 1973): "Vice and virtue, therefore, may be compar'd to sounds, colours, heat and cold, which, according to modern philosophy, are not qualities in objects, but perceptions in the mind: And this discovery in morals, like that other in physics, is to be regarded as a considerable advancement of the speculative sciences; tho', like that, too,

it has little or no influence on practice." See also Anthony T. Kronman, "A Comment on Dean Clark," 89 Columbia L. Rev. 1748, 1755 (1989): "[The view] that there are goods which are not the goods of any human beings at all, is likely to appear . . . wholly unintelligible, for it conflicts with what is perhaps the deepest and most widely shared orthodoxy of modern moral thought—the assumption that only the goods of human beings (or perhaps sentient beings) count in assessing different practices and institutions." Cf. Robin W. Lovin, "Empiricism and Christian Social Thought," Annual of Society of Christian Ethics 25, 41 (1982): "Ethics will never be like physics, chemistry, or certain types of sociology, because it understands the moral reality to be about an interaction between persons and the world which can only be known from the reports of those who experience that interaction."

Does Dworkin disagree? It is hard to tell. Cf. Dworkin, Life's Dominion, note 9, at 248 n. 1: "I do not mean to take any position on a further, very abstract philosophical issue not pertinent to this discussion: whether great paintings would still be valuable if intelligent life were altogether destroyed forever so that no one could ever have the experience of regarding paintings again. There is no inconsistency in denying that they would have value then, because the value of a painting lies in the kind of experience it makes available, while still insisting that this value is intrinsic because it does not depend on any creatures' actually wanting that kind of experience."

At one point in his discussion of "intrinsic" value, Dworkin writes: "David Hume and many other philosophers insisted that objects or events can be valuable only when and because they serve someone's or something's interests. On this view, nothing is valuable unless someone wants it or unless it helps someone get what he does want." Id. at 69. The second sentence here is a glaring non sequitur. It does not follow, from the Humean view, that nothing is valuable unless someone wants it or unless it helps someone get what he does want. It follows only that nothing is valuable unless it serves someone's or something's interests. That something serves my interests does not entail that I want it (or that it helps me get what I do want). After all, I might not know that something serves my interests, or I might not know what my real interests are. Indeed, that I want something (or that it helps me get what I do want) does not entail that it serves my interests: I might want things that are not good for me—indeed, that are bad for me.

78. To say that something has *merely* subjective value for someone is to say that she believes it to have value for her even though it does not. Considered in isolation something might have (objective and/or subjective) value for someone even if considered in context it does not: One thing that has value for someone might crowd out or preclude another thing that has even greater value for her.

79. Dworkin, Life's Dominion, note 9, at 78.

80. Id. at 82. See id. at 81–84.

81. Id. at 82.

82. Id. at 83.

83. Id. at 84.

84. Id. at 82.

85. Id. at 83.

86. Id. at 78.

87. Id. at 71.

88. Robert Grant, "Abortion and the Idea of the Sacred," Times Literary Supp.,

June 18, 1993, at 11. For another very critical comment, see Jenny Teichman, "What Is Sacred? Ronald Dworkin & His Answers," New Criterion, Nov. 1993, p. 8.

89. There are others. (See note 101 (mentioning the work of John Finnis and that of Jürgen Habermas).) A prominent secular argument for human rights—that is, a prominent secular argument that does not rely on the (ineliminably religious?) idea of human rights—is Alan Gewirth's. See Alan Gewirth, Reason and Morality, chs. 1–2 (1978); Alan Gewirth, The Community of Rights, ch. 1 (1996). Gewirth's argument has been extremely controversial, to say the least. See, e.g., Edward Regis, ed., Gewirth's Ethical Rationalism (1984); Brian Barry, Theories of Justice 285–88 (1989). For a careful restatement and defense of Gewirth's argument, see Deryck Beyleveld, The Dialectical Necessity of Morality: An Analysis and Defense of Alan Gewirth's Argument for the Principle of Generic Consistency (1991). For a skeptical review of Beyleveld's book, see Nick Fotion, 101 Ethics 579 (1993).

It bears emphasis that, as Garth Hallett has observed, "Gewirth does not argue that the [principle of generic consistency] is true, but only that any agent who wishes to be rational must accept it." Garth L. Hallett, Greater Good: The Case for Proportionalism 135 (1995). Hallett then writes, in a footnote: "In *The Dialectical Necessity of Morality*, 15, Deryck Beyleveld makes this point more clearly than does Gewirth: 'Use of the dialectically necessary method implies that Gewirth is not attempting to establish the PGC itself as a truth. What he attempts to establish as a necessary truth is the proposition "A PPA [prospective purposive agent] contradicts that it is a PPA if it does not accept/act in accordance with the PGC.'" " Id. at 184 n. 29.

90. Arthur Allen Leff, "Economic Analysis of Law: Some Realism About Nominalism," 60 Virginia L. Rev. 451, 454 (1974) (emphasis added).

91. James Griffin, Well-Being 239 (1987).

92. Williams, note 39, at 14.

93. David Tracy, "Theology, Critical Social Theory, and the Public Realm," in Browning & Fiorenza, note 61, at 19, 37.

94. Rorty, "Human Rights, Rationality, and Sentimentality," note 43, at 133.

95. James W. Nickel, Making Sense of Human Rights: Philosophical Reflections on the Universal Declaration of Human Rights 91 (1987).

96. See Stephen Scott, "Motive and Justification," 85 J. Philosophy 479, 499 (1988): "When he was deliberating about how to live, St. Augustine asked, 'What does anything matter, if it does not have to do with happiness?' His question requires explanation, because he is not advising selfishness nor the reduction of other people to utilities, and even qualification, because other things can have some weight. All the same, the answer he expects is obviously right: only a happy life matters conclusively. If I had a clear view of it, I could have no motive to decline it, I could regret nothing by accepting it, I would have nothing about which to deliberate further." Cf. Richard Taylor, "Ancient Wisdom and Modern Folly," 13 Midwest Studies in Philosophy 54, 57, 58 (1988): "The Greek *eudaimonia* is always translated 'happiness,' which is unfortunate, for the meaning we attach to the word *happiness* is thin indeed compared to what the ancients meant by *eudaimonia*. *Fulfillment* might be a better term, though this, too, fails to capture the richness of the original term.... The concept of happiness in modern philosophy, as well as in popular thinking, is superficial indeed in comparison." For an extended discussion of the "Why be moral?" problem from a neo-Aristotelian

perspective, see Rüdiger Bittner, What Reason Demands (Theodore Talbot trans., 1989).

97. Nickel, note 95, at 91.

98. See text accompanying note 43.

99. Nathan Stoltzfus, "Dissent in Nazi Germany," Atlantic, Sept. 1992, at 87, 94.

100. Taylor, note 96, at 87. Cf. id. at 3: "Much contemporary moral philosophy, particularly but not only in the English-speaking world, has given such a narrow focus to morality . . . . This moral philosophy has tended to focus on what it is right to do rather than on what it is good to be, on defining the content of obligation rather than the nature of the good life . . . . This philosophy has accredited a cramped and truncated view of morality in a narrow sense, as well as of the whole range of issues involved in the attempt to live the best possible life, and this not only among professional philosophers, but with a wider public." (Taylor's book is, among other things, a powerful argument for a different, larger understanding of "moral", an Aristotelian rather than a Kantian understanding. See id. at 4, 14–15, 63–64, 79, 87.)

The effort to evade the why-be-moral question by distinguishing between "reasons" and "motives" is unavailing—as, indeed, is implicit in Taylor's comments. See Henry B. Veatch, "Modern Ethics, Teleology, and Love of Self," 75 Monist 52, 60 (1992):

> [T]he stock answer given to this question has long been one of trying to distinguish between a *reason* and a *motive* for being moral. For surely, it is argued, if I recognize something to be my duty, then surely I have a reason to perform the required action, even though I have no motive for performing it. In fact, even to ask for a motive for doing something, when one already has a reason for doing it, would seem to be at once gratuitous and unnecessary—at least so it is argued. Unhappily, though, the argument has a dubious air about it at best. For does it amount to anything more than trying to prove a point by first attempting to make a distinction, implying that the distinction is no mere distinction, but a distinction with a difference—viz. the distinction between a reason and a motive. But then, having exploited the distinction, and yet at the same time insinuating that one might conceivably have a reason for doing something, but no motive for doing it, the argument draws to its conclusion by surreptitiously taking advantage of the fact that there possibly is no real distinction between a reason and a motive after all, so that if one has a reason for doing a thing, then one has a motive for doing it as well. In other words, it's as if the argument only succeeds by taking back with its left hand what it had originally given with its right.

101. John Finnis's argument in defense of a requirement "of fundamental impartiality among the human subjects who are or may be partakers of [basic human goods]" is simply unavailing. For the argument, see John Finnis, Natural Law and Natural Rights 106–08 (1980). "[John] Finnis has tried to do in two pages what . . . others have devoted entire books to: . . . [to] show that egoism is inherently self-contradictory or irrational. All of these attempts have failed. It is surprising that Finnis deals with such a problematic and contentious issue in such a brief and casual fashion." J.D. Goldsworthy, "God or Mackie: The Dilemma of Secular Moral Philosophy," 1985 American J. Jurisprudence 43, 75. See id. at 73–77. One of Finnis's most recent writings fares no better: John Fin-

nis, "Natural Law and Legal Reasoning," in Natural Law Theory: Contemporary Essays 134 (Robert P. George ed., 1992). (I criticize aspects of Finnis's argument in chapter 4.)

Given the current prominence in some circles of Habermasian "discourse ethics", this recent statement by Jürgen Habermas is worth reporting—a statement that should be very sobering for anyone tempted to believe that discourse ethics might supply an effective secular argument for human rights: "It is true that a philosophy that thinks postmetaphysically cannot answer the question that [David] Tracy . . . calls attention to: why be moral [i.e., impartial] at all?" Habermas, note 61, at 239. (For a recent effort to provide a grounding for human rights in Habermasian "discourse theory", see Robert Alexy, "Discourse Theory and Human Rights," 9 Ratio Juris 209 (1996).)

What Habermas then goes on to say is really quite remarkable:

> At the same time, however, this philosophy can show why this question does not arise meaningfully for communicatively socialized individuals. We acquire our moral intuitions in our parents' home, not in school. And moral insights tell us that we do not have any good reasons for behaving otherwise: for this, no self-surpassing of morality is necessary. It is true that we often behave otherwise, but we do so with a bad conscience. The first half of the sentence attests to the weakness of the motivational power of good reasons; the second half attests that rational motivation by reasons is more than nothing [*auch nicht nichts ist*]—moral convictions do not allow themselves to be overridden without resistance.

Id. Let's put aside the fact that "we" acquire our moral "intuitions" in many places besides (or in addition to) our parents' home—in the streets, for example. The more important point, for present purposes, is that we do not all acquire the same moral intuitions. Some of us acquire moral intuitions that enable us to ignore, and perhaps even to brutalize, the Other without any pangs of "conscience". It is incredible that in the waning days of this unbearably brutal century, Habermas—writing in Germany of all places—could suggest otherwise. We need not even look at the oppressors themselves; we need look only at those whose passivity makes them complicit—as the quote in the text accompanying note 99 confirms.

102. See Williams, note 39, at 103–04.

103. See Peter Vallentyne, ed., Contractarianism and Rational Choice: Essays on David Gauthier's *Morals by Agreement* (1991); David Gauthier & Robert Sugden, eds., Rationality, Justice and the Social Contract: Themes from *Moral by Agreement* (1993).

104. David Gauthier, "Rational Constraint: Some Last Words," in Vallentyne ed., note 103, 323, 330.

105. Peter Vallentyne, "Gauthier's Three Projects," in Vallentyne ed., note 103, at 1, 2. Cf. Robert Sugden, "The Contractarian Enterprise," in Gauthier & Sugden eds., note 103, at 1, 8: "At the core of [Gauthier's project] is the thought that traditional moral theory relies on the supposed existence of entities, such as God or goodness, which are external to human life yet somehow matter. A defensible morality should dispense with such mysterious entities, and accept that life has no meaning outside itelf."

106. Friedrich Nietzsche, "All Too Human," in Basic Writings of Nietzsche 148 (Walter Kaufmann trans., 1973). See note 147 and accompanying text.

107. Sugden, note 105, at 5. Gauthier has written that *Morals by Agreement* "is an attempt to challenge Nietzsche's prescient remark, "As the will to truth . . . gains self-

consciousness . . . morality will gradually perish". It is an attempt to write moral theory for adults, for persons who live consciously in a postanthropomorphic, posttheocentric, posttechnocratic world. It is an attempt to allay the fear, or suspicion, or hope, that without a foundation in objective value or objective reason, in sympathy or in sociality, the moral enterprise must fail." David Gauthier, "Moral Artifice," 18 Canadian J. Philosophy 385, 385 (1988). In the end, however, as the text accompanying this note confirms, Gauthier does not challenge Nietzsche so much as he embraces a Nietzschean conception of justice. See note 144 and accompanying text ( ).

108. Cf. Henry A. Kissinger, "Continuity and Change in American Foreign Policy," 15 Society 97, 99 (1977): "[O]ne of the basic challenges of foreign policy [is] the perennial tension between morality and pragmatism. Whenever it has been forced to wield its great power, the United States has also been driven to search its conscience. How does our foreign policy serve moral ends? How can the United States carry out its role as human example and champion of justice in a world in a world in which power is still often the final arbiter? How do we reconcile ends and means, principle and survival? How do we keep secure both our existence *and* our values? These have been the moral and intellectual dilemmas of the United States for two hundred years."

109. Warren Christopher, "Democracy and Human Rights: Where America Stands," 4 U.S. Department of State Dispatch 441, 442 (1993).

110. See Jerome J. Shestack, "An Unsteady Focus: The Vulnerabilities of the Reagan Administration's Human Rights Policy," 2 Harvard Human Rights Yearbook 25, 49–50 (1989) (footnotes omitted):

> What reasons should motivate an administration to afford human rights a central role in United States foreign policy as a matter of national interest? I believe that there are at least the following compelling motivations:
>
> 1. Human rights values advance national security. Nations that accept human rights are likely to be more stable and make better allies. Repression of human rights invites interventions and endangers stability. Conversely, human rights include responsiveness to the will of the people and restraints on aggressive action.
>
> 2. Human rights and world peace are interrelated. Peace and stability cannot be maintained in a world in which people are repressed and impelled to rise up against their oppressors. Afghanistan, Armenia, Burundi, Bangladesh, Haiti, the Philippines and many other places are stark examples.
>
> 3. Human rights are premised on the observance of rules of international law. Acceptance of the rule of law is a condition for a system of world order which, in turn, promotes world peace.
>
> 4. Human rights have become a central item on the global agenda, appealing to the expectations of people on every continent. The United States is perceived as having an immense potential to further human dignity and freedom. Championing human rights affords the United States the opportunity to be relevant to that agenda and responsive to the aspirations of peoples around the world.
>
> 5. Advancing economic and social human rights removes causes of tension and instability among less developed nations and promotes an equitable world order.
>
> 6. Human rights endeavors offer the United States the opportunity to act in concert with other nations to generate "coalitions of shared purposes."

7. Human rights address one of the world's most pressing problems: the enormous increase of refugees. The plight of refugees contributes to international tensions, and refugees impose huge burdens on nations to which they flee. Enforcing human rights will alleviate the suffering and number of refugees.

8. Including human rights in foreign policy formulation is favored by Congress. Without accommodation to this concern, the executive branch faces a polarized foreign policy marked by continuing disputes with Congress. A consensus with Congress on human rights issues advances the effectiveness and reliability of United States foreign policy initiatives.

9. Human rights policies command respect and support from this nation's citizenry. Conversely, foreign policies which ignore human rights are likely to be self-defeating by failing to sustain popular support.

10. Finally, advancing human rights reinforces this nation's own cohesion, its moral purpose and its appreciation of its own domestic liberties. Human rights have long been a focus for shared purpose in this nation's tradition, and a sense of shared purpose among its people is in the national interest.

111. Richard B. Bilder, "Human Rights and U.S. Foreign Policy: Short-Term Prospects," 14 Virginia J. International L. 597, 608 (1974). See also Richard B. Bilder, "Rethinking International Human Rights: Some Basic Questions," 1969 Wisconsin L. Rev. 171, 187–91.

112. Cf. Bilder, "Human Rights and U.S. Foreign Policy," note 111, at 608–09: "Moral compromises . . . may have real costs in terms of the way Americans view their own country and its role in the world. We are coming to see that national pride, self-respect, cohesion, and purpose are meaningful elements of both national power and domestic tranquility. It is true that there are practical limits to what the United States can reasonably attempt to accomplish in promoting the human rights of other peoples. But, in a period following Vietnam and Watergate, it may be worth some foreign policy risks to reassert historic American commitments to human worth and dignity."

113. See Christopher, note 109, at 441: "America's identity as a nation derives from our dedication to the proposition 'that all Men are created equal and endowed by their Creator with certain unalienable rights.'"

114. In his review of *Love and Power*, note 11, Ned Foley thought that I was denying that one can be moral without being religious. See Edward B. Foley, "Tillich and Camus, Talking Politics," 92 Columbia L. Rev. 954, 964–77 (1992).

115. See Foley, note 114.

116. Cf. Kristen R. Monroe, Michael C. Barton, & Ute Klingeman, "Altruism and the Theory of Rational Action: Rescuers of Jews in Nazi Europe," 101 Ethics 103 (1990); Neera Kapur, "Altruism v. Self-Interest: Sometimes a False Dichotomy," 10 Social Philosophy & Policy 90 (1993).

117. Leszek Kolakowski, Religion, If There Is No God: On God, the Devil, Sin, and Other Worries of the So-Called Philosophy of Religion 191 (1982) (emphasis added).

118. But cf. Jackson, note 50, at 9 ("Promethean self-creation and utterly gratuitous care for others risks collapsing into its (putative) opposite, a self-destructive and domineering hubris"); Fred R. Dallmayr, "Critical Theory and Reconciliation," in Browning & Fiorenza eds., at 119, 139:

If the world is totally corrupt and perverse, then this world must be destroyed and replaced by a completely new one through some kind of *creatio ex nihilo*; moreover, given the removal of absolutes, such creation can only be the work of human agents or producers. In this manner, reconciliation and redemption become the targets of goal-directed activity, that is, or purposive fabrication. . . . At the same time, being themselves part of the corrupt world, human agents can only perpetuate or re-create the state of corruption; thus, instrumentalism becomes inescapable and self-destructive.

119. Matthew 25:40.

120. For a series of meditations on Camus's work by one of the most important Christian (Catholic) writers of the late twentieth century—a writer who did not pretend that Camus was in any way an "anonymous" Christian—see Thomas Merton, "Seven Essays on Albert Camus (1966–68)," in The Literary Essays of Thomas Merton 179–301 (Patrick Hart ed., 1981).

121. Foley suggests that it would not have have arisen as between Paul Tillich and Albert Camus. He also explains that it need not arise as between someone who is "prochoice" on the issue of abortion and someone who is "pro-life". See Foley, note 114, at 973–75.

122. Cf. note 143.

123. Foley thinks that Camus's nonreligious (indeed, antireligious) response to the question of validity works, no less than a religious response. See Foley, note 114, 965–66. *Pace* Tinder (and Nietzsche), I am skeptical. I am inclined to say of any nonreligious response much the same thing Tim Jackson has said of antirealism:

> [T]he loss of realism . . . means the loss of any and all realities independent of or transcendent to inquiry. In this respect, God must suffer the same fate as any other transcendent subject or object. Because faith makes sense only when accompanied by the possibility of doubt, Rorty's distancing of scepticism means a concomitant distancing of belief in "things unseen." He, unlike Kant, denies both knowledge and faith; but for what, if anything, is this supposed to make room? Faith may perhaps be given a purely dispositional reading, being seen as a tendency to act in a certain way, but any propositional content will be completely lost. The pull toward religious faith is at best a residue of metaphysical realism and of the craving for metaphysical comfort. The taste for the transcendent usually associated with a religious personality will find little place in a Rortian world. Similarly, hope and love, if thought to have a supernatural object or source, lose their point. The deconstruction of God must leave the pious individual feeling like F. Scott Fitzgerald after his crackup: "a feeling that I was standing at twilight on a deserted range, with an empty rifle in my hand and the targets down." The deconstructed heart is ever restless, yet the theological virtues stand only as perpetual temptations to rest in inauthenticity. We live in a world without inherent *telos*; so there simply is no rest as Christianity has traditionally conceived it.

Timothy P. Jackson, "The Theory and Practice of Discomfort: Richard Rorty and Pragmatism," 51 Thomist 270, 284–85 (1987).

124. Habermas, note 61, at 239.

125. Jackson, "The Theory and Practice of Discomfort," note 123, at 289.

126. Rorty, "Human Rights, Rationality, and Sentimentality," note 43, at 116.

127. Id. at 124–25. Rorty is far from alone in reaching that conclusion. See, e.g., Jeffrie Murphy, "Afterword: Constitutionalism, Moral Skepticism, and Religious Belief," in Constitutionalism: The Philosophical Dimension 239, 243–45 (Alan S. Rosenbaum ed., 1988) (arguing that Kant failed in his effort to provide a secular foundation for the morality he wanted to defend). For a recent effort to provide (what he describes as) a Kantian foundation for human rights, see Alexy, note 101. See also Christine M. Korsgaard et al., The Sources of Normativity (1996).

128. Rorty, "Human Rights, Rationality, and Sentimentality," note 43, at 116.

129. Id. at 117. See id. at 117–18.

130. Id. at 126.

131. See Bernard Williams, "Auto-da-Fé," New York Rev., Apr. 28, 1983, at 33: "Rorty is so insistent that we cannot, in philosophy, simply be talking about human beings, as opposed to human beings at a given time.... Rorty ... contrasts the approach of taking some philosophical problem and asking ...'What does it show us about *being human?*' and asking, on the other hand,'What does the persistence of such problems show us about *being twentieth-century Europeans?*" (Emphasis in original.) See (in addition to Rorty, "Human Rights, Rationality, and Sentimentality," note 43) Richard Rorty, Contingency, Irony, and Solidarity, ch. 9 ("Solidarity") (1989).

132. See notes 105–07 and accompanying text.

133. Richard Rorty, "Fraternity Reigns: The Case for a Society Based Not on Rights but on Unselfishness," New York Times Mag., Sept. 26, 1996, at 155, 157.

134. Rorty, "Human Rights, Rationality, and Sentimentality," note 43, at 122.

135. Id. at 119.

136. Id. at 128.

137. Id. at 129 (referring to Annette C. Baier, A Progress of Sentiments: Reflections on Hume's Treatise (1991)).

138. See note 28 and accompanying text.

139. See Rorty, "Human Rights, Rationality, and Sentimentality," note 43, at 119.

140. See, e.g., Richard Rorty, "Religion as Conversation-Stopper," 3 Common Knowledge 1, 2 (1994).

141. Jackson, note 50, at 10.

142. Richard Rorty, Consequences of Pragmatism xlii (1982).

143. See Jeremy Waldron, "Religious Contributions in Public Deliberation," 30 San Diego L. Rev. 817, 844–45 (1992):

> Consider, for example, the issue of whether property owners are obliged by natural law to share their wealth with the poor. Locke's position on this is well known:
>
> > [W]e know God hath not left one Man so to the Mercy of another, that he may starve him if he please: God the Lord and Father of all, has given no one of his Children such a Property, in his peculiar Portion of the things of this World, but that he has given his needy Brother a Right to the Surplusage of his Goods; so that it cannot justly be denied him, when his pressing Wants call for it.

We might rephrase this as follows: "A needy person has a right to the surplus goods of a rich person if they are necessary to keep him from perishing." If we do, however, someone is likely to ask us for an *argument* to support this controversial proposition. In Locke, the argument is based on the seminal fact of God's creating the world for the sustenance of all men:

> God made Man, and planted in him, as in all other Animals, a strong desire of Self-preservation, and furnished the World with things fit for Food and Rayment and other Necessaries of Life, Subservient to his design, that Man should live and abide for some time upon the Face of the Earth, and not that so curious and wonderful a piece of Workmanship by its own Negligence, or want of Necessaries, should perish again presently after a few moments continuance. . . .

Once again, we might, at a pinch translate *that* into secular language: "That people have a right to make use of the goods that may help them to survive is common sense." It loses a little in the translation, though. Keeping hold of the idea that we were *meant* to survive, and that being denied access to the naturally available resources that we need is offensive to the fact of our existence is difficult in a secular tradition.

See also Rachel Mariner, "Burdens Hard to Bear: A Theology of Civil Rights," 27 Harvard Civil Rights–Civil Liberties L. Rev. 657 (1992).

144. Simone Weil, Waiting for God 139, 143 (Emma Crauford trans., 1973) (quoted at the beginning of Jackson, note 50).

145. See text accompanying note 125.

146. See notes 105–07 and accompanying text.

147. Nietzsche, note 10, at 159-60. See note 106 and accompanying text.

148. Cf. Thomas Nagel, "A Faith of the Enlightenment," Times Literary Supp., Dec. 14, 1990, at 1341 (stating that "a religious answer stands as much in need of defence and explanation as does a secular one").

149. Kent Greenawalt, Religious Convictions and Political Choice 6 (1988). See Perry, note, at 67 & 173 n. 1. Cf. Richard John Neuhaus, The Naked Public Square: Religion and Democracy in America 86 (1984): "In the minds of some secularists the naked public square [i.e., neutral/impartial political discourse] is a desirable goal. They subscribe to the dogma of the secular Enlightenment that, as people become more enlightened (educated), religion will wither away; or, if it does not wither away, it can be safely sealed off from public consideration, reduced to a private eccentricity."

150. See Goldsworthy, note 101; Arthur Allen Leff, "Unspeakable Ethics, Unnatural Law," 1979 Duke L.J. 1229; Murphy, note 127. See also Philip E. Johnson, "Nihilism and the End of Law," First Things, March 1993, at 19.

151. Text accompanying note.

152. Text accompanying note.

153. Murphy, note 127, at 248 (emphasis added).

154. Nietzsche, note 10, at 157.

155. Leff, note 90, at 1249.

After I had finished this chapter, I came across the speech delivered by Vaclav Havel, president of the Czech Republic, upon receipt of the Philadelphia Liberty Medal at Independence Hall on July 4, 1994: "The New Measure of Man," New York Times, July 8, 1994, at A15. Havel suggests, in the speech, that "the idea of human rights and freedoms" must be rooted in a religious vision of the world. Havel concludes his speech with this comment: "The Declaration of Independence, adopted 218 years ago in this building, states that the Creator gave man the right to liberty. It seems that man can realize that liberty only if he does not forget the One who endowed him with it."

CHAPTER 2

1. I put aside, for now, the question *for whom* is it wrong (or right) to do (or not to do) certain things. See note 14 and accompanying text.

2. Johannes Morsink, "World War Two and the Universal Declaration," 15 Human Rights Q. 357, 357 (1993).

3. Rebecca J. Cook, "Women's International Human Rights Law: The Way Forward," in Human Rights of Women: National and International Perspectives 3, 6–7 (Rebecca J. Cook ed., 1994). See, e.g., Velasquez Rodriguez Case, Inter-American Court of Human Rights, 1988, Ser. C, No. 4, reprinted at 9 Human Rights L.J. 212 (1988); Convention on the Elimination of All Forms of Discrimination Against Women; Declaration on the Elimination of Violence Against Women. For discussions of the point in the context of women's human rights, see Rebecca J. Cook, "State Responsibility for Violations of Women's Human Rights," 7 Harvard Human Rights L.J. 125 (1994); Kenneth Roth, "Domestic Violence as an International Human Rights Issue," in Cook ed., this note, at 326. For a general discussion of the point, and of related matters, see Andrew Clapham, "Opinion: The Privatisation of Human Rights," European Human Rights L. Rev., Launch Issue, at 21 (1995). See also Henry J. Steiner & Philip Alston, eds., International Human Rights in Context: Law, Politics, Morals 125 (1996): "The rights declared in the [International] Covenant [on Civil and Political Rights] are not by their terms restricted to rights against *governmental* interference, That is, interference by non-governmental, private actors (the rapist, say) could as destructively impair the right to 'security of person' (Article 9). The state's duty to provide effective remedies can then be read to attach to conduct (rape) that was initially non-governmental." For critical commentary on the public/private distinction, especially as it relates to the question of women's human rights, see the materials compiled in Steiner & Alston eds., this note, at 945–61.

4. In what sense of "binding" is international law binding? In what sense of "law" is international law law? For a discussion, see Anthony D'Amato, "Is International Law Really 'Law'?," 79 Northwestern U. L. Rev. 1293 (1985); Jonathan I. Charney, "Universal International Law," 87 American J. International L. 529 (1993).

5. Or perhaps to any human being "lawfully within the territory of the state". For example, Article 12 of the International Covenant on Civil and Political Rights provides, in part: "Everyone lawfully within the territory of a State shall, within that territory, have the right to liberty of movement and freedom to choose his residence."

6. See note 5.

7. Is the right a "human" right, then, or merely a "citizen" right? See note 15 and accompanying text.

8. According to the technical (procedural) vagaries of international law, it might be the case that only another state, or the UN, is legally empowered to enforce a human being's right against S (= S's duty to the human being), whether by suing in an international forum or by taking political action of some kind. In that sense, under D a human being might have a right against S but not the right to sue to enforce her right against S; under D the right to sue or to take other action to enforce her right against S might belong only to another state, or to the UN. But that under D a human being might not herself enjoy the right to sue to enforce her right against S does not mean that—and ought not to be confused with the different situation where—under D she does not have a right against S.

9. For an extended analytic discussion of different species of "rights" and of their correlatives, see Judith Jarvis Thomson, The Realm of Rights 37–78 (1990) (commenting and building on Wesley Newcomb Hohfeld, Fundamental Legal Conceptions (1919)).

10. See chapter 4.

11. See chapter 4.

12. John Finnis, Natural Law and Natural Rights 205 (1980).

Some rights theorists argue that the basic function of a moral right is to protect some aspect of the well-being of the persons who are the beneficiaries of the right. Other rights theorists contend that the basic function is to protect, not the well-being, but the autonomy of the beneficiaries of the right. Yet others argue—sensibly, in my view—that the basic function is not either/or but both/and: *sometimes* to protect well-being and *sometimes* to protect autonomy. See James W. Nickel, Making Sense of Human Rights: Philosophical Reflections on the Universal declaration of Human Rights 23–24 (1987). Compare L.W. Sumner, The Moral Foundation of Rights 203–05 (1987). Indeed, if autonomy is a particular, and particularly important, constituent of human well-being, then protecting autonomy is protecting (an important constituent of) human well-being and protecting human well-being in its entirety requires protecting autonomy. On "autonomy", see Gerald Dworkin, The Theory and Practice of Autonomy (1988). On the relation of well-being and autonomy, see Joseph Raz, "Liberalism, Skepticism, and Democracy," 74 Iowa L. Rev. 761, 779–86 (1989).

13. See chapter 1, note 5.

14. This is not to deny the existence of another, related right, which might be legal as well as moral: the right not to have anyone act for the purpose of interfering with one's enjoyment of the right (against one's own government) to vote.

15. See, e.g., Articles 2 & 26.

16. Cynthia Price Cohen, "United Nations Convention on the Rights of the Child: Introductory Note," 44 International Commission of Jurists Rev. 36, 38 (1990).

17. Steiner & Alston eds., note 3, at 908. The literature regarding the human rights of women is large and growing. For a citation to some of the literature, see ch. 3, note 65. On the human rights of children, see Cohen, n.ote 16, Dominic McGoldrick, "The United Nations Convention on the Rights of the Child," 5 International J.L. & Family 132 (1991); Lawrence J. LeBlanc, The Convention on the Rights of the Child: United Nations Lawmaking on Human Rights (1995).

18. See note 39 and accompanying text.

19. See, e.g., Joel Feinberg, Freedom and Fulfillment, ch. 8 (1992).

20. See, e.g., J.L. Mackie, "Can There Be a Right-Based Moral Theory," 3 Midwest Studies in Philosophy 350 (1978).

21. See note 45 and accompanying text.

22. Mary Ann Glendon, Rights Talk: The Impoverishment of Political Discourse x (1991).

23. Id.

24. Id. at xi, xii.

25. Id. at 12.

26. Id. at 14. (She also decries, in a passage less relevant to our present concerns, "its unapologetic insularity". Id.)

27. Id.

28. See, e.g., David Abraham, "Are Rights the Right Thing?: Individual Rights, Communitarian Purposes and America's Problems," 25 Connecticut L. Rev. 947 (1993); Janet E. Ainsworth, "Speaking of Rights," 37 New York Law School L. Rev. 259 (1992); Thomas D. Barton, "Reclaiming Law Talk," 81 California L. Rev. 803 (1993); Richard A. Epstein, "Rights and 'Rights Talk'," 105 Harvard L. Rev. 1106 (1992); Suzanna Sherry, "Rights Talk: Must We Mean What We Say?," 17 L. & Social Inquiry 491 (1992); Cass Sunstein, "Rightalk," New Republic, Sept. 2, 1991, at 33; Timothy P. Terrell, "When Duty Calls?," 41 Emory L.J. 1111 (1992).

29. Glendon, note 22, at 13.

30. Article 29.

31. See, e.g., International Covenant on Civil and Political Rights, Article 4; European Convention for the Protection of Human Rights and Fundamental Freedoms, Article 10(2); American Declaration of the Rights and Duties of Man, Article 28.

32. Glendon, note 22, at 13.

33. Article 20 also states: "Any propaganda for war shall be prohibited by law."

34. On the African Charter's (and the African human rights system's) emphasis on duties, see the materials compiled in Steiner & Alston eds., note 3, at 689–705.

35. There is also, for example, the UN Convention on the Rights of the Child. See notes 16 and 17.

36. David Hollenbach, S.J., "A Communitarian Reconstruction of Human Rights: Contributions from Catholic Tradition," in Catholicism and Liberalism: Contributions to American Public Philosophy 127, 142 (R. Bruce Douglass & David Hollenbach, S.J. eds., 1994).

37. Glendon, note 22, at xiii.

38. This language appeared in the preface of a draft of a book by Allan Hutchinson, but was dropped from the published version of the book. See Allan C. Hutchinson, Waiting for Coraf: A Critique of Law and Rights (1994).

39. Nancy Fraser, Unruly Practices: Power, Discourse, and Gender in Contemporary Social Theory 183 (1989). (Fraser is a feminist and critical theorist.) See also Amy Bartholomew & Alan Hunt, "What's Wrong With Rights?," 9 L. & Inequality 1 (1990); Hollenbach, note 36; Elizabeth Kingdom, What's Wrong With Rights?: Problems for Feminist Politics of Law 150–52 (1991); Jeremy Waldron, "Rights and Needs: The Myth of Disjunction," in Legal Rights: Historical and Philosophical Perspectives 87 (Austin Sarat & Thomas R. Kearns eds., 1996).

40. There is much more to Hutchinson's important critique of the liberal culture of rights than his (unfortunate, in my view) generalization across all rights talk.

41. What force does it have? See note 28 and accompanying text.

42. Nor does the force of Hutchinson's critique, for example, depend on whether or not the claims are expressed in the language of rights. See Hutchinson, note 38.

43. Finnis, note 12, at 210. However, rights talk "is often, . . . though not inevitably or irremediably, a hindrance to clear thought when the question is: What are the demands of justice?" Id. at 210. See Larry R. Churchill & José Jorge Simán, "Why the Abortion Debate Is Sterile: Abortion and the Rhetoric of Individual Rights," Hastings Center Report, Feb. 1982, at 9. Cf. Glendon, note 22, at 14 (claiming that "[a]ll of these traits promote mere assertion over reason-giving").

44. Hutchinson, note 38, at xi.

45. Finnis, note 12, at 209–10. Finnis continues: "Anthropologists studying certain African tribal regimes of law have found that in the indigenous language the English terms 'a right' and 'duty' are usually covered by a single word, derived from the verbal form normally translated as 'ought'. This single word (e.g. *swanelo* in Barotse, *tshwanelo* in Tswana) is thus found to be best translated as 'due', for 'due' looks both ways along a juridical relationship, both to what one is due to do, and to what is due to one. This is linked, in turn, with a 'nuance in tribal societies, in that they stress duty and obligation, rather than the nuance of modern Western society, with a stress on right[s]'." Id. (quoting Max Gluckman, The Ideas in Barotse Jurisprudence xxv (2d ed. 1972)). See Theodore M. Benditt, Rights 3 (1982):

> If we wish to determine whether we can come up with a useful notion of rights, we are immediately faced with the question "Why bother?" After all, the ancients and the medievals did not have the notion of a right—was their moral life stunted in some way as a result? Did they lack the tools for dealing with certain aspects of the moral enterprise? Among them moral questions were dealt with in terms of what is right and wrong, what is in accordance with or required by the natural law, what people ought to do or are obliged to do, but not in terms of what someone has a right to, or has a right to do.

For an essay "confess[ing] to a moderate skepticism about the necessity of the language of rights", see Martin P. Golding, "The Primacy of Welfare Rights," 1 Social Philosophy & Policy 119 (1984). (The quoted language appears at p. 121.) See also Richard B. Brandt, "The Concept of a Moral Right and Its Function," 80 J. Philosophy 29, 44 (1983). Cf. Benditt, this note, at 7–8 (arguing that duty talk, unlike rights talk, might be indispensable).

CHAPTER 3

1. Noam Chomsky, For Reasons of State 404 (1973).

2. John Paul II, Veritatis Splendor, 23 Origins 297, 314 (1993).

3. In the preceding chapter, we began to look at some of the things that, according to the views represented by the principal international human rights documents, ought not to be done to any human being and some of the things that ought to be done for every human being. The reader would find it useful to examine the international

human rights documents cited in this book to get a fuller picture of what, according to those documents, ought not to be done (by states, in particular) to any human being and what ought to be done for every human being.

4. See chapter 1, text accompanying note 66.

5. See chapter 1, text accompanying note 124.

6. See Cynthia Price Cohen, "United Nations Convention on the Rights of the Child: Introductory Note," 44 International Commission of Jurists Rev. 36, 39 (1990) (commenting on "[t]he carefully worded compromise language of article 1 which defines a child simply as 'every human being . . .' and leaves it to the State Parties to give their own meaning to the words 'human being' according to their national legislation"); Dominic McGoldrick, "The United Nations Convention on the Rights of the Child," 5 International J.L. & Family 132, 133–34 (1991) (same).

7. See Johannes Morsink, "World War Two and the Universal Declaration," 15 Human Rights Q. 357, 363 (1993).

8. Richard Rorty, "Human Rights, Rationality, and Sentimentality," in On Human Rights: The Oxford Amnesty Lectures 1993, at 111, 112 (Stephen Shute & Susan Hurley eds., 1993). See also id. at 125.

9. Martha C. Nussbaum, "Skepticism About Practical Reason in Literature and the Law," 107 Harvard L. Rev. 714, 718 (1994).

10. Id. at 744. See also Martha Nussbaum, "Compassion: The Basic Social Emotion," 1996 Social Philosophy & Policy 27 (1996).

11. See chapter 1, text accompanying note 99.

12. See chapter 1, text accompanying note 43.

13. See chapter 1, text accompanying note 43.

14. For an important argument about the nature of well-being (welfare), see L. W. Sumner, Welfare, Happiness, and Ethics (1996).

15. Something, G, can be good for someone in the sense that G serves her well-being even if she does not believe that G serves her well-being—indeed, even if she believes that G disserves her well-being—and does not want G. Similarly, something, B, can be bad for someone in the sense that it disserves her well-being even if she does not believe that B disserves her well-being—even if she believes that B serves her well-being—and wants B. In short, human beings can be mistaken about what is truly good for them or about what is truly bad for them or about both.

16. Let me pause to forestall a possible misreading. I do not mean to suggest that the fact that something is good for every human being somehow entails that it ought to be done for every human being. That something, B, is bad for every human being—that it disserves the well-being of every human being—does seems to entail (that is, in conjunction with the premise that every human being is sacred it seems to entail) that B ought not to be done, or at least that it conditionally ought not to be done, to any human being; it seems to entail, that is, that no one ought to act for the purpose, or at least that there is a strong presumption against anyone acting for the purpose, of doing B to any human being. (I discuss the matter of "conditional" vs. "absolute" or "unconditional" human rights in chapter 4.) However, that something, G, is good for every human being—that it serves the well-being of every human being—does not entail that G ought to be done, or even that it conditionally ought to be done, for every human being; it does not entail that someone (or someones) ought to act for the purpose, or

even that there is a strong presumption in favor of someone acting for the purpose, of doing G for every human being (or every human being lawfully within the jurisdiction, or every human being who is a citizen, etc.; see chapter 2, note 5). For example, G might not be something, like "help in trouble" (see text accompanying note 34), that someone can bestow on another human being. Or it might not be something that anyone can reasonably be thought to be required to bestow on another person just because the other person is a human being (and therefore sacred). Or, G might be something that every human being can achieve, if at all, only for himself or herself, or something that every human being is better off achieving for himself or herself, or, at least, something that the community is better off requiring everyone to achieve for himself or herself. In any event, that something is good for every human being does not by itself entail that it ought to be done for every human being, and I do not mean to suggest otherwise. Nonetheless, that something is good for every human being can be, depending on the nature of that something, part of an argument for concluding that it ought to be done for every human being. (Even if something is not good for every human being, or even for any human being, one might have an obligation to do it for some human beings[s]—if, for example, it is not bad for any human being and one has accepted consideration for a promise to do it.)

One more clarification. That something—for example, a democratic form of government—might *not* be good for each and every human being who has it does not entail that international law should not establish a right to that something as a human right; it does not entail that the international law of human rights should not make the choice of that something obligatory. That there is, as a moral matter, and that there should be, as an international-legal matter, a human right to X—freedom from torture, for example—might presuppose that something (torture) is bad for everyone who is subjected to it and that freedom from that something is good for every human being who has it; it might presuppose that any human being is better off for having X. But that there is, as a moral matter, and that there should be, as an international-legal matter, a human right to X—a democratic form of government, for example, or religious freedom—does not necessarily presuppose that X is good for every human being who has it. For whatever reason(s), there might be some who would be much better off, in one or more respects, if they did not have X. For example, there might be some poor souls, helplessly adrift in the spaces created by modern political and religious freedoms, who would be genuinely better off if, instead of living in a society that enjoyed such freedoms, they lived in a society in which they were told by a benevolent state what political and/or religious orthodoxies to accept. That there is a human right to X might presuppose only that most human beings in any existing society will be much better off (eventually if not right away) if they have X—and that a choice *against* X, which is a choice favoring the well-being of the few (the *genuine* well-being, let us assume) over the (genuine) well-being of the many, is therefore inconsistent with the premise that all human beings, and not merely some, are sacred.

17. The relativist might also claim that there is not even anything such that most people in any existing society will be better off, eventually if not right away, if they have it. (See note 16.) I concentrate, in this chapter, on the former claim. If the response I develop here to the former claim is sound—the response that some things *are* good and some things *are* bad for *every* human being—*a fortiori* the response works against the second claim as well: Some things are good, eventually if not right away, for most human

beings in any existing society. Even if the response I develop here is sound, there might still be serious disagreement about what things are good or about what things are bad for every human being, or about both—or about what things are good for most human beings in any existing society.

(A puzzle: Why might anyone who affirms that there is something about every human being in virtue of which every human being is sacred deny that there is anything about every human being in virtue of which some things are bad or some things are good, or both, for every human being?)

18. Elaine Sciolino, "Abuses by Serbs the Worst Since Nazi Era, Report Says," New York Times, Jan. 20, 1993, at A8.

19. Quoted in Stephen Shute & Susan Hurley, "Introduction," in Shute & Hurley eds., note 8, at 2.

20. Quoted in id.

21. Quoted in Rorty, "Human Rights, Rationality, and Sentimentality," note 8, at 112.

22. World News Tonight with Peter Jennings (Feb. 18, 1994), ABC News Transcript #4035.

23. For yet another report of horror from the former Yugoslavia, see Anthony Lewis, "The Level of Beasts," New York Times, June 27, 1994, at A17.

24. See, e.g., Mark Danner, The Massacre at El Mozote: A Parable of the Cold War (1994). I quote a passage from Danner's chronicle in the introduction to this book.

25. See text accompanying note 34.

26. I am referring here to wants or preferences the satisfaction of which is not antithetical to human flourishing or otherwise morally problematic.

27. David B. Wong, Moral Relativity 158 (1984).

28. Stuart Hampshire, Morality and Conflict 155 (1983).

29. Cf. Hilary Putnam, Reason, Truth and History 148 (1981):

> If today we differ with Aristotle it is in being much more pluralistic than Aristotle was. Aristotle recognized that different ideas of Eudaemonia, different conceptions of human flourishing, might be appropriate for different individuals on account of the difference in their constitution. But he seemed to think that ideally there was some sort of constitution that every one ought to have; that in an ideal world (overlooking the mundane question of who would grow the crops and who would bake the bread) everyone would be a philosopher. We agree with Aristotle that different ideas of human flourishing are appropriate for individuals with different constitutions, but we go further and believe that even in the ideal world there would be different constitutions, that diversity is part of the ideal. And we see some degree of tragic tension between ideals, that the fulfillment of some ideals always excludes the fulfillment of some others.

As Putnam goes on to emphasize, however: "[B]elief in a pluralistic ideal is not the same thing as belief that every ideal of human flourishing is as good as every other. We reject ideals of human flourishing as wrong, as infantile, as sick, as one-sided." Id. See id. at 140 (referring to "sick standards of rationality" and "sick conception(s) of human flourishing"), 147: "We have just as much right to regard some 'evaluational' casts of mind as sick (and we all do) as we do to regard some 'cognitional' casts of mind as sick."

30. See Bernard Williams, Ethics and the Limits of Philosophy 153 (1985):

[T]here are many and various forms of human excellence which will not all fit together into one harmonious whole, so any determinate ethical outlook is going to represent some kind of specialization of human possibilities. That idea is deeply entrenched in any naturalistic or . . . historical conception of human nature—that is, in any adequate conception of it—and I find it hard to believe that it will be overcome by an objective inquiry, or that human beings could turn out to have a much more determinate nature than is suggested by what we already know, one that timelessly demanded a life of a particular kind.

31. See Stuart Hampshire, Two Theories of Morality 48–49 (1977):

The correct answer to the old question—"why should it be assumed, or be argued, that there is just one good for man, just one way of life that is best?"—is . . . an indirect one and it is not simple. One can coherently list all the ideally attainable human virtues and achievements, and all the desirable features of a perfect human existence; and one might count this as prescribing the good for man, the perfect realization of all that is desirable. But the best selection from this whole that could with luck be achieved in a particular person will be the supreme end for him, the ideal at which he should aim. It is obvious that supreme ends of this kind are immensely various and always will be various. There can be no single supreme end in this particularized sense, as both social orders and human capabilities change. . . .

That there should be an abstract ethical ideal, the good for men in general, is not inconsistent with there being great diversity in preferred ways of life, even among men living at the same place at the same time. The good for man, as the common starting-point, marks an area within which arguments leading to divergent conclusions about moral priorities can be conducted. The conclusions are widely divergent, because they are determined by different subsidiary premises. Practical and theoretical reason, cleverness, intelligence and wisdom, justice, friendship, temperance in relation to passions, courage, a repugnance in the face of squalid or mean sentiments and actions; these are Aristotle's general and abstract terms, which do not by themselves distinguish a particular way of life, realizable in a particular historical situation. The forms that intelligence and friendship and love between persons, and that nobility of sentiment and motive, can take are at least as various as human cultures; and they are more various still, because within any one culture there will be varieties of individual temperament, providing distinct motives and priorities of interest, and also varieties of social groupings, restricting the choice of ways of life open to individuals.

32. Such differences have figured prominently in international political debates about human rights between proponents of liberal-democratic human rights of the sort emphasized in the "first" world and proponents of socialist human rights of the sort emphasized in the "second" world. See David Hollenbach, Claims in Conflict: Retrieving and Renewing the Catholic Human Rights Tradition, esp. ch. 1 (1979); Max L. Stackhouse, Creeds, Society, and Human Rights: A Study in Three Cultures (1984). Cf. note.

33. Stuart Hampshire, Innocence and Experience 90 (1989).

34. Philippa Foot, "Moral Relativism," in Relativism: Cognitive and Moral 152, 164

(Jack W. Meiland & Michael Krausz eds., 1982). For a more elaborate statement, see Martha C. Nussbaum, "Human Functioning and Social Justice: In Defense of Aristotelian Essentialism," 20 Political Theory 202 (1992). See also Jonathan Jacobs, "Practical Wisdom, Objectivity, and Relativism," 26 American Philosophical Q. 199 (1989); John Kekes, "Human Nature and Moral Theories," 28 Inquiry 231 (1985); Jane E. Larson, " 'Imagine Her Satisfaction': The Transformative Task of Feminist Tort Work," 33 Washburn L.J. 56 (1993); Bimal Krishna Matilal, "Ethical Relativism and Confrontation of Cultures," in Relativism: Interpretation and Confrontation 339, 357 (Michael Krausz ed., 1989) ("The common dispositions, constitutive of the concept of 'the naked man,' may be recognized as numerous simple facts about needs, wants, and desires, for example, removal of suffering, love of justice, courage in the face of injustice, pride, shame, love of children, delight, laughter, happiness.").

35. See Nussbaum, "Human Functioning and Social Justice," note 34. See also Martha C. Nussbaum, Aristotle on Human Nature and the Foundations of Ethics (1990); Martha C. Nussbaum, "Non-Relative Virtues: An Aristotelian Approach," in The Quality of Life 242 (Martha Nussbaum & Amartya Sen eds., 1993). (The anti-"essentialist" position denies that there are any needs or goods common to each and every human being simply *qua* human; it denies, in that sense, that there are any needs or goods that are "essentially" human; it denies that there is any human "essence".)

36. Richard Rorty, Contingency, Irony, and Solidarity xiii (1989). Rorty writes approvingly of "this historicist turn", which, he says, "has helped free us, gradually but steadily, from theology and metaphysics—from the temptation to look for an escape from time and chance. It has helped us substitute Freedom for Truth as the goal of thinking and of social progress." Id. For an excellent critique of this and related aspects of Rorty's views, see Timothy P. Jackson, "The Theory and Practice of Discomfort: Richard Rorty and Pragmatism," 51 Thomist 270 (1987).

37. Richard Rorty, "Solidarity or Objectivity?," in Post-Analytic Philosophy 3, 11 (John Rajchman & Cornel West eds., 1985) (emphasis added).

38. Bernard Williams, "Auto-da-Fé," New York Rev., Apr. 28, 1983, at 33 (emphasis in original).

39. Nussbaum, "Non-Relative Virtues," note 35, at 243 (emphasis added).

40. I concur in Martha Nussbaum's comment: "I grant that some criticisms of some forms of essentialism have been fruitful and important: they have established the ethical debate on a more defensible metaphysical foundation and have redirected our gaze from unexamined abstract assumptions to the world and its actual history. But I argue that those who would throw out all appeals to a determinate account of human being, human functioning, and human flourishing are throwing away far too much . . . ." Nussbaum, "Human Functioning and Social Justice," note 34, at 205. A comment by feminist legal theorist Robin West, though directed specifically to other feminist theorists, is relevant here: "What is of value in critical social theory for feminists? My suspicion is that what attracts many feminists to critical social theory is not its anti-essentialism, but more simply its skepticism: its refusal to accept any particular account of truth or morality as the essential true, moral or human viewpoint. This skepticism is entirely healthy and something we should treasure. The anti-essentialism of the critical theorist's vision, by contrast, is something we should reject. Surely we can have this both ways. A skepticism toward particular claims of objective truth, a particular

account of the self, and any particular account of gender, sexuality, biology or what is or is not natural, is absolutely necessary to a healthy and modern feminism. But that skepticism need not require an unwillingness to entertain descriptions of subjective and intersubjective authenticity . . . ." Robin West, "Feminism, Critical Social Theory, and the Law," 1989 U. Chicago Legal Forum 59, 96–97 (1989). For a more elaborate statement, see Robin West, "Relativism, Objectivity, and Law," 99 Yale L.J. 1473 (1990).

41. D.J. O'Connor, Aquinas and Natural Law 57 (1968).

42. See Michael J. Perry, Morality, Politics, and Law, ch. 1 (1988). If personal "autonomy" is a particular, and particularly important, constituent of human well-being, then protecting such autonomy is protecting (an important constituent of) human well-being and protecting human well-being in its entirety requires protecting personal autonomy autonomy. On the relation of human well-being and personal autonomy, see Joseph Raz, "Liberalism, Skepticism, and Democracy," 74 Iowa L. Rev. 761, 779–86 (1989).

43. One who holds the natural law position might also believe, and surely will believe: (1) that some things are good and some things are bad only for some human beings; and (2) that, nonetheless, whatever is good for a human being should be valued by that human being and whatever is bad for a human being should be disvalued by that human being. But the emphasis in the natural law tradition is on what is good/bad for every human being rather than on what is good/bad just for some human beings. (That something is good—sleep, for example—and should therefore be valued does not entail that one should value it more highly than something else with which, in the circumstances, it competes—for example, caring for one's sick child.)

Properly understood, the "should" ("should be valued", "should be disvalued") is hypothetical rather than categorical. See Perry, Morality, Politics, and Law, note 42, at 12–19.

44. See text accompanying notes 39 and 2.

45. See text accompanying note 1.

46. See Robin W. Lovin, "Perry, Naturalism, and Religion in Public," 63 Tulane L. Rev. 1517, 1532–33 (1989): "Perry speaks of 'human good' in nonrelativist terms, not because he thinks that there is universal agreement about what is good for persons, nor even because he believes that there is some single ideal of human flourishing that would satisfy everyone, but because he thinks that people who disagree about the human good understand that they are disagreeing about the same thing. They are not talking about, say, architecture and tennis, in which the terms are so different that we would wonder how two people arguing about the relative merits of a good lobby and a good volley got into the same conversation. An argument over the relative values of artistic and athletic achievement in a complete human life, by contrast, does make sense, even if we are not certain that there is one and only one best solution to the problem." Cf. Amélie Oksenberg Rorty, "Relativism, Persons, and Practices," in Krausz ed., note 34, at 418, 418–19 (emphasis added):

> [R]elativists are quite right to insist that even such dramatically basic activities as birth, copulation, and death, such basic processes as eating and sleeping, physical growth and physical decay, are intentionally described in ways that affect phenomenological experience. Events and processes are encompassed and bounded, artic-

ulated and differentiated, within the web of a culture's conceptual and linguistic categories; their meaning is formed by its primary practices and sacred books, songs and rituals. Even the conceptions of social practices and meaning are sufficiently culturally specific so that it is tendentious to refer to conceptions *of* culture practices [*sic*], as if *culture* or *practice* were Platonic forms, waiting to be conceptualized this way or that. Indeed the very practices of interpretation and evaluation are themselves culturally variable.

But nothing follows from this about the impossibility of crosscultural interpretation, communication, or evaluation, particularly among cultures engaged in practical interactions with one another. The core truth of relativism—the intentionality of practice and experience—does not entail that successful communication and justified evaluation require strict identity of meaning. *There are, furthermore, basic culturally invariant psychophysical and biosocial salience markers that set the boundaries of attention, however variously these foci may be identified, interpreted, or evaluated.*

47. Charles Taylor, Sources of the Self: The Making of the Modern Identity 61 (1989).

48. Id. at 61–62.

49. Jack Donnelly, "Post-Cold War Reflections on the Study of International Human Rights," 8 Ethics & International Affairs 97, 113 (1994). Where I have put the second ellipsis, Donnelly writes "and interdependence". Donnelly's reference to the "interdependence of internationally recognized human rights" is to the interdependence of "civil and political rights" on the one hand and "economic, social, and cultural rights" on the other. See id. at 111–13. With respect to the question of that interdependence, see note 62; see also note 32.

50. Alasdair MacIntyre, After Virtue 152 (1981).

51. Michael Moore, "Moral Reality," 1982 Wisconsin L. Rev. 1061, 1089–90 (1982).

52. Hampshire, Innocence and Experience, note 33, at 90.

53. Warren Christopher, "Democracy and Human Rights: Where America Stands," 4 U.S. Department of State Dispatch 441, 442 (1993).

54. It is a mistake, therefore, to think that such acts reflect a vision of human good, albeit a perverse vision. Rather, because everyone (not least, the perpetrators) understands that such acts—acts of calculated and gratuitous cruelty—are horrible for the victims, such acts constitute an existential, if not a reflective or self-conscious, denial that the victims are sacred. Some acts that violate one or another human right (or that are plausibly believed to do so)—some acts that do to a human being what ought not to be done to any human being, or that fail to do for a human being what ought to be done for every human being—can fairly be understood to reflect a (mistaken) vision of human good. (Female circumcision, which I discuss below, might be an example of such an act.) Moreover, some acts that violate one or another human right can fairly be understood to reflect, not the view that the victims of the act are not sacred, but only a (perhaps mistaken) judgment that the act, understood as a means, is justified by the end it serves. Some terrorist acts come to mind here—shootings and bombings—as do many acts of war. But it seems to me difficult to understand acts of calculated and gratuitous cruelty like those reported above as not reflecting, however

unself-consciously, the view that the victims of the act are somehow subhuman and therefore not sacred.

55. See Larson, note 34, at 60 n. 12: "Female genital surgeries include clitoridectomy (surgical removal of the clitoris), excision (surgical removal of the clitoris and labia) and infibulation (stitching up the vaginal opening after removal of the clitoris and labia). These practices are sometimes incorrectly called 'female circumcision,' but this analogy is seriously misleading. The consequences of female genital mutilation are not comparable to the far safer, less painful, non-mutilating (indeed, perhaps prophylactic) practice of removing the penile foreskin." See also "A Traditional Practice That Threatens Health—Female Circumcision," 40 World Health Organization Chronicle 31 (1986).

56. See generally Katherine Brennan, "The Influence of Cultural Relativism on International Human Rights Law: Female Circumcision as a Case Study," 7 L. & Inequality 367 (1989). "Female circumcision is practiced in over 20 African countries. . . . [It] is also found in Malaysia, Indonesia, the southern parts of the Arab peninsula, Pakistan, some sects in the Soviet Union, United Arab Emirates, Oman, Bahrain, and South Yemen. Although the operations are most prevalent in Africa and the Middle East, they are also done in Peru, Brazil, eastern Mexico, and among the aboriginal tribes of Australia." Id. at 373 n. 26. For recent stories about the practice in African countries, see Neil MacFarquhar, "Mutilation of Egyptian Girls: Despite Ban, It Goes On," New York Times, Aug. 18, 1996, at A8; Celia W. Dugger, "A Refugee's Body Is Intact but Her Family Is Torn," New York Times, Sept. 11, 1996, at A1; Celia W. Dugger, "African Ritual Pain: Genital Cutting," New York Times, Oct. 5, 1996, at A1; James C. McKinley, Jr., "At a Ceremony in Kenya, a Brother and Sister Painfully Enter Adulthood," New York Times, Oct. 5, 1966, at A5. See also Linda Burstyn, "Female Circumcision Comes to America," Atlantic, Oct. 1995, at 28.

57. For the data, see Christina M. Cerna, "Universality of Human Rights and Cultural Diversity: Implementation of Human Rights in Different Socio-Cultural Contexts," 16 Human Rights Q. 740, 746–48 (1994).

The language or vocabulary of rights, which I discussed in chapter 2, is mainly Western in origin, but like many other artifacts mainly or even solely Western in origin, "rights talk" has become an international currency.

58. Abdullahi Ahmed An-Na'im, "Human Rights in the Muslim World: Socio-Political Conditions and Scriptural Imperatives—A Preliminary Inquiry," 3 Harvard Human Rights L.J. 13, 15 (1990). But cf. Philip Alston, "The Universal Declaration at 35: Western and Passé or Alive and Universal," 31 International Commission of Jurists Rev. 60, 61 (1983) (explaining that although it "has some basis", the argument that Third World participation in the drafting of the declaration was negligible "is frequently overstated").

59. Cerna, note 57, at 747. However, to be a signatory to an international human rights convention is not necessarily to have signed on to everything decreed in the convention. A state might hedge its signing by including, in its signing, one or more "reservations" or "declarations". Indeed, in extreme cases, some signatories have so hedged their signing that they have signed on to very little. See id. at 748–49 (reporting troubling examples with respect to the Convention on the Rights of the Child).

60. But not without several controversial reservations and declarations. See gener-

ally "Symposium: The Ratification of the International Covenant on Civil and Political Rights," 42 DePaul L. Rev. 1167 (1993).

61. See Philip Alston, "U.S. Ratification of the Covenant on Economic, Social and Cultural Rights: The Need for an Entirely New Strategy," 84 American J. International L. 365 (1990).

62. See Antonio Cassese, Human Rights in a Changing World 63–67 (1990); Cerna, note 57.

I am not suggesting that there is unanimity. That there is widespread transcultural agreement does not entail that there is consensus. Widespread transcultural agreement about what human rights people have coexists with much disagreement about what human rights they have. But, typically, such disagreements are not intercultural: The dividing lines in such disagreements do not separate all the members of one or more cultures from all the members of one or more other cultures; instead, they separate some members of one or more cultures from some other members of the same culture or cultures. The Reagan administration's effort to paint the International Covenant on Civil and Political Rights as a "Western" document and the International Covenant on Economic, Social and Cultural Rights as a "non-Western", "socialist" document, though not surprising, was not at all persuasive. For an important discussion and development of the point, see Alston, "U.S. Ratification of the Covenant on Economic, Social and Cultural Rights," note 61, at 375–76, 386–88. "[T]he suggestion that the concept of economic and social rights is a 'Soviet-Third World' creation does a gross injustice to the Catholic and many other churches (at least since the late nineteenth century) and those many Western European states, not to mention Australia and New Zealand, which have consistently championed economic and social rights, at least since the creation of the United Nations in 1945 and, in most cases, since the establishment of the International Labour Organisation in 1919." Id. at 388. It is often the case, as the Reagan administration's effort to discredit the ICESCR illustrates, that "norms in societies are presumed to be ascertainable and cohesive; the multiply-constituted nature and competing understandings of any given culture are rarely discussed, and the tensions and contradictions within a society go unmentioned." Annie Bunting, "Theorizing Women's Cultural Diversity in Feminist International Human Rights Strategies," 20 J.L. & Society 6, 9–10 (1993). In particular, "the notion of 'Western' is rarely problematized by critics; while culture is seen as differentiated along the Western/non-Western lines, Western culture itself is not seen as heterogenous. Norms of morality within the West may be as diverse as norms found in non-Western contexts." Id. at 9. Not surprisingly, national leaders elsewhere have done in their political contexts what President Reagan did in his, namely, assert that some universally proclaimed human rights were more provincial than universal. Indeed, one prominent national leader, Chinese premier Li Peng, has mirror-imaged President Reagan: Whereas Reagan focused on "economic, social and cultural rights" of the sort protected by the ICESCR, Li Peng has focused on "political and civil rights" of the sort protected by the ICCPR. See Tom J. Farer & Felice Gaer, "The UN and Human Rights: At the End of the Beginning," in United Nations, Divided World 240, 294 & n. 114 (Adam Roberts & Benedict Kingsbury eds., 2d ed. 1993) (referring, in the text, to "the not infrequent claims of certain political leaders that many of the civil and political rights enumerated in the Universal Declaration [of Human Rights] and other sacred texts, rather than reflecting universally relevant demands and interests, are provincial products of the West's singular historical experience and the liberal ideology stemming therefrom" and citing, in the footnote, "the statement of Chinese Premier Li Peng to the first-ever heads-of-state meeting of the Security Council on 31 Jan. 1992. UN Doc. S/PV.3046, pp. 92–93."). See also Pieter van Dijk, "A Common Standard of Achievement: About Universal Validity and Uniform Interpretation of International Human Rights Norms," 13 Netherlands Q. Human Rights 105, 105, 118–19 (1995) (quoting Speech of Liu Huaqiu, head of Chinese delegation, Vienna, June 15, 1993).

63. For a useful collection of relevant articles, see Abdullahi Ahmed An-Na'im, ed., Human Rights in Cross-Cultural Perspectives: A Quest for Consensus (1992).

64. See, e.g., Brennan, note 56; Anna Funder, "*De Minimis Non Curat Lex*: The Clitoris, Culture and the Law," 3 Transnational L. & Contemporary Problems 417 (1993); Note, "What's Culture Got to Do with It?: Excising the Harmful Tradition of Female Circumcision," 106 Harvard L. Rev. 1944 (1993). See also the helpful compilation of materials in Henry J. Steiner & Philip Alston, eds., International Human Rights in Context: Law, Politics, Morality 240–54 (1996).

65. The literature on the human rights of women is large and growing. See, e.g., Charlotte Bunch, "Women's Rights as Human Rights: Toward a Re-Vision of Human Rights," 12 Human Rights Q. 486 (1990); Bunting, note 62; Noreen Burrows, "International Law and Human Rights: The Case of Women's Rights," in Human Rights: From Rhetoric to Reality 80 (Tom Campbell et al. eds., 1986); Hilary Charlesworth et al., "Feminist Approaches to International Law," 85 American J. International L. 613 (1991); Rebecca J. Cook, ed., Human Rights of Women: National and International Perspectives 3 (1994); Rebecca J. Cook, "State Responsibility for Violations of Women's Human Rights," 7 Harvard Human Rights L.J. 125 (1994); Ustinia Dolgopol, "Women's Voices, Women's Pain," 17 Human Rights Q. 127 (1995); Karen Engle, "International Human Rights and Feminism: When Discourses Meet," Michigan J. International L. 517 (1992); Karen Engle, "Female Subjects of Public International Law: Human Rights and the Exotic Other Female," 26 New England L. Rev. 1509 (1992); Hastings Law School Symposium, "Rape as a Weapon of War in the Former Yugoslavia," 5 Hastings Women's L.J. 69 (1994); Joanna Kerr, ed., Ours by Right: Women's Rights as Human Rights (1993); Nancy Kim, "Toward a Feminist Theory of Human Rights: Straddling the Fence Between Western Imperialism and Uncritical Absolutism," 25 Columbia Human Rights L. Rev. 49 (1993); Catharine A. MacKinnon, "Crimes of War, Crimes of Peace," in Shute & Hurley, eds., note 8, at 83; Catharine A. MacKinnon, "Rape, Genocide, and Women's Human Rights," 17 Harvard Women's L.J. 5 (1994); Johannes Morsink, "Women's Rights in the Universal Declaration," 13 Human Rights Q. 229 (1991); "No Justice, No Peace: Accountability for Rape and Gender-Based Violence in the Former Yugoslavia," 5 Hastings Women's L.J. 89 (1994); Julie Peters & Andrea Wolper, eds., Women's Rights, Human Rights: International Feminist Perspectives (1995); Steiner & Alston, eds., note 64, at 887–967; Fernando R. Tesón, "Feminism and International Law: A Reply," 33 Virginia J. International L. 647 (1993); Sarah C. Zearfoss, "The Convention for the Elimination of All Forms of Discrimination Against Women: Radical, Reasonable, or Reactionary," 12 Michigan J. International L. 903 (1991). See also note 64.

66. Celia W. Dugger, "New Law Bans Genital Cutting in United States," New York Times, Oct. 12, 1996, at A1.

67. See Larson, note 34, at 60 n. 12: "[T]he practice [of female genital mutilation] is designed to aid male sexual control over females and is designed to destroy female sexual pleasure, and thus represents a direct attack on female sexuality and a reflection of women's subordinate position." (Larson adds: "There is no credible argument that the practice of male circumcision in either non-Western or Western societies is a parallel mark either of hostility to male sexuality or of men's social inferiority." Id.)

68. On the Convention for the Elimination of All Forms of Discrimination against Women, see Zearfoss, note 65.

69. See Brennan, note 64, at 374. See also Maynard H. Merwine, "How Africa Understands Female Circumcision," New York Times, Nov. 24, 1993, at A24 (letter to the editor); Celia W. Dugger, "African Ritual Pain: Genital Cutting," New York Times, Oct. 5, 1996, at A1.

70. See chapter 1, text accompanying note 129.

71. See Michael J. Perry, Love and Power: The Role of Religion and Morality in American Politics, ch. 4 (1991).

72. Charles Taylor, "The Politics of Recognition," in Multiculturalism and "The Politics of Recognition," 25, 72 (Amy Gutmann ed., 1992). See id. at 66–73.

73. Id. at 72–73.

74. Id. at 73.

75. See Brennan, note 64, at 392.

76. Donnelly, note 49, at 115.

77. Philip E. Devine, "Relativism," 67 Monist 405, 412 (1984).

78. Richard Rorty, "Science as Solidarity," in Rhetoric of the Human Sciences: Language and Argument in Scholarship and Human Affairs 38, 43 (John S. Nelson, Allan Megill, & Donald N. McCloskey eds., 1987). Cf. Lynne Rudder Baker, "On the Very Idea of a Form of Life," 27 Inquiry 277, 279 (1984):

> [W]hen we think of forms of life as conventional, . . . "we are thinking of convention not as the arrangements a particular culture has found convenient, in terms of its history and geography, for effecting the necessities of human existence, but as those forms of life which are normal to any group of creatures we call human, any group about which we will say, for example, that they have a past to which they respond, or a geographical environment which they manipulate or exploit in certain ways for certain humanly comprehensible motives. Here the array of 'conventions' are not patterns of life which differentiate human beings from one another, but those exigencies of conduct and feeling which all humans share." This passage makes it clear that—the amorphousness of life notwithstanding—most fundamentally, the human species is the locus of forms of life. For specific purposes, "form of life" is sometimes applied to practices that are not universal, as when writers take religion (or a particular religion) to be a form of life, or when writers speak of different societies as exhibiting different forms of life. Although I think that these narrower uses of "form of life" illustrate the elasticity of the idea, and suggest that forms of life, though not clearly demarcated, are thoroughly interwoven and even

"nested", they do not tell against the point that Wittgenstein's first concern is with human practices, not with local options.

(Quoting Stanley Cavell, The Claim of Reason: Wittgenstein, Skepticism, Morality and Tragedy 111 (1979).) See also W.W. Sharrock & R.J. Anderson, "Criticizing Forms of Life," 60 Philosophy 394, 395, 398 (1985):

> Whether there are insuperable obstacles to mutual understanding (and, therefore, to external criticism) is not, then, something to be determined *a priori*, for the simple reason that the answer will depend on the nature of the differences and disagreements involved. . . .
>
> There is no basis in Wittgenstein's numerous comments on the nature of human beings and their lives for supposing that understanding between them must be either impossible or inevitable. He seems to try to maintain a perspicuous view of the balance of homogeneity and heterogeneity among human beings. He tries not to lose sight of the fact that human beings are, after all, human beings, members of the same species with their animal constitution (which has ramifying consequences for the lives they do lead) in common. At the same time he emphasizes how much the practices which they create may diverge from one another. Human lives develop in very different directions from the common "starting points" provided by their species inheritance. It is the fact that human beings are the kinds of creatures that they are which lets them take to training, to learn language and other practices. The fact that a human being might, with equal ease, have been inducted into either of two ways of life does not, however, mean that having been drawn into the one he can now adopt the other with the same facility as if he had been brought up to it—learning a second language is not the same as learning a first and, of course, a language like ours makes Chinese harder to learn than French. Two ways of life might, then, be organized in such ways that the grasp of one is inimical to the understanding of the other.

79. Williams, Ethics and the Limits of Philosophy, note 30, at 158. See also Rorty, "Solidarity or Objectivity?," note 37, at 8–9: "It is a consequence of this holistic view of knowledge . . . that alternative cultures are not to be thought of on the model of alternative geometries. Alternative geometries are irreconcilable because they have axiomatic structures, and contradictory axioms. They are *designed* to be irreconcilable. Cultures are not so designed, and do not have axiomatic structures."

80. Williams, Ethics and the Limits of Philosophy, note 30, at 158. For an extended argument in support of this claim, see Chandran Kukathas, "Explaining Moral Variety," 11 Social Philosophy & Policy 1 (1994).

81. Amélie Oksenberg Rorty, note 46, at 418. See also Richard Rorty, "Solidarity or Objectivity?," note 37, at 9: "[T]he distinction between different cultures does not differ in kind from the distinction between theories held by members of a single culture. The Tasmanian aborigines and the British colonists had trouble communicating, but this trouble was different only in extent from the difficulties in communication experienced by Gladstone and Disraeli."

82. See note 62.

83. Kim, note 65, at 88–90. See also Amy Gutmann, "The Challenge of Multi-

culturalism in Political Ethics," 22 Philosophy & Public Affairs 171, 172–78 (1993); Thandabantu Nhlapa, "Cultural Diversity, Human Rights and the Family in Contemporary Africa: Lessons from the South African Constitutional Debate," 9 International J.L. & Family 208, 213 (1995).

84. See text accompanying note 79.

85. Lee Yearley, "The Author Replies," 21 J. Religious Ethics 385, 392 (1993).

86. Association of African Women for Research and Development, "A Statement on Genital Mutilation," in Third World—Second Sex: Women's Struggles and National Liberation 217 (Miranda Davies ed., 1983). Cf. Dugger, note 66, at A6 (reporting that in 1996 World Bank provided grants to the Inter-African Committee on Traditional Practices Affecting the Health of Women and Children, based in Addis Ababa).

87. See Brennan, note 64.

88. See text accompanying note 9B.

89. An-Na'im, "Human Rights in the Muslim World," note 58, at 15. See also these writings by An-Na'im: "Religious Minorities Under Islamic Law and the Limits of Cultural Relativism," 9 Human Rights Q. 1 (1987); Toward an Islamic Reformation: Civil Liberties, Human Rights and International Law (1990); "Civil Rights in the Islamic Tradition: Shared Ideals and Divergent Regimes," 25 John Marshall L. Rev. 267 (1992); "Cultural Transformation and Normative Consensus on the Best Interests of the Child," 8 International J.L. & Family 62 (1994).

90. An-Na'im, "Human Rights in the Muslim World," note 58, at 15. "An-Na'im . . . consider[s] that efforts to promote respect for international human rights standards are often likely to remain superficial and ineffective until such time as they relate directly to, and where possible are promoted through, local cultural, religious and other traditional communities." Philip Alston, "The Best Interests Principle: Towards a Reconciliation of Culture and Human Rights," 8 International J.L. & Family 1, 8 (1994).

91. The quote is from the editorial introduction accompanying the reprinting of the declaration in *Concilium*, vol. 3, at 140–50 (1994). For three recent articles on Islam and human rights, see Abdullahi A. An-Na'im, "Islamic Law and Human Rights Today," 10 Interights Bulletin 3 (1996); Mona Rishmawi, "The Arab Charter on Human Rights: A Comment," 10 Interights Bulletin 8 (1996); Hatem Aly Labib Gabr, "Shari'a as Principal Source of Legislation: Rulings of Egypt's Supreme Constitutional Court," 10 Interights Bulletin 43 (1996).

92. Kukathas, note, at 10.

93. Id. See also Bruce B. Lawrence, "Woman as Subject/Woman as Symbol," 22 J. Religious Ethics 163, 180–83 (1994).

94. See, e.g., Leila Ahmed, Women and Gender in Islam (1992); Kari Elisabeth Borresen and Kari Vogt, Women's Studies of the Christian and Islamic Traditions: Ancient, Medieval and Renaissance Foremothers (1993); Fatima Mernissi, The Veil and the Male Elite (1991). I am grateful to my colleague Jane Larson for bringing these works to my attention. See also Seth Mydans, "Blame Men, Not Allah, Islamic Feminists Say," New York Times, Oct. 10, 1996, at A4.

95. Riffat Hassan, "Women in Islam and Christianity: A Comparison," 3 Concilium 18, 22 (1994).

96. Peter Waldman, "Leap of Faith: Some Muslim Thinkers Want to Reinterpret Islam for Modern Times," Wall Street J., Mar. 15, 1995, at A1. For an indication of some

of the arguments Islamic reformers, including Islamic feminists, make from within the Islamic tradition, see Carla Makhlouf Obermeyer, "A Cross-Cultural Perspective on Reproductive Rights," 17 Human Rights Q. 366, 376–80 (1995).

97. Foot, note 34, at 164. (For Foot's perceptive explanation why "relativists, and subjectivists generally," are not able to take the whole journey, see id. at 165–66.) See also Ronald Beiner, Political Judgment 186 n. 17 (1983):

> The question here is not whether there is some ascertainable moral-political framework that will guarantee a resolution in all cases; but rather, whether there is, in principle, any limit to the possibility of overcoming incommensurability. . . . [T]here is no such limit: at no point are we justified in terminating an unresolved argument, for it always remains open to us to persevere with it still further. The next stage of argument may yet bring an enlargement of moral vision to one of the contending parties, allowing this contender to integrate the perspective of the other into his own in a relation of part to whole. . . . Therefore at any point there remains the possibility, though not the guarantee, of resolving deep conflict. . . . Confronted with apparent stalemate, there is no need to give in to moral or intellectual "pluralism", for it always remains open to us to say "Press on with the argument".

98. Christopher, note 53, at 442.

99. For a discussion of some of the different meanings of the term, see Alison Dundes Renteln, International Human Rights: Universalism v. Relativism 61–87 (1990). See also Douglas Lee Donoho, "Relativism Versus Universalism in Human Rights: The Search for Meaningful Standards," 27 Stanford J. International L. 345 (1991).

100. See text accompanying note 72.

One or more of the three positions I am about to criticize might be embedded in an antiimperialist or anticolonialist sensibility. Nothing I am about to say is meant to disparage such a sensibility, which might, after all, reflect an embrace of the conviction that every human being—and not just the privileged citizens of the imperial or colonial powers—is sacred.

101. Richard Rorty, "Postmodernist Bourgeois Liberalism," 80 J. Philosophy 583, 589 (1983).

102. See note 47.

103. See generally Geoffrey Harrison, "Relativism and Tolerance," in Meiland & Krausz eds., note 34, at 229. See also Joseph Raz, The Authority of Law 271 (1979); Samuel Scheffler, "Moral Scepticism and Ideals of the Person," 62 Monist 288, 300–01 (1979); Simon Blackburn, "Rule-Following and Moral Realism," in Wittgenstein: To Follow a Rule 163, 176 (Stephen H. Holtzman & Christopher M. Leich eds., 1981). But cf. Gilbert Harman, "Human Flourishing, Ethics, and Liberty," 12 Philosophy & Public Affairs 307, 321 (1983): "[We can] condemn other people as evil, bad, or dangerous by our lights, or take them to be our enemies. Nothing prevents us from using our values to judge other people and other moralities. But we only fool ourselves if we think our values give *reasons* to others who do not accept those values."

104. See note 83 and accompanying text.

105. See notes 92–93 and accompanying text.

106. See Devine, note 77, at 405, 406:

[R]elativism is not individualistic subjectivism, for which anything goes intellectually; nor is it collective subjectivism, which would settle intellectual questions by voting. The analogy with law makes this point clear: while law is relative to a particular society, law and public opinion are not the same thing. Not anything goes by way of legal argument—the precedents and statutes have to be taken into account. But one can say, so long as one does not do so too often, that the decision of the courts, even those of the last resort, are legally and not just morally or politically wrong. Likewise a moral relativist who finds his basic standards in the ethos of a given society can disagree with the majority of that society (though perhaps not the overwhelming majority) on some moral issue, so long as he is prepared to defend his disagreement on grounds whose relevance the majority is prepared to accept. In brief, while the standards we employ are (according to the relativist) grounded in the fact of their acceptance by a group to which we belong, the application of these standards is objective and not a matter of what people think.

Cf. Meiland & Krausz eds., note 34, at 4: "[J]ust as our ordinary conception of truth allows a person to hold beliefs which are false, so too the notion of relative truth must allow an individual to hold beliefs which are false *for him* or *her*. If it were not possible for an individual to hold beliefs which were false for him or her, then the notion of relative truth would be superfluous; for then to say that a belief is true for Jones would only be a roundabout way of saying that it was one of Jones' beliefs. And we do not need a new way of saying *that*."

107. Joseph de Maistre, quoted in Edmund Leach, Social Anthropology 56 (1982).

108. On the "coherentist" or "holist" nature of justification, see Perry, Love and Power, note 71, ch. 4.

109. See Alston, "The Best Interests Principle," note 90, at 18: "If human rights norms in general can be said to be inherently indeterminate, the best interests principle is located by most of its critics at the most indeterminate outer margins even of that body of norms." For discussions of the Convention on the Rights of the Child, see, in addition to Alston's essay, Cynthia Price Cohen, "United National Convention on the Rights of the Child: Introductory Note," 44 International Commission of Jurists Rev. 36, 38 (1990); Dominic McGoldrick, "The United Nations Convention on the Rights of the Child," 5 International J.L. & Family 132 (1991); Lawrence J. LeBlanc, The Convention on the Rights of the Child: United Nations Lawmaking on Human Rights (1995).

110. Basic Law: Human Dignity and Freedom, enacted by the Knesset on 12th Adar B 5752 (Mar. 17, 1992). The bill and explanatory comments were published in *Hatza'ot Hok* 2086, of 6th Kislev 5752 (Nov. 13, 1991), p. 60.

111. There can be little doubt about the practical necessity of establishing normatively indeterminate—or, more precisely, underdeterminate—norms both in domestic, especially constitutional, law and, above all, in the international law of human rights. For a helpful presentation of the point in the context of the international law of human rights, see Alston, "The Best Interests Principle," note 90. For a presentation in the context of domestic (American) constitutional law, see Michael J. Perry, The Constitution in the Courts: Law or Politics? 76–78 (1994).

112. Cf. Benjamin N. Cardozo, The Nature of the Judicial Process 67 (1921):

"[W]hen [judges] are called upon to say how far existing rules are to be extended or restricted, they must let the welfare of society fix the path, its direction and its distance." Hans-Georg Gadamer observed, in *Truth and Method*:

> In both legal and theological hermeneutics there is the essential tension between the text set down—of the law or of the proclamation—on the one hand and, on the other, the sense arrived at by its application in the particular moment of interpretation, either in judgment or in preaching. A law is not there to be understood historically, but to be made concretely valid through being interpreted. Similarly, a religious proclamation is not there to be understood as a merely historical document, but to be taken in a way in which it exercises its saving effect. This includes the fact that the text, whether law or gospel, if it is to be understood properly, i.e., according to the claim it makes, must be understood at every moment, in every particular situation, in a new and different way. Understanding here is always application.

Hans-Georg Gadamer, Truth and Method 275 (1975). In *The Federalist* No. 37, James Madison wrote: "All new laws, though penned with the greatest technical skill and passed on the fullest and most mature deliberation, are considered as more or less obscure and equivocal, until their meaning be liquidated and ascertained by a series of particular discussions and adjudications." The Federalist Papers 229 (Clinton Rossiter ed., 1961). See also Kim Lane Scheppele, Legal Secrets 94–95 (1988): "Generally in the literature on interpretation the question being posed is, What does a particular text (or social practice) *mean*? Posed this way, the interpretive question gives rise to an embarassing multitude of possible answers, a cacophony of theories of interpretation. . . . [The] question that (in practice) is the one actually asked in the course of lawyering and judging [is]: what . . . does a particular text mean *for the specific case at hand?*"

113. Neil MacCormick, "Reconstruction after Deconstruction: A Response to CLS," 10 Oxford J. Legal Studies 539, 548 (1990). Where I have used the term "specification", MacCormick uses the Latin term *determinatio*, borrowing it from John Finnis. "John Finnis has to good effect re-deployed St Thomas' concept of *determinatio*; Hans Kelsen's translators used the term 'concretization' to much the same effect." Id. (citing J.M. Finnis, "On the Critical Legal Studies Movement," 30 American J. Jurisprudence 21, 23–25 (1985), and Hans Kelsen, The Pure Theory of Law 230 (1967)).

114. Anthony T. Kronman, "Living in the Law," 54 U. Chicago L. Rev. 835, 847–48 (1987).

115. See Perry, The Constitution in the Courts, note 111, chs. 5–6.

116. Alston, "The Best Interests Principle," note 90, at 9 & 23.

117. Id. at 5.

118. Id. at 22. "Nor is the reference to these predominantly Third World-focused case studies intended to suggest that the situation in the industrialized countries is radically different. Even within the common law tradition, American and English law have been shown to function very differently, in large part because of the different legal, political and institutional cultures in which the law operates." Id. at 22–23.

119. Id. at 19. "In cultural terms, . . . the Convention [on the Rights of the Child], while by no means perfect, is probably more sensitive to different approaches and perspectives than most of the principal human rights treaties adopted earlier." Id. at 7. (The convention was adopted in 1990.)

120. Donnelly, note 49, at 113.

121. John Paul II, note 2, at 314 (emphasis added). See Alston, "The Best Interests Principle," note 90, at 20:

> Perhaps the best way to understand the role that culture can and does play in this regard is by analogy to the concept of the margin of appreciation within the jurisprudence developed under the European Convention on Human Rights. The analogy also serves to emphasize that the cultural dimension is a universal one and not only something which comes unto play when we are considering non-Western cultural factors. The margin of appreciation concept is nowhere to be found in the text of the European Convention. Rather, it is a doctrine which has been developed by the European Commission and Court of Human Rights to enable an appropriate degree of discretion to be accorded to national authorities in their application of the provisions of the Convention. Cultural considerations have figured very prominently in the factors for which the European supervisory organs have been prepared to make some allowance. Moreover, many of the cases in which the doctrine has been most clearly applied and explored have concerned the notion of permissible restrictions upon rights, the organs have also made considerable use of the doctrine in determining the actual scope of many of the rights.

On the "margin of appreciation" doctrine in the European Convention system, see Steiner & Alston eds., note 64, at 615–17 & 626–36.

122. Christopher, note 53, at 442 (passages rearranged).

123. Alston, "The Best Interests Principle," note 90, at 20.

124. Philip Alston, "The UN's Human Rights Record: From San Francisco to Vienna and Beyond," 16 Human Rights Q. 375, 384 (1994). See also Anne F. Bayefsky, "Cultural Sovereignty, Relativism, and International Human Rights: New Excuses for Old Strategies," 9 Ratio Juris 42 (1996). Cf. Michael Posner, "Rally Round Human Rights," 97 Foreign Policy 133, 137–38 (1994–95):

> Many of the Asian governments, like those of China and Singapore, that are most critical of U.S. human rights policy and seek to characterize it as Western-based and culturally biased are among the declining number of regimes that absolutely prevent any independent human rights groups from operating. Their claims of cultural relativism can only be sustained if they continue to prevent their own people from raising human rights issues. But they are fighting a losing battle. Recent experience in countries as diverse as Chile, Kuwait, Nigeria, South Africa, and Sri Lanka leave no doubt that where people are allowed to organize and advocate their own human rights, they will do so. The common denominators in this area are much stronger than the cultural divisions.

For a recent example of the Chinese government's effort to deflect the West's emphasis on human rights, see the Speech of Liu Huaqui, head of the Chinese delegation, Vienna, June 15, 1993, quoted in Dijk, note 62. See also "Human Rights in China," a statement issued in 1991 by the Information Office of the State Council of the Peoples' Republic of China, excerpted in Steiner & Alston eds., note 64, at 233–34. For a kindred statement on behalf of the countries of East and Southeast Asia, including Singapore, see Bilhari Kausikan, "Asia's Differing Standard," 92 Foreign Policy 24 (1993). For a skeptical look at the claim "that there is a distinct Asian approach to human rights", see Yash Ghai, "Human Rights and Governance: The Asia Debate," 15 Australian Yearbook International L. 1 (1994).

125. Alston, "The Best Interests Principle," note 90, at 20.

CHAPTER 4

1. Charles Fried, Right and Wrong 10 (1977).

2. John Finnis, Moral Absolutes: Tradition, Revision, and Truth 12, 20 (1991).

3. See, e.g., the European Social Charter (1991), reprinted in Basic Documents on Human Rights 363 (Ian Brownlie ed., 1992); Additional Protocol to the American Convention on Human Rights in the Area of Economic, Social and Cultural Rights (1988), reprinted in id., 521.

4. This is not to deny that the imperatives set forth in the ICESCR are meaningful standards against which the behavior of states can, to some extent, be evaluated.

5. See note 7.

6. Not even under the Constitution of the United States is the right to freedom of religious practice, or the right to freedom of expression, unconditional—or determinate in every context in which the right is implicated.

7. That such provisions are indeterminate—for example, that informed persons can reasonably disagree about whether a measure is "necessary" to protect the public morals, or even about what "the public morals" require—is undeniable. In a famous case involving a claim that the United Kingdom had violated Article 10 of the European Convention, the European Court of Human Rights stated:

> 48. These observations apply, notably, to Article 10 :88 2. In particular, it is not possible to find in the domestic law of the various Contracting States a uniform European conception of morals. The view taken by their respective laws of the requirements of morals varies from time to time and from place to place, especially in our era which is characterised by rapid and far-reaching evolution of opinions on the subject. By reason of their direct and continuous contact with the vital forces of their countries, State authorities are in principle in a better position than the international judge to give an opinion on the exact content of these requirements as well as on the "necessity" of a "restriction" or "penalty" intended to meet them. . . . [I]t is for the national authorities to make the initial assessment of the reality of the pressing social need implied by the notion of "necessity" in this context.
>
> Consequently, Article 10 :88 2 leaves to the Contracting States a margin of appreciation. This margin is given both to the domestic legislator ("prescribed by law") and to the bodies, judicial amongst others, that are called upon to interpret and apply the laws in force.

Handyside Case, European Court of Human Rights, 1976, Ser. A, No. 24, 1 EHRR 737. On the "margin of appreciation" doctrine in the European Convention system, see Henry J. Steiner & Philip Alston, eds., International Human Rights in Context: Law, Politics, Morals 615–17 & 626–36 (1996).

8. H.L.A. Hart, The Concept of Law 128 (2d ed. 1994).

9. Id.

10. They can. One way to do so, writes Hart, "is to freeze the meaning of the rule so that its general terms must have the same meaning in every case where its application is in question. To secure this we may fasten on certain features present in the plain case and insist that these are both necessary and sufficient to bring anything which has them within the scope of the rule, whatever other features it may have or lack, and whatever may be the social consequences of applying the rule in this way." Id. at 129.

11. Id. at 129–30.

12. See chapter 3, notes 109–23 and accompanying text. See Hart, note 8, at 129:

When we are bold enough to frame some general rule of conduct (e.g. a rule that no vehicle may be taken into the park), the language used in this context fixes necessary conditions which anything must satisfy if it is to be within its scope, and certain clear examples of what is certainly within its scope may be present to our minds. They are the paradigm, clear cases (the motor-car, the bus, the motor-cycle); and our aim in legislating is so far determinate because we have made a certain choice. We have initially settled the question that peace and quiet in the park is to be maintained at the cost, at any rate, of the exclusion of these things. On the other hand, until we have put the general aim of peace in the park into conjunction with those cases which we did not, or perhaps could not, initially envisage (perhaps a toy motor-car electrically propelled) our aim is, in this direction, indeterminate. We have not settled, because we have not anticipated, the question which will be raised by the unenvisaged case when it occurs: whether some degree of peace in the park is to be sacrificed to, or defended against, those children whose pleasure or interest it is to use these things. When the unenvisaged case does arise, we confront the issues at stake and can then settle the question by choosing between the competing interests in the way which best satisfies us. In doing so we shall have rendered more determinate our initial aim, and shall incidentally have settled a question as to the meaning, for the purpose of this rule, of a general word.

13. Id. at 130–31. See id. at 130 et seq.

14. But, Article 6(2) states: "In countries which have not abolished the death penalty, sentence of death may be imposed only for the most serious crimes in accordance with the law in force at the time of the commission of the crime and not contrary to the provisions of the present Covenant and to the Convention on the Prevention and Punishment of Genocide. This penalty can only be carried out pursuant to a final judgment rendered by a competent court."

15. See Articles 2, 3, & 4. Consider, too, Article 5 the Statute of the International Tribunal for the Prosecution of Persons Responsible for Serious Violations of International Humanitarian Law Committed in the Territory of the Former Yugoslavia, which states: "The International Tribunal shall have the power to prosecute persons responsible for the following crimes when committed in armed conflict, whether international or internal in character, and directed against any civilian population: (a) murder; (b) extermination; (c) enslavement; (d) deportation; (e) imprisonment; (f) torture; (g) rape; (h) persecutions on political, racial, or religious grounds; (i) other inhumane acts."

16. Serge Schmemann, "Israel Allows Use of Physical Force in Arab's Interrogation," New York Times, Nov. 16, 1996, at A7.

On the controversy, both in and out of Israel, about the Israeli secret police's use of force in the interrogation of prisoners, see Serge Schmemann, "In Israel, Coercing Prisoners Is Becoming Law of the Land," New York Times, May 8, 1997, at A1. For a defense of Israel's policy, by the father of a girl killed in the terrorist bombing of a bus in Israel, see Stephen Flatow, "Israel's Fine Line," New York Times, May 19, 1997, at A13. For a critique of the policy, see Gordon Marino, "Justifying Torture: Why the Israelis Are Wrong," Commonweal, June 6, 1997, at 9.

17. Michael Tanner, Nietzsche 29 (1994).

18. Choosing to kill P should not be confused with choosing to do something else that has as one of its foreseeable but unintended consequences that P or some other innocent person (or persons) dies. The philosophical literature defending the "killing vs. letting die" distinction (and/or the related "doctrine of double effect"), criticizing it, or simply commenting on it, is voluminous. For a recent piece, see Tracy L. Isaacs, "Moral Theory and Action Theory, Killing and Letting Die," 32 American Philosophical Q. 355 (1995).

19. Fried, note 1, at 10.

20. See chapter 1, notes 28–60 and accompanying text. Even one who does not accept that all human beings are sisters/brothers to one another should be able to understand the basic idea: that the life of one human being (e.g., my child) can be, not just for her but for me too (her parent), an intrinsic value.

21. John Finnis, Natural Law and Natural Rights 118–19 (1980).

22. For a persuasive critique of the approach on which Finnis relies—the of-itself-does-nothing-but approach of Finnis's mentor, Germain Grisez—see Jean Porter, "'Direct' and 'Indirect' in Grisez's Moral Theory," 57 Theological Studies 611, 627–31 (1996).

23. Id. at 122–23.

24. See id. at 85–90.

25. Id. at 119, 121.

26. 3 Oxford English Dictionary 549 (2d ed. 1989). See also Oxford American Dictionary 125 (1st ed. 1980) ("able to be measured by the same standard").

27. Finnis, Natural Law and Natural Rights, note 21, at 111–12.

28. John Finnis, Fundamentals of Ethics 90 (1983). See also Robert P. George, "Does the 'Incommensurability Thesis' Imperil Common Sense Moral Judgments?," 37 American J. Jurisprudence 185, 189 (1992). Cf. Cass R. Sunstein, "Incommensurability and Valuation in Law," 92 Michigan L. Rev. 779, 857 (1994):

> Suppose that a society is deciding whether to sacrifice a number of jobs in return for protecting an endangered species. . . . [P]erhaps the people entrusted with the power of decision will ask, as part of the inquiry, about the society's prevailing ideals, about ways minimally to damage relevant goods, and about what decision fits best with the community's self-understanding as this has been established over time. This is not merely a descriptive inquiry. It asks what choice puts that self-understanding in its best or most attractive light. On this view, choice among incommensurables is an act of interpretation, one that involves a dimension of fidelity to the past, but that is also constructive. In law and politics, a diverse set of standards—liberty, equality, property, excellence, all of these umbrella terms—will be brought to bear on hard cases.

29. Finnis, Fundamentals of Ethics, note 28, at 90–91, 92.

30. Id. at 91.

31. See Finnis, Natural Law and Natural Rights, note 21, at 111–12.

32. Cf. J.L. Mackie, Ethics: Inventing Right and Wrong 243 (1977): "D.D. Raphael, in 'The Standard of Morals', in Proceedings of the Aristotelian Society 75 (1974–75) follows Edward Ullendorff in pointing out that whereas 'Thou shalt love thy neighbor as thyself' represents the Greek of the Septuagint (Leviticus 19:18) and of the New Testament, the Hebrew from which the former is derived means rather 'You shall treat your neighbor lovingly, for he is like yourself.'"

33. That every basic human value should be regarded as of equal importance to every other such value, none more important than another, is not inconsistent with the assumption that no basic human value should be regarded as more important than a human life.

34. See, e.g., Robert P. George, "Proportionalism and the Catholic Moral Tradition," U. Detroit Mercy L. Rev. 1, 10 (1992). For an important discussion and thoughtful, careful defense of proportionalism, see Garth L. Hallett, Greater Good: The Case for Proportionalism (1995).

35. A fundamental point that Robert George's discussion (see note 34) overlooks.

36. For a discussion of the point, in the context of a critique of Germain Grisez's absolutist position, see Hallett, note 34, at 98–99. See also id. at 95–97.

37. See H. David Baer, "Proportionalism Defended," First Things, May 1994, at 3–4. (This illuminating short piece is a letter to the editor, and Baer is identified as a graduate student in the Department of Theology at the University of Notre Dame.) See also Hallett, note 34.

38. Cf. Richard A. McCormick, S.J., "*Veritatis Splendor* and Moral Theology," America, Oct. 30, 1993, 8, 10: "Let me return, then, to John Paul II's language. He cites as an objection to proportionalist tendencies the notion that some acts are intrinsically evil from their object. I believe all proportionalists would admit this *if the object is broadly understood as including all the morally relevant circumstances.*"

39. I owe the term "deserved reverence" to R. George Wright.

40. Eric Rakowski, "Taking and Saving Lives," 93 Columbia L. Rev. 1063, 1065 (1993).

41. Id. at 1156.

42. Imagine, for example, that S3 takes place in the context of a society almost all of whose citizens accept, on religious grounds, that choosing an act that foreseebly does nothing of itself but destroy a human life is always—unconditionally—a violation of the law of God and never, therefore, to be countenanced. In such a society, would choosing to kill P to save millions *necessarily* deny the sacredness of P? Cf. Hallett, note 34, at 117 (commenting on a hypothetical, which Hallett calls "TRANSPLANT", discussed by Judith Thomson):

> The young man in TRANSPLANT [who, though healthy, is being asked to sacrifice his vital body parts so that five others may live] says, "I deeply sympathize, but no." Suppose he went on to explain: "I wish I could help, I really do. I would willingly give my life for those five fine people—for Mr. Rawlins, the outstanding civic leader; for widow Delaney, with all her kids; for young Jimmy, so

full of promise; for Sue, the only child of doting parents; for Bishop Giesling, a blessing to his flock. But I was told in school that organ transplantation is mutilation and that mutilation is a sin. I'm caught between my desire to help and the dictates of my conscience, and I'm afraid I must follow my conscience." Poor man, he's deluded. A familiar fallacy blocks his altruistic preferences. So may we not act as he truly desires and disregard his erroneous conscience? Does his regretful, misguided "No" carry more weight than these five people's deaths, with all their ramifications?

For Hallett's critique of the absolutist position Judith Thomson defends in *The Realm of Rights* (1990), see id. at 113–27.

43. See Hallett, note 34, at 74 (quoting Alan Donagan, The Theory of Morality 66 (1977)): "In *The Theory of Morality*, Alan Donagan examined the Hebrew-Christian tradition and from it elicited the fundamental principle: 'It is impermissible not to respect every human being, including oneself or any other, as a rational creature.'" Donagan defends an absolutist position on the basis of that fundamental principle. Hallett argues against Donagan's absolutism. See id. at 74–88.

44. Fried, note 1, at 10.

45. Finnis, Moral Absolutes, note 2, at 12, 20. For a thoughtful discussion of Finnis's theology and its relation to his argument, see Thomas W. Smith, "Human Finitude, Providence, and Morality," 55 Rev. Politics 723, 724–26 (1993) (reviewing Finnis's *Moral Absolutes*).

46. Cf. "The Bible and Christian Theology," 76 J. Religion 167–327 (1996) (several articles).

47. Who accepts, for example, Finnis's belief that it is better that "the whole people perish" than that "one innocent person be put to death"? See Finnis, Fundamentals of Ethics, note 28, at 95 (recalling "Caiaphas's question 'Is it not better that one innocent person be put to death than that the whole people perish?'").

48. See notes 14–15 and accompanying text.

49. That the law forbids an act does not entail that choosing (with full knowledge of the law) to commit the act is immoral; and that the law requires an act does not entail that choosing not to commit the act is immoral.

50. Indeed, one might think that it makes good sense, as a practical matter, for the articulated morality of human beings, or of some of them, to compromise at least some unconditional moral rights and duties. As Garth Hallett has put the point, "[P]roportionalist grounds might support the exceptionless wording and unquestioning application of certain negative precepts." Hallett, note 34, at 51. See also Joel Kupperman, "A Case for Consequentialism," 18 American Philosophical Q. 305, 305–06 (1981): "[The consequentialist argument is that in] any case in which it is not true that one should do what has the best consequences, the reason for this has to be based on some judgment of consequences. . . . [According to this claim,] some form of consequentialism is correct, . . . the only valid reason for not doing what has the best consequences . . . is that the optimific act in question is ruled out by some moral rule, motive, or system of attitudes which itself is shown to be desirable by virtue of its consequences."

51. There is a substantial affinity between my argument in this chapter and Kent Greenawalt's discussion of the general justification defense in criminal law. I am grate-

ful to Greenawalt for calling his article to my attention. See Kent Greenawalt, "Natural Law and Political Choice: The General Justification Defense—Criteria for Political Action and the Duty to Obey the Law," 36 Catholic U. L. Rev. 1 (1986) (1986 Pope John XXIII Lecture at the Catholic University of America). Greenawalt comments critically on John Finnis's moral absolutism at a number of points in his article. Jean Porter's recent, powerful critique of fundamental aspects of Germain Grisez's moral theory is also highly relevant and very important. See Porter, note 22.

Index

159